# SCHNEIDER TROPHY AIRCRAFT
## 1913–1931

The Schneider Trophy.

# SCHNEIDER TROPHY AIRCRAFT
## 1913–1931

## DEREK N. JAMES
### A.M.R.Ae.S.

PUTNAM

LONDON

BY THE SAME AUTHOR

*Gloster Aircraft since 1917*

Published to commemorate the
50th anniversary
of the
last Schneider Trophy Contest

ERRATA

*Page 154 line 8* For 'S1596' read 'S1595'
*Page 154 caption* For '407.5 mph' read '379.05 mph'
*Page 297* The aircraft housed in the Mitchell Memorial
Hall, Southampton, is the S.6A N248, not the
S.6B S1596. N248 was the reserve aircraft in the
1931 contest.

© 1981 Derek N. James
ISBN 0 370 30328 8
Printed in Great Britain for
Putnam & Company Ltd
9 Bow Street London WC2E 7AL
by Thomson Litho Ltd
East Kilbride, Scotland
*First published 1981*

# CONTENTS

# Preface

Man is, and always has been, a competitor. From the dawn of time, when competing for and winning the means of life was a necessity fundamental to the continuance of life itself, mankind has progressed on the back of the need to win. Too often, war has provided the contest and the urgent need for victory; yet it also has played a leading part in the stimulation of invention and the acceptance of new ideas. When men are faced with an alternative to extermination, it is astonishing how they will open their purses and their minds. Yet in the absence of war, man has invented peaceful combat to satisfy that innate desire to be the first in the field—to whom accrues the prestige, the laurels and the benefits.

In the air, however, peaceful contest between powered aircraft came five years before the beginning of the First World War and balloons had locked in amicable and silent combat some half-century earlier. With the advent of the hydro-aeroplane in 1910, it was to be expected that soon there would be competitions for this type of aircraft. They were not long in coming, and the Monaco Hydro-Aeroplane Meeting of 1913 was the first venue for the greatest of them, La Coupe d'Aviation Maritime Jacques Schneider. This book endeavours to chart the course of the many designers, engineers and pilots who set out to win the Schneider Trophy in the twelve contests which were held, to describe the aeroplanes which were created as a means to accomplish victory, and to identify the benefits which they and the competing countries reaped from participation.

But no historical reference work, such as this book, can be prepared through the efforts of the author alone. He is not required to make a single-handed voyage across the years, for, happily, there are always fellow-travellers who, having made a similar journey before, prospecting the same deserts and waterholes for information, are ready at hand with much needed help of the type which sweetens labour.

Thus much of the reward from the creation of this book's original manuscript stemmed from the personal contacts established and renewed with others of similar interests in many parts of the world. Their co-operation and willing assistance with advice and constructive criticism, guidance and information has been unstinting and without it this latest chronicle of what was, arguably, a major stimulus to aviation progress between the wars could not have been completed. Their names are a roll-call of engineers, writers, pilots, designers and total aviation personalities of the past 75 years, and it is with pride and gratitude that their names are recorded here.

First are those who were personally involved with the Schneider Trophy contests; Air Commodore F. R. Banks, the late Hubert Broad, Hugh Burroughes, the late W. George Carter, the late Basil Fielding, the late Jack Johnstone, Arthur Rubbra, and Air Vice-Marshal S. N. Webster. These all gave much to this great aero-maritime adventure, and their combined documentary material was of great value in the preparation of a number of sections of this book.

The route to the source of many of the details of Schneider Trophy aeroplanes, and of the contests, was pointed out for me by very many friends; among them are John Blake and Michael Hooks (Society of British Aerospace Companies), Eric Folland and John Waghorn, both sons of famous fathers, William Green, Arnold Nayler and Michael FitzGerald (Royal Aeronautical Society), Julian Partridge (Gloster Design Services), Robert Roux and Stephen Wolff. I was also very appreciative of the friendly and rewarding contacts made with Michael Davis, Michael Evans, Steve Hannaway and Terry Jones before and during a visit to Thorpe Park.

It was invaluable to receive many fine photographs, and I am exceedingly grateful to Russell Adams, R. Barker (RAF Museum), Ken Brookes, Ron Brown, Charles W. Cain, Jim Cownie (Rolls-Royce), Herbie Edgar (Short Brothers), John Gray (British Aerospace – Manchester), Mike Hall, Jacques Marmain (*Aviation Magazine International*), Stephen Piercey (*Flight International*), Jay P. Spenser (National Air and Space Museum, Smithsonian Institution), Michael Stroud (British Aerospace – Kingston), Richard Ward, and Brian Wexham (Vickers Ltd) for their most generous help with prints. My thanks go, too, to Charles Andrews for his kind permission to use drawings of Supermarine projects. Information, drawings and photographs from overseas were of particular interest and value, and I am much indebted to Louis Casey (United States), B. Duperier (Aéro-Club de France), Centro Storico Fiat, Harry Hutcherson (Dowty – North America), Evan Kiousis (United States), S. Nicolau and Yvan Kaiser (Musée de l'Air), Gerhard Patt (Dornier GmbH), Dr Gianflorio de Santis (Aeronautica Macchi), Industrie Aeronautiche e Meccaniche Rinaldo Piaggio, SIAI-Marchetti Società per Azioni and Pierre Sers (Techlia).

Archival research which involves the scanning and reading of published works on the same and allied subjects is the foundation on which histories are built, and the bibliography on page 300 gives credit to the work of all those authors whose many publications and narratives have provided such an insight to the Schneider Trophy contests, the aircraft, and the personalities involved. Chief among these is Thomas Foxworth's monumental *The Speed Seekers* which is, unquestionably, the definitive work on the early history of air racing and a model for all those who essay the detailed chronicling of the past.

Finally, I must record the debt of gratitude I owe to Patricia and John Stroud for their practical help and guidance throughout the past year and for their encouragement during the dog-days; to Clem Watson whose fine drawings do so much to enhance the following pages; and to my wife who has toiled with me as she prepared the final typescript and an endless supply of revivifying coffee.

Barnwood, Glos, 1981                                                D.N.J.

# Introduction

Before aerial combat added a third dimension to war, before the gas-turbine allowed aircraft to travel faster than the sun, before space travel enabled man to see sixteen sunrises in one day, there was the Gordon Bennett Aviation Cup and the Coupe Deutsch de la Meurthe. There was also the Schneider Trophy. But even before that there was Jacques Schneider himself who began it all.

Jacques Schneider was born near Paris on 25 January, 1879. As the bright adventurous son of the wealthy owner of the Schneider armament factory at Le Creusot, he was expected to follow in his father's footsteps in this important factory. Certainly he trained as an engineer, but it was in the field of coal mining that he decided to carve out a career for himself. Coal mining was an industry without glamour, a battle between the strength and skill of colliers wielding picks and shovels, and the hard barely-yielding coal seams. An environment full of danger where roofs were supported on wooden props and bars, where coal tubs were hand

Jacques Schneider, the donor of the trophy and originator of the contests which bore his name, pictured at the controls of one of his high-speed racing hydroplanes. (*Musée de l'Air*)

propelled and where fire damp was a constant menace. It was to the solution of many of the underground problems that young Jacques Schneider addressed himself during his practical and theoretical training on the surface and in the pit at Courrières.

His father's wealth and life-style, however, brought him into contact with people of other engineering disciplines, among them Louis Blériot; and yet it was another man and a flying machine which enabled him to use that wealth to exchange the dangers of the pit for those of the air.

The man who wrought such a fundamental change in Jacques Schneider's life was Wilbur Wright who, in August 1908, brought his new Model A aircraft to France and demonstrated it in flight at Le Mans on the 8th of that month. As an engineer Schneider initially was fascinated not only by the manoeuvres and operation of Wright's flying machine but also by its design and construction. Soon, however, this fascination grew into a passionate interest in everything associated with aviation. From this deep interest grew a determination to add the experience and skill of an aeroplane pilot to those which he had earlier acquired as a hydroplane driver. It was while taking part in this high-speed waterborne sport at Monte Carlo in 1910 that he sustained injuries which left him partially handicapped in one arm for the remainder of his life. This did not deter him, however, and in the same year he became a member of the Aéro-Club de France at the age of 31. The following year he qualified for his aeroplane pilot's licence, and swiftly thereafter acquired a free-balloon pilot's licence. Then, less than two years later, flying his balloon, *Icare*, he established a new French altitude record of 10,081 metres. But the accident and his injuries prevented young Jacques Schneider from taking an even more active part in the developing aviation scene in France; as a result, he concentrated to a growing extent on the organization of flying meetings and races, and became increasingly involved in the administrative side of sporting aviation.

His pre-occupation with this particular aspect of aviation did not prevent him from making flights of fancy, and one of these was the allying of his new airborne interests to those of his hydroplane racing days. Schneider believed that, as 70 per cent of the earth's surface is covered by water, the seaplane—or hydro-aeroplane as it was then known—could be developed as an almost universal form of transport to provide a communications system linking most parts of the world. It was the creation of another Frenchman, 27-year old Henri Fabre, who came from a ship-owning family, which had sparked-off Schneider's vision of the future for air transport. This was a seaplane of somewhat alarming design and construction. While the airframe was of unusual design, particularly the horizontal aerofoil surfaces, Fabre's marine experience produced highly effective floats of a type which were used subsequently on a number of early hydro-aeroplanes.

Fabre, born in Marseilles and three years younger than Schneider, was the first man to design, build and successfully fly a hydro-aeroplane. This was in March 1910 and was all the more remarkable in that Fabre's knowledge of aircraft design was minimal, having culled what he knew from a study of French landplanes, and that he had no practical experience of flying. Such was the spirit and courage of the aviation pioneers in Europe.

But France was not alone in spawning such men; in the United States a young enthusiast, named Glenn Curtiss, also foresaw the use of water as an almost limitless surface from which to operate aeroplanes, and in 1910 he began a series of experiments in the creation of hydro-aeroplanes. Curtiss' experience was a good deal wider than that of Fabre when, on 26 January, 1911, he first flew his hydro-aeroplane from San Diego Bay in California. A flimsy pusher biplane, it featured a stubby central float and had cylindrical tanks on the wingtips to act as stabilizing floats.

Glenn Curtiss had, by then, become known as an accomplished racing pilot, having won the world's first international air race for the James Gordon Bennett Aviation Cup at Reims in 1909, at a speed of 47 mph.

Some fourteen years later, in 1923, Curtiss racing seaplanes made history by winning the Schneider Trophy for the United States for the first time, repeating this success in 1925. After that, the US effort and will to compete in this important international event ran out of steam and the challenge from across the Atlantic never equalled the capabilities and achievements of the European creators and pilots of Schneider Trophy Contest floatplanes.

The year 1911, when Curtiss first got airborne in his hydro-aeroplane, also saw the first flight of a British aircraft of this type piloted by Commander Oliver Schwann (later Air Vice-Marshal Sir Oliver Swann KCB, CBE) a Royal Navy officer. This aircraft was the first of the six Avro Type D biplanes and was powered by a 35 hp Green four-cylinder, inline water-cooled engine. Schwann bought it for £700 in June 1911 and despatched it by rail from Brooklands to Barrow-in-Furness for testing.

Commander Oliver Schwann taxi-ing his much modified Avro Type D floatplane at Barrow-in-Furness during August 1911. Numerous float designs were tried before the aircraft would take off. (*Courtesy Royal Aeronautical Society*)

There the wheels were removed and the aircraft was fitted, in turn, with seven or eight different sets of alighting gear, including floats designed by Schwann and his associates and built by Royal Navy artificers. After protracted trials in Cavendish Dock at Barrow, during which the Avro capsized once, Schwann, who was not a qualified pilot, took it into the air rather unexpectedly on 18 November, 1911—only to alight abruptly and rather heavily and capsize again. However unpromising this short flight may have appeared, this was the first occasion that a British seaplane had flown from British waters. While France, the United States, and Great Britain, ploughed a pioneering furrow of marine aviation, Germany and Italy had to await the stimulus of war to bring their development of floatplanes and flying-boats to a similar level of advancement. But the pace of development, even in these three countries, was slow and to Jacques Schneider it seemed that the seaplane was being neglected by designers and manufacturers in favour of the landplane. This was not altogether surprising for the combination of the problems and risks facing the designers and pilots of aircraft—who were often one and the same—operating from water stretched their ingenuity, skill and courage.

In an effort to speed the progress of seaplane development, Schneider determined to establish a special contest limited to this type of aeroplane. On 5 December, 1912, at the customary banquet following the fourth Gordon Bennett Aviation Cup race at Chicago, he announced his intention to present a trophy which was to be for international competition by seaplanes. The trophy, which bore the name 'La Coupe d'Aviation Maritime Jacques Schneider', was valued at £1,000 and was to be the premier award in an annual contest between aeroclubs rather than individual pilots. Schneider and his small team of advisers took much care in drawing up a set of rules for the contest, for which he had also offered to provide £1,000 annually for the first three years. The rules were aimed at producing not simply high-speed racing 'freaks' but practical aircraft which were capable of operation from the open sea, were reliable and had a good range. Thus they stipulated that the contests—which were not, as so many people still refer to them, races in that the entrants did not all take-off at the same time—must take place on a course over the open sea and be over a distance of the equivalent of at least 150 nautical miles. For this reason the competing aircraft would be required to undergo quite complex seaworthiness trials.

Any aeroclub affiliated to the Fédération Aéronautique Internationale could issue a challenge to the trophy-holding club, which would then have the responsibility of organizing the next contest to defend its title. The FAI had been formed in Paris during 1905 as the governing body for sporting aviation and, as such, was and still is the internationally recognized authority for the regulation of flying competitions and the ratification of air records.

A most important rule was that the country which succeeded in winning the trophy three times in five years would be declared its permanent holder and the series of contests would then officially be terminated. It is clear that Schneider had thought long and deeply about the rules governing the contests for his magnificent trophy. With each participating club allowed a maximum of three entries, the teams were compact and not of such a size as to be too unwieldy to move around the world to the various venues envisaged. Finally, the rule regarding the nomination of a permanent holder meant that there was not only an added incentive for a sustained effort in the development of seaplanes for the contest, but there was a distinct possibility—which was to be realized in 1931—that the series of contests would prove to be only a launching pad for a more comprehensive programme of seaplane and engine development and not simply an interminable tussle for supremacy in this one annual event. Schneider's belief in the national authority and power of 'l'Aéro-Club' system is apparent in the promotion of this competition as being an international inter-club event.

Fashionably dressed Armand Deperdussin (*left foreground*) who financed the construction of the first Schneider contest winner, greets friends at an early French air meeting. (*Musée de l'Air*)

That Schneider's original vision of a world-embracing transport system operated with floatplanes and flying-boats would never become fact could not have been countenanced in those far-off days during the dawn of aviation when almost anything seemed capable of being achieved—ultimately. Sadly, Jacques Schneider's splendid bronze trophy failed to motivate seaplane designers to serve the ends he sought. Their creations, while rarely warranting the 'freak' classification, were solely for high-speed flying at low level, were, almost without exception, single-seaters and were powered by engines which had been 'tweaked' to deliver maximum output for comparatively short durations. Hardly the globe-encircling passenger transport aircraft which were Schneider's dream and goal. But the series of contests were of inestimable value in many other ways, principally because they provided a stimulus, a raison d'être, for research and development programmes which might not otherwise have been pursued with such vigour or with the same rate of achievement. As a result, not just marine aircraft but many other aspects of aviation were advanced and benefited from the creation of floatplanes for the contests.

Nowhere was the fall-out more marked or more beneficial than in the development of aero-engines of high power and low specific weight, and of the special fuels which they required. These particular benefits were longer lasting and of more moment possibly than any other which resulted from the Schneider contest series.

However, with the passing years and contests, as each one failed to move marine aviation toward Schneider's goal, he seemed to slip further from the centre of the contest stage. It is not clear whether he began to lose interest in this international event which he had fathered, or whether those involved in it began to regard the Frenchman almost as irrelevant to the cut and thrust of the annual encounter. His name appeared with less frequency and the last contest which he attended was in 1926. During the summer of the following year he underwent an operation for appendicitis which did not allow him to see the British victory in Venice. Then, on 1 May, 1928, Jacques Schneider died at Beaulieu-sur-Mer near Nice. His death went almost unnoticed and unremarked, and he died, in reduced circumstances, at the early age of 49, knowing neither the ultimate winner of his splendid trophy nor the changes and benefits it brought to those nations who had fought to own it.

Roland Garros starting at Monaco in 1913. The three-float alighting gear of the Morane-Saulnier is seen to advantage. (*Courtesy Jacques Gambu*)

# The Contests

## Monaco 1913

Having in mind the overwhelming lead in aviation which France had established at this time, it is not surprising that no less than eight French pilots and their aircraft aspired to membership of the French team for the first Schneider contest at Monte Carlo on 16 April, 1913. In the event this number was reduced to the required total of three entrants by the combined effects of bad weather, mechanical failure and pilot error during the Monaco Hydro-Aeroplane Meeting at which the contest for the new Schneider Trophy ended the two-week programme of competitive flying. The three were Dr Gabriel Espanet in a Nieuport, Maurice Prévost flying a Deperdussin and Roland Garros in a Morane-Saulnier. All their aircraft were monoplanes. The only other competitor was Charles Weymann who, although born in Haiti, educated in France and was to fly a Nieuport aircraft, was representing the United States.

Thus, although there was no need for eliminating trials, all three Frenchmen and their aircraft successfully completed two laps of the 10 km (6·21 miles) course laid out in Baie de Roquebrune between Monte

Carlo and Cap Martin in France. In addition, as proof of seaworthiness, they alighted once and taxied 500 m (1,640 ft) on the sea. Of Weymann there is no record of his having undergone the same trials, such was the relaxed manner in which this first contest for the new Schneider Trophy was conducted. The day of the contest was brilliantly sunny with little wind, which suited the contestants admirably as they had to taxi over the starting line and continue on the water for half of the first lap before getting airborne. Having drawn lots, Prévost was first away and completed the first of the required 28 laps in 11·25 min: by which time Garros had begun his taxi-ing run, only to swamp the Morane's engine with water thrown up by its porpoise-like passage, and had to be towed back to land. Meanwhile, Weymann and Espanet were in hot pursuit of Prévost, with the superior speed of the Nieuports being offset by Prévost's more skilful rounding of the four turning points. When Espanet alighted with engine trouble, Garros, who had completed his taxi-ing test, saw Prévost and Weymann flying so well that he decided to abandon his attempt to win the Trophy. With three-quarters of the contest over, the American was more than three minutes in the lead; but soon Prévost's earlier start meant that he had completed his 28 laps and he alighted 500 m short of the finishing line and taxied across it to return a total time of 2 h 50 min. Sadly, Prévost had not read his contest rules, for he should have flown over the finishing line and was therefore disqualified. He refused advice to go out again and simply comply with the rule he had violated. Then, with only four laps to

Standing, it is hoped, on a strongpoint of the fuselage this unidentifiable man gives scale to the little Morane-Saulnier Hydro-monoplane, at Monaco in 1913. (*Musée de l'Air*)

Most of the Nieuport's design features are visible in this view of Espanet's aircraft at Monaco in 1913. (*Musée de l'Air*)

complete, Weymann's Nieuport alighted with a burst oil pipe. Back on land the Gnome engine was found to need replacing, which put the US entrant out of contention. Immediately, the Morane was started, completed the navigability test and began lapping the course in Garros' skilled hands. But Prévost had been alerted to the situation; he saw the sense of the earlier advice and quickly took off to fly over the finishing line to be declared the winner. Thus a Frenchman in a French aircraft with a French engine won the first contest for the Schneider Trophy, presented by a Frenchman.

## Monaco 1914

The course for this contest was the same as the previous year, with the same number of laps to be flown. It attracted entrants from France, Germany, Great Britain, Switzerland and the United States, including the four pilots who had participated in 1913. The eliminating trials surprisingly ruled out Prévost, leaving Garros in the 160 hp Morane-Saulnier, and Espanet and Pierre Levasseur flying similarly-powered Nieuports, to represent France. Weymann had a new Nieuport with a 160 hp Le Rhône eighteen-cylinder rotary engine; Ernst Stoeffler in an Aviatik Pfeil (Arrow) was the German entrant; Switzerland sent Ernest Burri in an FBA flying-boat with a 100 hp Monosoupape Gnome engine; while a second US entrant was William Thaw whose second choice of

3

aircraft was a 160 hp Le Rhône-powered Deperdussin. Britain's hopes were pinned firmly to the Sopwith Tabloid with a 100 hp Gnome Monosoupape engine and the experienced Howard Pixton; Lord Carbery with his Le Rhône-engined Morane was competing very much in a supporting role.

The contest day, 20 April, dawned bright and dry with a light wind. Carbery and Stoeffler had been forced to withdraw from the contest due to mishaps the previous day; however, Carbery managed to borrow a Deperdussin from one of the French reserves and was back in the lists.

With the rules calling for two alightings and take-offs during the first lap, the two Nieuports flown by Levasseur and Espanet were first away. Burri, in the FBA flying-boat, followed them after a long bouncing take-off run, with Pixton getting airborne a few minutes afterwards. At once the superior speed of Pixton's little Tabloid was apparent as he completed his first lap in half the Frenchmen's time and proceeded to build up a 13 min lead over them. Then, as the Nieuports were pressed to keep from slipping further behind, the rear cylinder banks of their twin-row Gnome engines overheated and both aircraft dropped out of the contest with seized pistons, leaving Pixton and Burri to battle it out. Weymann and Garros played a waiting game, refusing to start unless Pixton failed to complete the course. But they waited in vain for although on its 15th lap the Tabloid's Gnome began to misfire on one cylinder and, initially, its speed gradually fell, the eight remaining cylinders continued to fire efficiently and Pixton's lap times improved again. When he crossed the finishing line after completing the required 28 laps in 2 hr and 13 sec, he did so to an enthusiastic reception from the predominantly French crowd—and kept flying for a further two laps to establish a new world seaplane record of 139·36 km/h (86·6 mph) over a 300 km (186·41 miles) course to add to his Schneider Trophy winning speed of 139·66 km/h (86·78 mph).

The Swiss flying-boat, meanwhile, had had to alight in quite rough water to refuel on its 23rd lap, and had some problems in taking-off to resume the contest. Weymann and Garros realized that they had lost their gamble, but both Prèvost and Levasseur shared an idea to try and better Pixton's performance. Neither was successful. Prévost's Deperdussin suffered engine failure almost as soon as it was launched, and although Levasseur got airborne in Weymann's Nieuport, he retired after nine laps with engine trouble. Burri continued to trundle round his remaining five laps, which he completed in 3 hr 24 min, to take second place.

There was much rejoicing among the British party in Monaco, even though this victory of Sopwith's little biplane and its Australian pilot went virtually unremarked in the daily newspapers in Britain. Sopwith was also ready to acknowledge not only the debt he and the team owed to the Tabloid's French Gnome Monosoupape engine but to claim that it was a major factor in aviation progress of that prewar era. In addition, he did

Howard Pixton under way in the Sopwith Tabloid in front of the exotic casinos and hotels of Monaco. (*British Aerospace – Kingston*)

not overlook the fact that Government orders for the Tabloid had provided the support he had needed to redesign and construct the seaplane racer version.

# Bournemouth 1919

Four years of war clearly had left a series of apparently contradictory marks on aviation by the time it fell to Great Britain to organize its first Schneider Trophy contest. While engine powers, reliability, and power-to-weight ratios, had advanced out of all recognition beyond those of the rotary engines used in the 1914 contest, there was what appeared to be a retrograde step in airframe development in that all the entrants were biplanes. Two events contributed to the continuing dominance of the biplane over the monoplane; one was the Tabloid's victory in the 1914 contest, the other was the crash of the Coanda military monoplane at Wolvercote, Oxford, on 10 September, 1913, in which both the crew were killed. This accident followed a number of others involving monoplanes and led to a War Office ban on aeroplanes of this configuration for the RFC Military Wing. Although this hasty decision was rescinded some five months later, it prejudiced monoplane development in Great Britain for many years thereafter. France, rather surprisingly, followed suit, and when the Allies went to war in 1914 it was with biplanes which, undeniably, enjoyed certain advantages over the monoplanes. A more rugged construction, better take-off and climb performance and greater manoeuvrability were among them, and these, allied to more powerful engines, gave the biplane the edge. So it was that Italy, Great Britain, and France, sent a total of six such aircraft to Bournemouth in September 1919 to compete for the Schneider Trophy over ten laps of a 20 nautical mile (37·06 km) three-leg course, starting and finishing off Bournemouth Pier, with turning points at Swanage Bay and Hengistbury Head. Four British aircraft flew in the preliminary trials on 8 September and as a result the Avro 539 floatplane (G-EALG) flown by Capt H. A. Hamersley, who had joined A. V. Roe and Co earlier in the year when it had started a joyriding operation at Hamble, was withdrawn. This left a Sopwith seaplane (G-EAKI) powered by a 450 hp Cosmos Jupiter II engine, and a Fairey III seaplane (G-EALQ) and the Supermarine Sea Lion flying-boat (G-EALP) each powered by a 450 hp Napier Lion. Harry Hawker flew the Sopwith, Vincent Nicholl the Fairey III and Basil D. Hobbs the Sea Lion. Hamersley, Nicholl and Hobbs were all much-decorated veteran war-pilots.

France had entered two 300 hp Hispano-Suiza-engined Nieuports, both based on the military Type 29 and float mounted, and a Spad-Herbemont powered by a 340 hp Hispano-Suiza engine. The Nieuports' pilots were Lieut Jean Casale, a Corsican and renowned wartime pilot,

The Avro 539 Falcon taking off during the elimination trials for the 1919 contest. The large amount of 'down' aileron on the port mainplanes and the way the port float is digging in make an interesting comparison with the photograph of the Nieuport on page 55 (*British Aerospace – Manchester*)

and Henri Malard, and the equally renowned Sadi Lecointe was to fly the Spad. The lone Italian entry, a Savoia S.13 flying-boat with a 250 hp Isotta-Fraschini engine, had Sgt Guido Jannello of the Italian Air Force as its pilot.

Both Nieuports were damaged during pre-delivery trials on the Seine but were repaired and when Casale arrived alone to alight in the Medina estuary in the Isle of Wight, he hit a buoy. Only determined efforts by the Saunders company in rebuilding the aircraft enabled it to be ready for the contest on 10 September. Malard set out for Bournemouth but came down in the English Channel and, having clung to the still floating Nieuport for some 24 hr, was picked up by the Royal Navy. The Spad was delivered safely by sea and after its trials at Cowes, André Herbemont, its designer, decided to crop about 15 in (38 cm) off each upper wingtip to obtain more speed.

If the competitors and their aircraft were well prepared for the contest, this was not the case with its organizers, who had overlooked the provision of such fundamental facilities as launching slips, roped-off areas of a public beach where the aircraft could receive final preparations, safety boats to keep the starting area clear, or any catering facilities for the pilots and teams of mechanics. Moreover, a thick sea mist shrouded the whole course and the 2.30 p.m. start was postponed until 6 p.m., whereupon the French team started some repair work on their floats which were holed. Then, at 5 p.m., a slight improvement in the visibility prompted the Royal Aero Club race committee to change their minds and sent a launch to tell competitors the contest would begin in 15 minutes time, only to follow it with a second launch to advise them the start would be in 30 minutes! There was confusion, too, over the precise starting signals and when Nicholl took off in the Fairey III he did so 15 sec too early. It mattered very little for, having groped his way into Swanage Bay in the mist, narrowly avoiding hitting the mast of the red and white mark boat and being hit by another aircraft, Nicholl returned to Bournemouth and beached the Fairey.

The Nieuport and the Sopwith had drawn second and third starting places but neither was ready or prepared to take-off, so Hobbs set off in the Sea Lion. Meanwhile the French had given up hope of making their aircraft seaworthy and had withdrawn from the contest. Then Hawker decided to get airborne whether the official starter was ready or not, leaving Jannello in the S.13 flying-boat to make the only completely correct start. While he was out on his first lap, Hawker alighted and gave up the unequal struggle with the sea fog. Then Hobbs, who, on his first lap, had alighted in Swanage Bay for fear of flying into the cliffs, decided to return to Bournemouth to get his bearings and make a fresh start. Unfortunately, he hit a floating object while taking-off and, although he made a perfect rounding of the Christchurch mark boat, when he attempted the first of the mandatory two first lap alightings to prove seaworthiness, the Sea Lion's hull—which had been badly holed—filled with water and the flying-boat inverted with its tail in the air. Hobbs was rescued by a launch.

Above all these scenes of failure and disaster, Jannello lapped steadily, but a timekeeper noticed his lap times were too short for the known speed of the S.13. When he had completed his final lap and alighted he was advised to fly an additional one to make sure he had covered sufficient distance to allow the last ten uninterrupted laps to count as an attempt on the 200 nautical miles (370·6 km) seaplane record. Jannello set off again—though doubtful that he had sufficient fuel to complete the 20

Guido Jannello in his moored Savoia S.13 at Bournemouth during a short spell of sunshine before the 1919 contest. The short-span, narrow-chord racing mainplanes and the four-blade pusher propeller are clearly seen. (*Flight*)

miles (37·06 km). He was correct, and when he came down out on the course there was a long delay before a launch could be organized to search for him. Worse was to come for, while the Christchurch mark-boat crew had recorded Jannello's ten laps, the Swanage boat said they had never seen him at all!

When the race committee disqualified the Italian entry and declared the race void, Jannello insisted he had seen and rounded the Swanage boat each lap. When he was asked to indicate on a map where he had seen the boat, he pointed to Studland Bay—where a reserve mark boat had been moored! The Italians protested and it seemed that the world supported them, seeing the justness of their case. With British sportsmanship at stake, at a Royal Aero Club committee meeting on 22 September it was decided to award the Trophy to Italy. This decision was not wholly fair to the pilots who had been prevented from flying the correct course due to the weather conditions. Thus, the Fédération Aéronautique Internationale reversed this award on 24 October, but asked the Royal Aero Club of Italy to organize the next contest.

Rarely can there have been such a demonstration of amateur bungling in the organization of an international sporting event. How sad that it should have been Great Britain which failed to measure up to the required standards of organizing skill and so prevented what could have been a British victory. Much of this could have been avoided by better pre-contest planning, but the decision to base the aircraft servicing facilities at Cowes and the assembly and starting areas at Bournemouth, with the contest committee aboard a motor yacht in the Solent, was a prime factor in making the entire event farcical.

# Venice 1920

The grace-and-favour decision of the FAI to allow Italy to organize the 1920 Schneider contest, but not to receive the Trophy, ultimately had a direct bearing on the whole course of the contest series. Immediately, it had the effect of removing the venue a very long way from Britain and from other potential entrant countries. Both France and Britain were heading for the inevitable postwar economic crisis following a few heady years, and though, traditionally, Britain saw the future of its aircraft industry as closely allied to its maritime interests and its role within the Empire, there was little if any money for competition flying, even where seaplanes were involved. The Royal Aero Club's proferred £500 prize money to be shared among the three best placed British aircraft did not attract any entrants; the United States and France preferred to make a major effort in the Gordon Bennett Cup event at the more convenient Étampes venue; and Swiss interest in the Schneider contest had waned after its one appearance at Monaco before the war. Thus Italy, which had arranged a change in the rules so that all participating aircraft had to carry

300 kg (661 lb) of ballast as a representative payload, which favoured the Italian flying-boat entries, found itself without competition after the French Spad-Herbemont was withdrawn. Four biplane flying-boats of the light bomber or reconnaissance type were entered for the contest; a Savoia S.12 bomber powered by a 550 hp Ansaldo water-cooled engine driving a pusher propeller; a Savoia S.19 built for the contest and fitted with a similar 550 hp Ansaldo engine with a conventional tractor propeller; a Macchi M.12 pusher-type reconnaissance aircraft powered by a 430 hp Ansaldo engine; and a Macchi M.19 two-seater, with a 680 hp Fiat water-cooled engine, which had been built for the contest with the new regulations in mind.

In the event, due to mechanical problems and failures, all but the S.12, which had been specially developed and prepared for racing, failed to come to the starting line on 20 September for the contest.

The triangular course over the Adriatic was from Porto di Lido in the north down to Porto di Malamocco in the south and eastwards to a point over the sea—all turning points being marked by captive balloons. All that was required of Lieut Luigi Bologna, an Italian naval pilot, was that he should complete the 370 km (200 nautical miles) course correctly and this he did at an average speed of 172·561 km/h (107·224 mph) in 2 hr 10½ min and took the Trophy. Following the highly unsatisfactory nature of the preceding year's contest at Bournemouth, this Italian 'fly-over' victory was heavily criticized in certain quarters, but there were no appeals and this time the glory and the Trophy were Italy's for the first time.

# Venice 1921

Apart from the fact that Italy moved another step toward laying permanent claim to the Schneider Trophy, the two major outcomes of the 1921 contest in Venice were that it proved conclusively that novelty was no substitute for sound design and engineering and, secondly, that the high cost of participation in terms of time, effort and money was severely limiting the number of entries. Italy had agreed to another change in the rules concerning the carriage of 300 kg (661 lb) of simulated payload so that speed—coupled with reliability—was the essential feature; however, in a move to discourage the creation of stripped high-power aircraft of outlandish design, a new rule was substituted requiring participating aircraft to be moored out, fully loaded, as a test of float qualities and the structural strength of the alighting gear generally. In addition, for every entrant, a 5,000 franc registration deposit, plus the entry fee, was required to be paid to the contest organizers to prevent frivolous entries. This 'no-show' deposit was refunded if the aircraft took part in the contest.

On the closing date for registration the list of entries was a repeat of the previous year—Italy versus France. The host country had mustered sixteen flying-boats, produced by Macchi and Savoia, of various sizes, designs and power; they were five M.7 pusher biplanes, two M.18s and the M.19 two-seater produced for the previous year's contest, six S.13s similar to the aircraft which, flown by Jannello, initially had been declared the winner of the 1919 contest at Bournemouth, an S.21 and an S.22. These last two aircraft were unusual in that the upper wing of the single-engined S.21 was shorter than the lower wing, and the S.22 had its two engines in tandem. The lone challenge to this fleet of Italian aspirants was a French Nieuport-Delage powered by a 300 hp Hispano-Suiza engine and specially built for the contest. Not surprisingly, Italian design and engineering skills proved to have been spread too thinly and too quickly, with the result that the S.21, due to the illness of Jannello, its pilot, was withdrawn; so were the two M.18s which suffered engine trouble, plus three M.7s and the S.22 crashed during test flying. This left nine Italian aircraft in the team selection trials, out of which came the old M.19 flown by Arturo Zanetti, and two M.7s with Piero Corgnolino and Giovanni de Briganti as their pilots. Opposing them was Sadi Lecointe in the Nieuport-Delage, but its alighting gear failed during the contest's navigability tests on 11 August, making a gift of the Trophy to Italy which again had only to complete the course to secure it for the second successive time. Even then the crankshaft in the M.19's Fiat engine failed and caused a fire, forcing Zanetti to alight hurriedly, and Corgnolino's old M.7 ran out of fuel only two kilometres (1·2 miles) from the finishing line, leaving de Briganti, in the slowest M.7, to complete the required 16 laps of the 24·6 km (15·28 miles) course at an average speed of 189·677 km/h (117·859 mph) and be declared the winner.

## Naples 1922

It was agreed that the 1922 contest, to be held on 10–12 August, should be flown over 13 laps of a 28·5 km (17·7 miles) course at Naples, much to the relief of the people of Venice who twice had been assailed by the ear-shattering roar of the seaplanes' high-powered engines above their tranquil lagoons and canals. This year, with Italy fully expecting to win the contest for the third successive time and take permanent possession of the Trophy, there were entries by Great Britain and France. A major difference between the teams was that both the Italian and French teams were supported by their respective Governments, whereas the British entry, the Supermarine Sea Lion II G-EBAH was privately financed by Hubert Scott-Paine, managing director of Supermarine Aviation Works. He was supported by the Napier engine company—through the enterprise of its managing director H. T. Vane—which agreed to provide the 450 hp Lion engine, and by the Shell petroleum and Wakefield oil companies, who promised to give all the fuel and lubricants required.

An unidentified CAMS 36 taking off. The examples entered for the 1922 contest had I interplane struts. The 'boat illustrated resembles more closely the CAMS 36bis of 1923. (*Courtesy Jacques Gambu*)

The Sea Lion II was of the same basic biplane configuration as the Sea Lion I of 1919; however, the hull shape had been refined, the tail unit redesigned, and the Lion engine turned a four-blade rather than the earlier two-blade propeller. Italy had given early notice of its intentions with the design and construction of two new aircraft by Savoia, the S.50 seaplane 2031 and S.51 flying-boat I-BAIU. These were to be supported by an M.7 (I-BAFV) similar to the previous contest winner, and an M.17 flying-boat (I-BAHG) developed from the M.7. The S.51 was powered by a 300 hp Hispano-Suiza engine and the two Macchi aircraft by 260 hp Isotta-Fraschini engines. France was represented by two CAMS 36 military flying-boats (F-ESFA and 'B) with 300 hp Hispano-Suiza tractor power units in place of the pusher installation of the standard aircraft. Built by Chantiers Aéro-Maritimes de la Seine, these flying-boats had been extensively modified in preparation for the contest. Inevitably it seemed, one of Italy's entrants, the S.50, crashed during its test flying programme, killing the pilot.

In Naples, during the pre-contest flight testing, all three teams were intent upon finding out as much as they could of the other competitors' capabilities while revealing as little as possible of their own. Capt H. C. Biard never flew the Sea Lion II to its limits or showed any skill at rounding marks when he believed that French or Italian eyes were on him or stop-watches being consulted. In this way, he induced the opposition to credit his aircraft with a maximum speed a good deal less than it could achieve.

The French team was even more successful in hiding its light and the first tangible piece of information came on 12 August when both their aircraft were withdrawn after one of the CAMS 36 flying-boats capsized during the preliminary trials. It was not alone with this problem, for the S.51 suffered a similar fate during the mandatory six-hour flotation test; however, contrary to the contest rules, it was righted, and as there were no protests from either France or Great Britain, the S.51 was included in the Italian team.

Two legs of the triangular course crossed the Bay of Naples eastbound and northwestbound, with turning points just south of Naples, further south along the coast at Cabo di Posillip and across the bay at Torre del Greco.

The prototype Macchi M.17 seen at Monaco in 1920 before it was destroyed in a very heavy and uncontrolled alighting. Its appearance afloat makes an interesting comparison with the second M.17, I-BAHG, shown on page 83. (*Aeronautica Macchi*)

The day of the contest was extremely hot and the start was not until 4 p.m. Biard had drawn the first start position and, once airborne, he had decided to push the Sea Lion's throttle wide open and keep it there, so that he could compare his top speed with that of the other aircraft. His first lap was the fastest he was to fly, being completed in 7 min 10 sec. Corgnolino in the M.7 was second to start, with Zanetti third starter in the M.17. Last away was Passaleva flying the S.51. At the ends of their first laps only the S.51's time was anywhere near to the Sea Lion's, being 22 sec slower than the British entry. But the contest had a long time to run and soon Biard found that being a one-man team had its problems, particularly at the turning points where the three Italian pilots managed to bunch together and so prevent him from passing them. However, he used his speed advantage and after flying close behind the trio he suddenly pushed the throttle wide, leap-frogged over them then dived for the next turning point, leaving them bumping about in his slipstream.

The Lion engine responded magnificently to the demands Biard was making upon it as, for the next seven laps—half the contest distance—he flew flat out. But when Biard throttled back to ease the strain on the engine, Passaleva in the S.51 began to overhaul him, but he too had problems with vibration caused as the bonding between the laminations of his propeller failed and they opened up, a direct result of the previous day's capsize. Slowly he made up the seconds which separated him from the Sea Lion, but the S.51 was simply not fast enough to pull back the enormous lead built up by Biard who came home the winner by two minutes.

Biard and Napier's Lion engine had proved that the apparently impossible could be achieved. The pilot's skilful handling of the engine, his contest strategy and the tactical handling of his aircraft—an old design which had responded to the magic touch of a young designer named R. J. Mitchell who had been responsible for many performance-improving airframe modifications—had proved an unbeatable combination, whatever the Italians had tried to do, either singly or as a team. Most significantly, this convincing British victory kept the entire contest series alive, for had Italy taken the Trophy it would have become Italian property for all time and the results of much subsequent research and experimental work would have been lost.

# Cowes 1923

The 1922 Naples contest victory gave Great Britain the privilege of hosting the 1923 contest. The Royal Aero Club was charged with the responsibility of organizing the event and, with the experiences of the 1919 Bournemouth contest still clearly in mind, it was decided that it

Three of the 1923 contestants entering the Medina from S. E. Saunders' slipway at Cowes. From the left they are Irvine's Curtiss CR-3 (No. 3), Biard's Supermarine Sea Lion III (No. 7), and Hurel's CAMS 38 (No. 9).

should take place at Cowes. The five lap course, starting and finishing off Cowes, with turning points at Selsey Bill and Southsea, was unique in that it provided not only the longest lap of any of the twelve contests, but also the longest single leg; these were 37·2 nautical miles (68·89 km) and 18·52 nautical miles (34·299 km) respectively. In addition, this contest was flown over the smallest number of laps, and the contest distance of 186 nautical miles (344·47 km) was shorter than any other.

This year's contest had another unique feature; it was that, for the first time, the United States entered the list of nations aspiring to win the Schneider Trophy. With typical US efficiency and thoroughness, four aircraft and a large team of pilots and mechanics were sent to Britain a month in advance of the contest to acclimatize themselves and to thoroughly practice their flying techniques over the Solent. The seaplanes were crated and shipped aboard a US Navy carrier but the air and ground crews travelled in the *Leviathan*.

The aircraft selected for this first US crack at Europe's much vaunted Schneider Trophy were two Curtiss CR-3 biplanes (A6080 and 6081) built as racing aircraft for the US Navy, a new NW-2 which was a USN racer produced by Wright Aeronautical Co, plus a TR-3A, built by the Naval Aircraft Factory, as a reserve aircraft for practice flying. The CR-3s had new 465 hp Curtiss D-12 engines driving Reed metal propellers, the NW-2 had a 600 hp Wright T-2 twelve-cylinder inline engine while the reserve aircraft had a modest 300 hp Wright engine. The US Navy pilots for these aircraft were nominated some three months before the 28 September contest date. Led by Lieut F. W. Wead—known to his teammates as 'Spig'—they were Lieuts A. W. Gorton, Rutledge Irvine and David Rittenhouse. These three were experienced test pilots from Anacostia Naval Air Station on Long Island, and Gorton had the additional advantage of having flown racing seaplanes in the 1922 Curtiss Marine Trophy, which he had won. Because of this experience, it was only to be expected that he should fly the most fancied and the fastest aircraft, which was the NW-2, and accordingly, after some joint preliminary training with the other pilots, he went to the Naval Aircraft Factory at Philadelphia where, operating from the Delaware, he started familiarization and handling flights with this powerful seaplane. Meanwhile, Irvine and Rittenhouse were doing the same thing with the Curtiss CR-3s at the Curtiss factory on Long Island.

All three were excited by the high speeds they attained during these trials but did their best to keep the figures secret. But inevitably during the voyage in the *Leviathan*, the pilots revealed their top speeds to each other, much to the amazement of Gorton who discovered that his teammates in their lower-powered Curtiss aircraft were topping the 200 mph mark, some 20 mph faster than his best speed. In an effort to improve the NW-2's performance, Wead arranged for the Wright engine company to test a T-2 engine to destruction by running it on the testbed at maximum revolutions, something Gorton had rarely done. It ran for five hours before failing, but this was enough for Wead and Gorton who changed the pitch of the NW-2's metal propeller to get every ounce of thrust out of it. Four days before the contest Wead decided to let Gorton try some full-throttle trials over the course in the NW-2, but having successfully completed three-quarters of a lap at very high speed, while flying low down at around 220 mph (354·04 km/h) from Southsea toward the finishing line at Cowes, the engine blew up. The aircraft hit the water, Gorton was thrown out but was unhurt and was picked up by a fishing boat.

The wisdom of bringing a reserve aircraft was apparent and Wead began practising his high-speed circuit flying in the TR-3A with even more determination. In the event, during the navigability trials, a back-fire wrecked the starting gear and, as the engine could not be started by hand-swinging the propeller, team-leader Wead and his aircraft were withdrawn; thus the two CR-3s were to carry the entire responsibility for taking the Schneider Trophy back to the United States for the first time.

Rutledge Irvine taking-off in his Curtiss CR-3 at the start of the 1923 contest.

But the USA was not alone with its problems; Great Britain, France and Italy were to suffer their own before the contest was over. France had chosen five aircraft, including reserves, for the journey to Cowes. They were a new CAMS 38 flying-boat (F-ESFD) powered by a 360 hp His-pano-Suiza engine, two Latham L.1 flying-boats (F-ESEJ and F-ATAM) each fitted with two 400 hp Lorraine-Dietrich engines mounted in tandem, a Blanchard-Blériot C.1 (F-ESEH) with a 450 hp Cosmos/Bristol radial engine licence-built in France, and a CAMS 36 flying-boat (F-ESFC), having a 360 hp Hispano-Suiza engine, as the reserve aircraft. During the cross-Channel flight to Cowes by the two Latham L.1s, F-ATAM flown by M Benoist had engine trouble and diverted to Little-hampton, where it was damaged by surf and by the subsequent beaching operations by enthusiastic but amateur local people. As a result, it was withdrawn from the contest. While the other L.1 (F-ESEJ) arrived safely at Cowes, back in France the 450 hp Jupiter-powered Blanchard-Blériot

Three of the 1923 French entrants moored out for the navigability trials. The Latham L.1 F-ESEJ (No. 11) is nearest with, beyond, the CAMS 36 F-ESFC (No. 10) and CAMS 38 F-ESFD (No. 9).

aeroplane had failed to measure up to its forecast top speed, and so a second aircraft with a 550 hp Jupiter was being test flown. Unfortunately, this aircraft collided with another in flight and crashed. This left the CAMS 36 and 38 and one Latham L.1 to form the French team. But there were more difficulties and near-disasters still to come for them. Meanwhile one British entrant was also meeting with misfortune. This was the Blackburn Pellet G-EBHF which had capsized almost immediately after its initial launching, had been repaired, transported to the Hamble but, during its first flight, had proved almost impossibly nose-heavy and suffered overheating of its Napier Lion engine. Following hurried overnight modifications, its pilot, R. W. Kenworthy, nevertheless seemed full of confidence when he began his navigability trials, which, as usual, consisted of taxi-ing over the starting line, taking-off, alighting and further taxi-ing out on the circuit, then taxi-ing over the finish line. Sadly, when a rowing boat moved into the take-off area as the Pellet began to get under way, Kenworthy rammed open the throttle with the result that the aircraft left the water in an exaggerated nose-up attitude, bouncing off the surface several times before finally putting its nose in and turning turtle. Fortunately, its pilot was rescued but the Pellet was beyond repair and was withdrawn.

This left only the Supermarine Sea Lion III, to be flown again by Biard, to sustain Britain's hopes of another Schneider victory. But this was the previous year's winning aeroplane G-EBAH which, having been bought by the Air Ministry after the Naples contest, had been returned to Supermarine, on loan, for extensive modifications to bring it up to an acceptable aerodynamic standard and for the installation of a more powerful 525 hp Napier Lion engine.

An alteration to the contest rules allowed the competing aircraft to start as a team or group within a 15 minute period. This rule was unique to the 1923 contest, as was the start which, because of the prevailing wind on 28 September, the day of the contest, and the requirement for entrants to begin by taxi-ing across the starting line, meant that the aircraft had to

Rutledge Irvine, in shirt sleeves, shares a few words with his CR-3's handling crew before coming ashore after a flight.

take-off in a westerly direction and on a reciprocal course from the first leg of the contest circuit. The US team had drawn first start, and Rittenhouse in A6081 and Irvine flying A6080, got off the water smartly together, before gaining altitude and turning left and right through 180 deg to bring them back onto their first lap. Biard was scheduled to start in the second 15 minute period but his take-off coincided with the unexpectedly early completion of the first lap of the two Curtiss CR-3s. For this reason the starting line judges were unsure whether Biard had executed a correct start by taxi-ing over the line; but he was not to know of this, or of the fact that he had been disqualified, and hurriedly swung round into the first lap in an effort to catch the speeding US aircraft.

As recorded earlier, the French were not finished with their misfortune. When the time came for them to move out to the starting area, the CAMS 36, piloted by Lieut Pelletier d'Oisy, damaged its hull when it hit a moored yacht and was withdrawn from the contest. Lieut de Vaisseau Maurice Hurel, flying the pusher CAMS 38, made a satisfactory start; but the magnetos failed on one of the L.1's Lorraine-Dietrich engines and Jacques Duhamel, its pilot, was forced to scratch it from the contest. Finally, the CAMS 38 came down on its second lap with engine trouble and had to be towed in. The French challenge had collapsed.

Meanwhile, the two CR-3s lapped with monotonous consistency and alarmingly regular increases of their lap speeds, outpacing the Sea Lion III which was itself flying faster than any previous Schneider contest winner. And while this lone British entrant flew on, by now aware that he could not hope to improve on the Curtiss' performance, down below the managing director of Supermarine, Mr J. Bird, was enlisting the help of officials and contest observers in an attempt to get Biard's disqualification set aside. Eventually, after written confirmation that the Sea Lion III had been in contact with the water at the moment it crossed the starting line, the judges agreed to reverse their initial decision. It made little difference to the contest result: Rittenhouse's CR-3 came home in triumph with a final lap speed of 291·34 km/h (181·029 mph) to take first place with an average speed of 285·457 km/h (177·374 mph). Irvine followed him in, averaging 278·97 km/h (173·35 mph), and Biard was third—and last— with a contest average of 252·93 km/h (157·17 mph). That the Sea Lion III with its reliable Napier Lion engine had improved on its previous year's performance by about 12 mph was no consolation to Biard, Supermarine or Great Britain. As the Schneider Trophy went across the Atlantic to the National Aeronautic Association in the United States for the first time, there were many people in Europe who believed that it would remain there for all time.

Irvine and Rittenhouse (*right*) shake hands, a little self-consciously, for the cameras after their 1923 victory.

19

Irvine's CR-3, A6080, sweeps into a turn around the two mark boats at the start and finish line in the 1923 contest.

# Baltimore 1924

If the Americans' pre-Cowes confidence in their aircraft's potentialities had appeared, to European minds, like gross exaggeration, and if their high-powered planning and meticulous attention to detail had smacked of State-aided professionalism, then their clear-cut victory justified both their faith in the aircraft designers and constructors and their awareness that flying high-speed aeroplanes successfully was a co-ordinated effort by men on the ground as well as in the air.

Any remaining unpopularity of the US victory was removed, as will be seen, by a strikingly sporting and generous gesture by the National Aeronautic Association shortly before the 1924 contest was scheduled to take place in Chesapeake Bay, Baltimore, on 24 and 25 October.

In preparation for the defence of the Schneider Trophy, the United States team, aircraft and engine manufacturers, and the Baltimore Flying Club, the organizers of the contest, all set about their tasks with their expected thoroughness. The US Navy arranged for the Curtiss company to convert to a seaplane one of the two specially built R2C-1 landplane racing biplanes powered by Curtiss D-12 engines, which had taken first and second place in the 1923 Pulitzer Trophy race. The winning aircraft, A6692, had been stored since that event in readiness for conversion for the Schneider contest. The two Curtiss CR-3s which had won at Cowes were also prepared for Baltimore, although it was anticipated that only one—probably Rittenhouse's A6081—would compete. A fourth aircraft, a Wright F2W-2 with a 750 hp T-2 engine and developed from the ill-fated NW-2 in which Gorton had crashed the previous year, completed the US group of entries.

20

Gorton had the unnerving experience of being asked to fly the F2W-2 at the Philadelphia Naval Aircraft Factory. After initial taxi-ing trials, during which a larger rudder was fitted to help control the enormous torque of the big T-2 engine, he managed to get airborne. However, the fore-and-aft trim was bad and Gorton decided to alight again. As he did so, steam from a wrongly-positioned vent in an upper-wing radiator hit him in the face, causing him to touchdown at high speed, bounce, and become inverted before plunging back into the water. Fortunately, he was rescued unhurt but his aircraft was a total write-off. Lieuts G. T. Cuddihy and R. A. Ofstie, meanwhile, were flying the two CR-3s and Rittenhouse had averaged 227·49 mph (366·12 km/h) over a measured course in the newly converted Curtiss aircraft which had been redesignated R2C-2.

While the United States worked up to a fine pitch of preparedness, in Europe there was considerable gloom. France had begun it by deciding to pull out some four months before the scheduled date of the contest. There was much conjecture over a possible monoplane entry from the Adolphe Bernard stable but it failed to materialize. Italy, too, was experiencing great difficulties, initially with its engines, and purchased two Curtiss D-12s from the United States for dismantling and study by Fiat. A new seaplane was designed and built for the contest by Cantieri Riuniti Dell'Adriatico (CRDA) but it sank twice during preliminary taxi-ing trials and never got off the water. Piaggio fared no better with its P.c.3 monoplane project—designed to be powered by the second D-12—which was abandoned.

In Britain, while the Royal Aero Club appealed for financial assistance to support a British entry, the Air Ministry gave a £6,000 order for two Gloster II biplane seaplane racers powered by 585 hp Napier Lion VA engines and a second for a Supermarine racing flying-boat. This aeroplane, which was also to have been powered by a 585 hp Napier Lion, featured an unusual propulsion system, having the engine mounted inside the hull with a geared shaft-drive to the propeller. It was too complex, with the threat of power loss through the gears and the shaft length, so it was abandoned early in 1925. The Italians' ill fortune continued and early in September they too withdrew their entry from the contest. The Gloster II manufacture went ahead and the first one (J7504) was delivered to Felixstowe for flight trials by Hubert S. Broad, an experienced seaplane pilot. Unfortunately, at the end of its first flight when it alighted, it began to porpoise, one of the front float struts collapsed and the aircraft capsized and sank. Broad escaped unhurt. The second aircraft (G-EBJZ) was not ready for the contest and Britain had no reserve to fly.

With no foreign competitors, the United States only had to fly round the Baltimore course to claim the Trophy. In a most sporting way, the National Aeronautic Association declared the contest to be cancelled for that year.

21

The primitive nature of the accommodation at Bay Shore Park, Baltimore, in 1925, is well illustrated by this view of the canvas shelters and the wooden track to the slipway. Visible are the Gloster III, Supermarine S.4 and a US Navy Curtiss F6C Hawk. (*RAF Museum*)

# Baltimore 1925

An unusual feature of the 1925 contest, which was to be flown over the same three-legged course within Chesapeake Bay planned for the previous year's cancelled contest, was Great Britain's entry of the 700 hp Napier Lion engined Supermarine S.4 seaplane (N197/G-EBLP) and Italy's Macchi M.33 flying-boat powered by a 435 hp Curtiss D-12A engine. Both aircraft were cantilever monoplanes, the first to break the succession of biplane entrants since the 1914 Monaco appearances of the Deperdussins and Nieuports which had been beaten most convincingly by the biplane Tabloid. Additionally, the S.4 was the first seaplane to be designed by R. J. Mitchell for the Schneider series, all his earlier designs having been flying-boats, and Mario Castoldi had embodied the unusual feature of mounting the engine high above the hull on struts in his design of the M.33.

The Curtiss R3C-2 seaplanes, with 565 hp Curtiss V-1400 engines, chosen to equip the US team, followed the pattern of contemporary Army and Navy pursuit aircraft and were biplanes; so too was Great Britain's other team type, the 700 hp Lion-powered Gloster IIIs (N194—5) designed by Folland.

There was one other important feature of this contest; for the first time the British effort to regain the Trophy was meticulously planned and was

Reginald Mitchell and Henri Biard maintained close contact with the production stages of the S.4. They are seen in the Woolston factory, with the aeroplane nearing completion in the background.

H. P. (Harry) Folland, with his ever-present pipe, and Larry Carter, Gloster's pilot, who had many flying hours in the Gloster I.

Hubert Broad taxies away from the Bay Shore Park slipway at Baltimore in the Gloster IIIA in 1925. (*Flight*)

well supported by the Air Ministry, which provided funds for the purpose. Conversely, the Italian Government's support was limited to lending the Macchi company the two D-12 engines bought a year earlier from Curtiss, leaving Macchi to organize and finance Italy's entry.

During preliminary flight trials before they were shipped to Baltimore, both the S.4, flown by Biard, and the Gloster III, flown by Hubert Broad, experienced problems. The S.4's wing appeared to flutter very slightly during turns, and the Gloster III proved directionally unstable; but Biard

The Supermarine S.4's Lion engine being run at Baltimore in 1925. Note the twin hold-back ropes and the tail hold-down strop. (*Flight*)

24

dismissed the wing 'shiver' as being 'all in the mind' and although increased dihedral on the Gloster III's wings was the preferred solution, lack of time allowed Folland only to increase the area of the dorsal and ventral fins which much improved the stability. The reserve Gloster III was flown only once by Bert Hinkler before the team set out for the United States. The teams arrived at Baltimore to find little done for their reception and appalling weather. Canvas hangars leaked and were almost wrecked in a gale—which caused a support pole to fall and damage the S.4's tailplane—the crew accommodation left much to be desired and Biard fell ill with influenza. However, both he and Broad managed to fly their respective aircraft in spite of the rough weather.

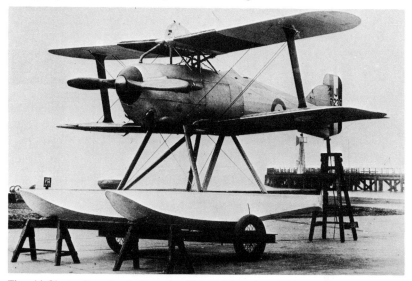

The old Gloster Bamel, rebuilt as the Gloster I floatplane J7234, was used for practice flying by the British team pilots during 1925. It was taken to Baltimore as a reserve or hack aircraft but was not uncrated. It is pictured at Felixstowe with surface radiators and a coolant header tank fitted on the upper centre section.

The US team, Navy Lieuts Cuddihy and Ofstie, Army Lieut J. H. Doolittle, reserve Navy Lieut F. Conant, led by Lieut-Cmdr H. C. Wick, also began trials, as did the Italians, Briganti and Morselli. On 23 October the Italian Giovanni de Briganti in an M.33, Broad in a Gloster III and Ofstie in R3C-2 were followed into the air by Biard in the S.4. It was to be his last flight in the all-white monoplane, but the true reasons for his subsequent crash into the sea are not known. The official report stated that the S.4 had stalled and entered a series of uncontrolled sideslips before hitting the water.

Another report, credited to Biard, clearly indicated that he believed that wing or aileron flutter in a turn had been the primary cause of the accident. A guide to the truth can perhaps be seen in Mitchell's designs for the subsequent S.5 and S.6 seaplanes, both of which employed wire-braced rather than pure cantilever structures for the wing and alighting gear. Had Mitchell, in his quest for speed, ventured into a flight regime about which little was known at that time? It appeared so.

The second Gloster III was hastily readied to fill the gap but when Hinkler alighted in rough water after a trial flight, a float strut fractured, the nose dropped and the propeller chopped into the float, causing the aircraft to be withdrawn. Great Britain's hopes rested on one aircraft; and so did those of Italy when engine trouble forced Riccardo Morselli's M.33 to withdraw.

Fortunately, improved weather conditions on 26 October, the contest day, allowed the five remaining entrants to get airborne without much trouble; first Doolittle, then Broad, Cuddihy, Ofstie and de Briganti in that order. It was soon clear that Doolittle's experience as a test pilot used to withstanding high-g conditions was invaluable, for he flew the R3C-2 fast and made very tight turns, unlike the Navy pilots who took their Curtiss racers wide and lost time. The M.33's 435 hp D-12 engine was simply not powerful enough and it flew steady laps, with tight turns, but without a hope of victory. But speed and engine power were not all that was needed; when the 565 hp V-1400 engines of the two Navy pilots' R3C-2s put them out of the contest—one through mechanical failure and the second through oil loss and a fire—the contest became a procession. In the event, Doolittle's R3C-2 was first with an average speed of 374·274 km/h (232·562 mph), only 4·02 km/h less than his last and fastest lap; the Gloster III, with a fastest lap of 323·95 km/h (201·53 mph) averaged 320·53 km/h (199·167 mph) to take second place, and the M.33 came third averaging 271·08 km/h (168·44 mph). The Schneider Trophy was to remain in the New World for at least another year.

# Hampton Roads 1926

The victories of the United States entrants at Cowes in 1923 and at Baltimore in 1925 had resulted in 1926 being a watershed year in the Schneider Trophy contests. It was then that Britain realized its own design deficiencies when compared with the US industry, and accepted the need for pilots to be trained in the techniques of high-speed flight in landplanes and seaplanes.

Another important feature of the 1926 contest year was that Britain was first to voice the opinion that, with the growing complexity of high-speed seaplane design, the annual nature of the contests gave insufficient time to evolve the special aircraft required. The Royal Aero Club's request to the US National Aeronautic Association that the contest be postponed until 1927 was, naturally enough, refused. The United States needed only one more victory to lay permanent claim to the Trophy. The

Italian request for a postponement met with the same refusal. Similarly, the FAI turned down French and Italian proposals requiring the competing aircraft to carry loads of up to 400 kg (881 lb)—even though Jacques Schneider's original aim had been to encourage the development of seaplanes and flying-boats traversing the world in the interests of commerce.

In Britain, although aviation enthusiasts and the Press tried hard to whip up support for a British entry of one kind or another, and there were persistent rumours of private venture aircraft being built by the Short and Supermarine companies, a new world speed record for seaplanes, an average of 245·71 mph (395·43 km/h) set by Jimmy Doolittle in a Curtiss R3C-2 on 27 October confirmed the enormity, and impossibility, of the task. There would be no British entry. In Italy, however, Il Duce, Benito Mussolini, saw an opportunity to prove that Fascism could achieve the impossible and he issued an edict that, with his government providing the money and all other facilities, Italy must win back the Trophy at all costs.

Arturo Ferrarin in one of the Macchi M.39 trainers. The surface radiators and the very broad-chord tailplane can be seen well. (*Aeronautica Macchi*)

Macchi and Fiat, because of their experience, were charged with building the aircraft and engine. The airframe designed by Mario Castoldi, began to take shape in April 1926. Five M.39 monoplanes were to be built, three for the contest and two for training. The team, led by Commandant the Marchese Vittorio Centurione, was Maj M. de Bernardi, Capt A. Ferrarin and Lieut A. Bacula, with Capt G. Guasconi as reserve. Sadly, Centurione was to lose his life when he stalled a practice M.39 into Lake Varese, the team's base. When Italy asked for a short postponement of the contest—until 11 November—the United States agreed, much to the chagrin of the Royal Aero Club.

27

In the United States it was a wholly Navy team which was to defend the Trophy with the three Curtiss R3C-2s (A6978, A6979 and A7054) from the previous year, two being re-engined. A6979 was powered by a 685 hp Curtiss V-1550 twelve-cylinder water-cooled inline vee engine and designated R3C-4; A6978 had a 650 hp geared Packard Model 2A-1500 of similar configuration installed and was designated R3C-3; A7054, fitted with the older Curtiss V-1400 of 565 hp, became the R3C-2. The reserve aircraft was a Curtiss F6C-3 Hawk biplane fighter mounted on floats and powered by a 520 hp Curtiss D-12 engine. The US Navy pilots were Lieuts G. Cuddihy, F. Conant and W. Tomlinson with Marine Corps Lieut H. Norton—with their aircraft they were a formidable, and confident, combination. But on 13 September Norton stalled while practising in CR-3 (A6081), the 1923 contest winning aircraft, and was killed when it dived into the water. Six weeks later, on 30 October, Conant's aircraft hit an obstruction standing out of the shallow water of Winter Harbor, Anacostia, and he, too, was killed. Replacements were hurriedly sought and a Marine Corps pilot, Lieut C. F. Schilt, succeeded Norton, with Navy Lieut C. Champion coming in as the reserve. Engine trouble with the R3C-4 did nothing to restore the team's confidence which these accidents had shattered.

When the Italian M.39s arrived at Hampton Roads, the contest venue, they, too, had troubles with engines, and when bad weather delayed the customary navigability trials, there was much despondency in both camps. This mounted when trials began on 11 November; de Bernardi had a float holed by the boat detailed to tow him to his moorings for the mooring-out test, and connecting rods in the AS.2 engine in Ferrarin's M.39 failed, wrecking the crankcase. Then, with Champion ill in bed, Tomlinson managed to get airborne in the R3C-3, coping manfully with the unusual opposite-hand rotation of the Packard-driven propeller, but stalled on alighting and ended up inverted in the water. Fortunately, Tomlinson was unhurt and bravely took-off in the Hawk later on to complete the trials.

The 31·06 mile (50 km) course started in Willoughby Bay near to Norfolk Naval Air Station and ran northwest to a pylon in Chesapeake Bay, back to Newport News headland and returning to the start point. The day of the contest, 13 November, was sunny with clear skies and little wind. Both the US and Italian teams were at full strength and Bacula's M.39 was first away on the seven laps of the course, followed by Tomlinson's Hawk. Ferrarin should have been third to start but he feigned starting problems and Cuddihy, in the R3C-4, was waved off—only to have Ferrarin immediately start up and follow the US aircraft into the air where he could cover its movements. De Bernardi and Schilt started in that order.

The Hawk lapped at more than 132 mph (212 km/h) and Bacula's M.39 initially attained only 209·58 mph (337·3 km/h). Cuddihy then put in a 232·42 mph (374·04 km/h) lap which was beaten by some 2 mph on Ferrarin's first lap, before de Bernardi's M.39 shattered these with 239·44 mph (385·34 km/h). But this killing pace was too much for Ferrarin's AS.2 engine and a fractured oil pipe put his aircraft out of contention. Cuddihy's engine was suffering fuel starvation through partial failure of engine and hand pumps, and de Bernardi had increased his altitude to find cooler air for his overheating engine. Entering the last lap either could have won—but fuel starvation hit Cuddihy's R3C-4 first and, for the second successive year, he was beaten on this ultimate lap. De Bernardi risked all, kept the throttle open and came home at a winning average speed of 396·698 km/h (246·496 mph), trailed by Schilt's R3C-2 at 372·34 km/h (231·36 mph), Bacula at 350·84 km/h (218 mph) and, finally, Tomlinson's Hawk at only 220·406 km/h (136·953 mph). Thus the Italian team not only won the Trophy in accordance with Mussolini's orders and had prevented it from becoming the permanent property of the United States but, in so doing, had added new life to the contest series and opened up the possibilities of advancing Europe's knowledge of high-speed flight yet again.

# Venice 1927

In spite of the United States' preference for a biennial contest, Italy and Britain voted for a 1927 contest at a meeting called by the FAI in Paris on 25 January of that year, and this was accepted. With Italy holding the Trophy, the venue was Venice again, with a course of seven laps of 50 km (31·06 miles) each above the inshore waters of the Adriatic from the Porto di Lido in the north to Porto di Chioggia in the south, with the third turning point midway between at Porto di Malanocco. Britain had made an early decision to enter a team through its encouragement in 1925 of the Supermarine, Gloster and Short design teams and by its formation, in October 1926, of an RAF High Speed Flight at Felixstowe—if only in

Capt Arturo Ferrarin flying fast in the Macchi M.52 (No. 7) before he was forced to retire at Venice in 1927. (*Flight*)

embryonic form. The United States Navy announced early in 1927 that it would not contest ownership of the Trophy, while the US Army reserved a decision for a later date. However, the National Aeronautic Association made a provisional entry, and before the final acceptance date there was a private-venture entry by US Navy Lieut A. J. Williams of his Kirkham-Williams biplane racer built with his own money and that of countless individuals, who also donated time and equipment to create a potential Trophy winner. There was little likelihood that France would be able to provide a contender, but in Italy, the host nation, work was pressed ahead to refine the design of the victorious Macchi M.39 and to extract even more power from Fiat's AS.2 engine. Designated M.52, it was expected that these modifications to airframe and power unit would give this aircraft a maximum speed of more than 485 km/h (301·36 mph). At Felixstowe the one full-time member of the High Speed Flight, Flt Lieut O. E. Worsley, was joined by Flt Lieut S. N. Webster and Flg Off H. M. Schofield; all under the command of Sqn Ldr L. J. Slatter. They were eager to fly the new aircraft which were being prepared for them. These were three Supermarine S.5s (N219, N220 and N221) designed by R. J. Mitchell, three of H. P. Folland's Gloster IVs (N222, N223 and N224), and the Short-Bristow Crusader (N226) designed by W. G. Carter. This was the largest number of aircraft ever built for a single contest by one nation and reflected the importance Britain placed on regaining the Trophy. A fourth type, designed by S. E. Saunders and P. Beadle remained a drawing-board project.

The Crusader, powered by a 650 hp Bristol Mercury nine-cylinder air-cooled radial engine, and nicknamed *Curious Ada* by the High Speed Flight pilots, was first to arrive at Felixstowe, in late April, but, much to

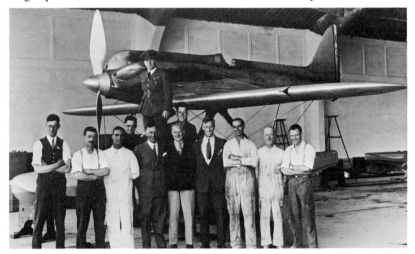

S. N. Webster and R. J. Mitchell (centre) with the S.5 and the Supermarine team in the hangar at San Andrea. (*Flight*)

The British contingent at San Andrea Naval Air Station, during the 1927 contest. Backed by the Gloster IVB and Supermarine S.5, seated are (*left to right*) L. E. Coombes, Capt Forsyth (Air Ministry), Flt Lieuts H. M. Schofield and S. M. Kinkead, Wing Cdr Fletcher, Flt Lieut O. E. Worsley, Air Vice-Marshal F. R. Scarlett (team commander), Flt Lieut S. N. Webster, Sqn Ldr L. S. Slatter (team leader), Flg Off T. H. Moon (engineering officer), Maj Buchanan (Air Ministry), Messrs L. Ransome (AID) and Reason; standing centre second row are Mr Scott, Sir Harry Brittain (Director of D. Napier), H. T. Vane (Managing Director of D. Napier), H. P. Folland (Chief Designer, Gloster Aircraft), R. J. Mitchell (Chief Designer, Supermarine Aviation), Sir James Bird (Managing Director of Supermarine Aviation), Mr J. Smith. Standing second row, fifth and eighth from left are J. B. Johnstone (Gloster experimental department), and Basil Fielding (Gloster inspector) who provided material used in this book.

the pilot's chagrin, Bert Hinkler arrived to make the first test flight. After some increase in rudder size at his insistence, he took off in this unusual looking aeroplane to average 232 mph (373 km/h) over a measured mile. Unfortunately, when alighting, the Crusader's port float dug into the water and the support struts were bent. These were repaired but on subsequent flights intermittent cutting out by the Mercury engine gave the pilots a rough ride, and this problem was not cured before the Crusader was shipped to Venice in August with an S.5 (N219) and the Gloster IVA N222, both of which had had minimal flying. In August, one, possibly two, more S.5s and the Gloster IVB N223 were also despatched to Italy.

By then, it was clear that progress with the Kirkham-Williams racer and its 1,200 hp Packard twenty-four-cylinder inline water-cooled X engine, was failing, and when a US request for a 30-day postponement of the contest was turned down by the Italian organizing committee when Britain objected, Williams withdrew his entry.

In Venice the British team, under the overall command of Air Vice-Marshal F. R. Scarlett, was joined by Flt Lieut S. M. Kinkead and began practice flying in the S.5 and Gloster IVA on 10 September. The following day the Crusader, with the fully-rated 960 hp Mercury engine, was

31

prepared for a test flight with Schofield as pilot. As he taxied out he opened and closed the throttle to check the Mercury's response, and after a sluggish take-off run the Crusader became airborne. Then, when it was about 15 ft (4·5 m) above the water, the port wing dropped. Schofield applied corrective aileron, but this increased the rate of roll, the wingtip hit the water and the Crusader plunged in. Fortunately, the wooden fuselage split open at the cockpit and Schofield was thrown clear, to be rescued by an emergency boat. When the Crusader was salvaged several days later—it had been located by the bubbles rising to the surface as the result of sea water action on the magnesium crankcase—it was discovered that control cables in the aileron circuit had been crossed so that movement of the control surface was the opposite of that expected.

When the Italian's three scarlet M.52s arrived at Venice, Mario Castoldi's design changes were discernible, with the slightly swept wings of reduced span and area, smaller floats and a reduced frontal area fuselage plus a 1,000 hp Fiat AS.3 engine, the most powerful then used in a Schneider contest entrant.

The pilots were Maj M. de Bernardi, the winner of the 1926 contest at Hampton Roads, and Capts F. Guazetti and A. Ferrarin. Opposing them were Worsley in an S.5 with a 900 hp direct-drive Napier Lion VIIA engine, Webster flying another S.5 with an 875 hp geared Lion VIIB, and Kinkead in the Gloster IVB having a similar engine.

Following a 24 hr delay due to bad weather, the contest was declared 'on' for 26 September, and first away was the Gloster IVB. It was followed at five minute intervals by de Bernardi trailing black smoke from his M.52's AS.3 engine, Webster's S.5, Guazetti in the AS.2-powered M.52, and Worsley's S.5. Last off was Ferrarin in the third M.52, but as he crossed the starting line the engine coughed out smoke and flame and Ferrarin was forced to retire almost before he had begun. There was even worse to come for at the start of his second lap, after completing the first at an average of 442·45 km/h (275 mph), de Bernardi

For the later contests in the Schneider series, competing aircraft were towed to the take-off area on special pontoons. Here the Italian officer in charge of the operation signals the towing launch to stop as it carries a Macchi M.52. (*Flight*)

Shirt-sleeved Flt Lieut Sam Kinkead in the Gloster IVA N222 at Venice in 1927.

withdrew when a connecting rod in the AS.3 failed and punched a hole in the crankcase, leaving Guazetti to carry the hopes of the Italian crowd.

Meanwhile, the three British aircraft roared powerfully around the course with its two nearly-180 deg turns, and it was apparent that even if the sole M.52 completed the seven laps, it would be outpaced. The Italian technique of banking vertically and climbing at each turn was causing them to lose speed which was not recovered in the ensuing dive onto the next leg. The steep bank around the pylon during the steady low-level turns of the British team was much more effective. During the fourth and fifth laps, the Gloster IVB began to falter and Kinkead retired in the sixth. Back in its hangar, the propeller was removed to reveal a crack three-quarters of the way round the Lion's splined propeller shaft.

Then Guazetti's M.52 veered off the course at the end of its sixth lap when a fuel line fractured, spraying petrol around and into the cockpit. This left the two S.5s to complete the course, take first and second place and regain the Trophy for Great Britain. This they did, Webster's aircraft averaging 453·282 km/h (281·655 mph) to set a new world speed record for seaplanes, with Worsley's S.5 close behind with an average speed of 439·45 km/h (273·07 mph).

In spite of all the engineering and administrative skills which had brought the Trophy to Great Britain, there appeared to be no foolproof method for the pilots to count the number of laps as they flew them. In each British machine was fitted a board with paper-covered holes, one of which could be pushed out as each lap was completed. Webster had carefully poked his finger through seven holes but had glanced at his watch on the finishing straight and found he had another five minutes to go on the anticipated time for seven laps. To make sure, he flew an eighth lap, fortunately having enough fuel to be able to go around the 50 km course once more.

| SCHNEIDER TROPHY CONTEST | | | | | | | | | |
|---|---|---|---|---|---|---|---|---|---|
| COMPETITORS NUMBER | | COMPLETED LAPS — TIME IN MINUTES & SECONDS, SPEED IN M.P.H. DECIMALS OMITTED | | | | | | | SPEED OF RACE M.P.H. |
| | | 1 | 2 | 3 | 4 | 5 | 6 | 7 | |
| U.S.A. 1 | TIME | | 17·2 | | | | | | |
| GREAT BRITAIN 2 | TIME | 5·45 | 11·25 | | 22·43 | 28·22 | 34·4 | 39·42 | 328 |
| | SPEED | 324 | 329 | 331 | 328 | 330 | 327 | 331 | |
| ITALY 4 | TIME | 6·30 | 13·0 | 19·37 | 26·8 | 32·43 | 39·10 | 45·34 | 294 |
| | SPEED | 286 | 287 | 285 | 283 | 293 | 283 | 282 | |
| GREAT BRITAIN 5 | TIME | 6·34 | 13·10 | 19·47 | 26·24 | 33·2 | 39·39 | 46·13 | 282 |
| | SPEED | 284 | 282 | 282 | 281 | 281 | 281 | 293 | |
| ITALY 7 | TIME | 6·34 | | | | | | | |
| | SPEED | 284 | | | | | | | |
| GREAT BRITAIN 8 | TIME | 6·9 | 11·54 | 17·33 | 23·10 | 28·50 | 34·28 | 40·5 | 325 |
| | SPEED | 302 | 324 | 330 | 332 | 328 | 331 | 332 | |
| ITALY 10 | TIME | 6·11 | | | | | | | |
| | SPEED | 301 | | | | | | | |

Clear evidence that this great adventure in the air was not a race! An official lap speed and time board set up on Ryde Pier, Isle of Wight, for the 1929 contest. (*Flight*)

# Calshot 1929

At a meeting of the FAI in Paris on 5 January, 1928, the need for a biennial contest was discussed and unanimously agreed by all the participating nations. With growing emphasis on engines of increased power, aerodynamic refinement, and advanced structural techniques and materials, one year between contests was insufficient to enable research and development programmes to be carried through properly. Thus the rules were amended to read 'The winner to be the country which shall have gained three victories out of five successive contests, the contests to be held every two years.' In this context the term 'winner' can be interpreted as becoming the permanent holder of the Trophy.

The meeting was historic in that it was the last at which Jacques Schneider was present. He had attended to offer his congratulations to the Royal Aero Club representative on Britain's victory at Venice in 1927. Schneider died on 1 May, 1928, at Beaulieu-sur-Mer near Nice. He would never know that his aims of promoting the design and creation of fast, reliable, passenger-carrying flying-boats would be met only in part; that the development and use of floatplanes would be comparatively limited; or that, as far as Great Britain would be concerned, its Trophy-winning airframes and aero-engines would be of such ultimate military importance. That was all in the future. But before that meeting, a curious situation had arisen in Britain in which the expected refusal of the

Treasury to fund the British entry in the 1929 contest did not materialize; instead, it was the Air Council which raised objections to RAF participation again, offering merely to loan whatever high-speed aircraft were available. It was not until 25 February, 1928, that, with full Government backing assured, the Air Ministry settled to the task of organizing British participation to ensure another victory.

The RAF High Speed Flight was re-formed having been disbanded soon after the 1927 contest victory. It was to suffer its first loss on 12 March, 1928, when Flt Lieut Kinkead was killed in the S.5 N221 while attempting to establish a new world speed record at Calshot. Impatient after a long period of bad weather, Kinkead took off in misty conditions with a glassy calm on the water and no horizon visible. The S.5 climbed, turned into its approach dive towards the measured mile and never pulled out. Kinkead's replacement was Flt Lieut D. D'Arcy A. Greig.

Meanwhile, in Italy, Mario Castoldi had refined the design of the Macchi M.52 powered by a reworked and more reliable Fiat AS.3 engine. With the designation M.52R or M.52bis, Maj de Bernardi set a new world speed record of 512·69 km/h (318·57 mph). This was exceeded by D'Arcy Greig in the S.5 N220 on 4 November when he averaged 514·308 km/h (319·57 mph). It was a British record but was not a sufficiently large increase over the M.52R's speed to be homologated as a world record.

A new team of High Speed Flight pilots was named in January 1929. They were commanded by Sqn Ldr A. H. Orlebar, and, in addition to D'Arcy Greig, were Flt Lieut G. H. Stainforth, Flg Offs R. L. R. Atcherley, H. R. D. Waghorn and T. H. Moon, the latter being Engineer Officer.

Royal interest in the Schneider Trophy. HRH The Prince of Wales with the 1929 British team at Calshot. Left to right are Flg Off H. R. Waghorn, Flt Lieut G. H. Stainforth, Sqn Ldr A. H. Orlebar, His Royal Highness, Flt Lieut D. D'Arcy A. Greig, Flg Off R. L. R. Atcherley, an unidentified Wing Commander, Flg Off T. H. Moon, and an un-identified civilian. Behind is the Gloster IVA practice aircraft N222. (*Flight*)

Pilots of the 1929 Italian team with a Macchi M.52R. Pictured (*left to right*) are Capt A Canaveri, Lt-Col M. Bernasconi (team commander), Lieut R. Cadringher, Lieut G. Monti and Sgt Maj F. Agello. Warrant Off T. Dal Molin is not in the group. (*RAF Museum*)

The Gloster and Supermarine companies, meanwhile, were designing and building new contest aircraft. Folland had finally abandoned the biplane configuration, though not from choice, and created the beautiful Gloster VI racing monoplanes (N249 and N250). Mitchell at Supermarine was concentrating on producing basically an enlarged version of the S.5 but of low weight. Designated S.6, it was to be powered by the new 1,900 hp Rolls-Royce R twelve-cylinder liquid-cooled inline vee engine. Folland had stayed with the latest Napier Lion VIID promising 1,320 hp.

In Italy Gen Balbo, recognizing the opportunity for technical advances which participation in the contest offered, established a high-speed flying school at Desenzano on Lake Garda to study not only flying techniques but every aspect of high-speed flight. So thorough was the research that the 1929 contest course was reproduced on the lake for practice flying.

In addition, four aircraft manufacturers were instructed to produce new designs of racing seaplanes. They could not have differed more widely. The three Macchi M.67s (103, 104 and 105) of mixed wood and metal construction, with 1,800 hp Isotta-Fraschini direct-drive eighteen-cylinder inline liquid-cooled broad-arrow engines, seemed quite orthodox with unswept symmetrical wings. The tiny Fiat C.29s (129 and 130) had all-metal structures and, as powered by the 1,000 hp Fiat AS.5 engine, the world's best power/weight ratio. Most distinctive and revolutionary were the Savoia Marchetti S.65 and the Piaggio-Pegna P.c.7 (127). The pilot of the S.65 sat in a central nacelle between two 1,000 hp Isotta-Fraschini engines mounted in tandem. The tail unit was carried on twin booms braced to the rear of the very long floats. Most revolutionary was Ing Pegna's design which dispensed with the traditional heavy drag-producing floats. Instead, the fuselage and elliptical plan form wing were made watertight so that the aircraft could float, with hydrofoils to provide lift in the water. An 850 hp Isotta-Fraschini engine drove through clutch and shaft mechanisms either a metal two-blade variable-pitch water propeller or a two-blade tractor propeller for conventional flight. Change-over from the water propeller to the airscrew was to be effected through this mechanism when the fuselage had risen high enough on its hydrofoils to provide sufficient propeller clearance.

Government support for an entry was not forthcoming in the United States and it was left to Lieut Al Williams to drum up private backing for his attempt to regain the Trophy. However, his mid-wing monoplane developed from the Kirkham biplane of 1927 was designed by the Navy Department and built in the Naval Aircraft Factory at Philadelphia, using the same Packard engine from the earlier design. Mercury Flying Corporation was formed by a group of flying enthusiasts to provide the necessary funds. But money alone was not enough, and on test, Williams was unable to get the overweight Mercury racer off the water. When he finally managed a short flight of a few hundred yards, the Packard engine overheated and lost power and he was soon back on the water. A new engine developing some 1,500 hp was prepared and Williams made plans to install it during the sea journey to Britain, but the Navy Department refused further support of the venture and refused to allow Williams to compete.

Although France had not entered a Schneider Trophy contest since 1923, the French Government believed that the time was ripe for a new attempt to be made. Accordingly, in the spring of 1928, the Ministry for Marine ordered two racing seaplanes from Société des Avions Bernard and two from Société Anonyme Nieuport-Delage. From Bernard came the H.V.40 and H.V.42 mid-wing monoplanes, the H.V. meaning Haute Vitesse (high speed). Power for the H.V.40 was reported to come from a new 550 hp Gnome-Rhône Mistral nine-cylinder air-cooled radial engine but its very low output made this unlikely. More credible was the 800 hp Mistral Major eighteen-cylinder radial, but even this was not in the power range of contemporary contest entrants. The H.V.42 was to be fitted with a new 1,680 hp Hispano-Suiza 18R eighteen-cylinder water-cooled broad-arrow engine of complex design and temperamental performance.

Nieuport-Delage produced a pair of low-wing monoplanes of clean design but with floats longer than the fuselage. The engine chosen was the Hispano-Suiza 18R but long delays in its development and that of the Mistral Major ruled out a French presence in the 1929 contest. Italy, too, had problems with the unorthodox S.65 and P.c.7 aircraft. Engine and airframe snags hit the former aircraft and the impossibility of providing an efficient drive to the P.c.7's water propeller to get the aircraft under way made them both non-starters. The Italian team, led by Lieut-Col

M. Bernasconi, comprised Lieuts R. Cadringher and G. Monti, Warrant Officer T. Dal Molin and Sgt Maj F. Agello. The last named was lucky to escape serious injury when his Fiat C.29 caught fire in the air and then, on a later flight, stalled and crashed into Lake Garda. Sadly, on 22 August, 1929, Capt G. Motta was killed in an M.67 which also plunged into the lake after a high-speed low-level run. As a result of these accidents, Italy asked for a postponement of the contest but this was refused by the Royal Aero Club, a decision supported by the FAI.

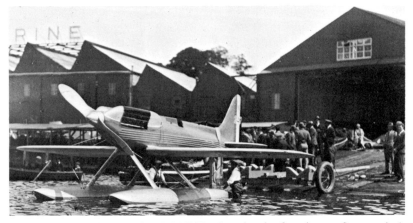

The 1929 winner, Supermarine S.6 N247, afloat for the first time at Supermarine's Woolston works.

When the British pilots received the first S.6 (N247) at Calshot, their initial enthusiasm was short-lived for Orlebar found the port float digging in on take-off and causing the aircraft to progress in semi-circles. Emptying the port float fuel tank helped a bit but it was not until the surface water began to ripple in a light air that the S.6 would unstick and get airborne. Other small snags which appeared were quite quickly cured, even an engine overheating problem was cured by adding radiators on the float top surfaces. The Gloster VI (N249), too, had engine problems stemming mainly from fuel starvation which caused the Lion to cut out, especially on turns. This fault continued to plague the Golden Arrow, as this aircraft was named, and it was withdrawn. This left only two S.6s to defend Britain's still temporary ownership of the Trophy and so S.5 (N219) was prepared for the contest.

No less than six aircraft accompanied the Italian pilots when they arrived at Calshot; two M.67s, the speed-record-holding M.52R, an M.52 practice aircraft, the second C.29, and the S.65—warts and all. Monti flew in an M.67 on 4 September and had a generally successful handling flight but Dal Molin hit a floating object as he was taking-off in the M.52R and holed a float. The following day, in glassy calm conditions, all the British and Italian aircraft satisfactorily completed their navigability and six-hour mooring-out tests, even though one S.6 (N248) began to take water in one float before it was finally beached for repairs. Then, during a final check of the Rolls-Royce engine in Waghorn's S.6 (N247) a mechanic spotted a small speck of metal on a sparking plug as he was removing it from the cylinder head. He took it to Flg Off Moon, the Engineer Officer, who called A. C. Lovesey, a senior experimental engineer at Rolls-Royce. He decided that the piston was picking up and that the remedies were either a complete engine change or a change of cylinder block. The rules precluded a change of engine once it was installed for the contest, but the Royal Aero Club contest committee agreed that components could be changed.

Fortunately, several hundred Rolls-Royce employees, who had built and tested the engines, had come down from Derby to watch the contest and were spread all over Southampton in pubs and hotels. It took time to track down those with the specialist skill required to change the cylinder block concerned, but, eventually, a team was gathered with Lovesey in charge. They worked through the night, removed the block, changed the offending piston, replaced the block and had had an engine run by 8 a.m. the following day.

The contest day, 7 September, was perfect for the occasion; sunny, blue sky, excellent visibility and a light breeze. The quadrilateral course laid out had the starting and finishing line off Ryde Pier, with the first turn pylon off Seaview. The next leg led to a destroyer-mounted pylon some four miles south of Hayling Island and thence to Southsea Pier, and on, westward, to another destroyer off Cowes where an acute 150 deg turn put the aircraft back on a long run to Ryde. First off its pontoon was the S.6 (N247) flown by Waghorn who made a skilful take-off, first tacking out of wind to counteract the swing to port caused by the float digging in as a result of propeller torque, then ruddering into wind as the floats began to lift and run on top of the water. His initial flight path to the first turn was somewhat erratic, as he was at first unable to pick out the destroyer carrying the pylon. However, Waghorn soon settled on course, making impeccable steeply banked turns to complete the first lap at a speed of 521 km/h (324 mph), slower than anticipated, but the next was better at 529 km/h (329 mph), with the third at 532 km/h (331 mph) being the fastest of all.

While N247 was breaking record after record, the first Italian aircraft, the M.52R flown by Dal Molin, got airborne. With two aircraft out on the course, excitement mounted, particularly when it was seen that the S.6 was overhauling the M.52R, passing the Italian as it completed its first lap. Dal Molin's lap speed of 460 km/h (286 mph) was far too slow to worry the British team.

Third away was the S.5 (N219) flown by D'Arcy Greig who, although going flat out, could record only 456 km/h (284 mph) on his first lap. Meanwhile, Waghorn had pushed out the sixth of the paper-covered holes in his lap-counter and was on course for the first turn of his last

D'Arcy Grieg in the S.5 N219 (No. 5) en route to the 1929 finishing line off Ryde. (*Flight*)

lap—when N247's engine began to falter and although he throttled back, it continued to misfire. Somehow, he managed to climb to some 800 ft (245 m) hoping he could glide to the finishing line if the engine cut out completely; it did so as he turned onto the final leg and forced him to alight off Old Castle Point. His utter disappointment at this failure to finish the course and self-criticism for possibly over-taxing the engine left him drained of strength—until a motor launch came alongside to take N247 in tow, with a wildly enthusiastic crew aboard. Apparently, Waghorn, like Webster at Venice, had miscounted the completed laps and had run out of fuel on the extra lap.

In the air there was a running battle between the old warriors, the S.5 and the M.52R, with both still going at full throttle in case the S.6 had failed to finish. But the main Italian challenge to Waghorn's speed came when the first M.67 got airborne flown by Cadringher. However, it did not last long. The cockpit began to fill with exhaust fumes on each left-hand turn and the Isotta-Fraschini engine had had its maximum revolutions reduced by some 400 rpm to prevent failure. Thus Cadringher, half choked and blinded by the fumes and unable even to overtake Dal Molin in the elderly M.52R, decided to alight out on his second lap.

Atcherley, in S.6 N248 also had vision problems caused when he pushed up his goggles after they became obscured with dirty sea water, and lost them in the slipstream. Unable to put his spare pair into position, he crouched down in the cockpit and decided to fly on. With little outside vision, it was not surprising that he turned inside the first pylon and was disqualified.

Last hope for Italy was the second M.67 flown by Monti. He made a good take-off and appeared to be flying very fast, just ahead of Atcherley, but only a few feet above the water. Both were making good turns and it seemed possible that both could do better than Waghorn, but Monti was suffering the effects of exhaust fumes in the cockpit. Then as he began his second lap, a joint in the engine cooling system failed and he was badly scalded when steam and boiling water sprayed over his leg and arm. He was fortunate, and skilful enough, to be able to put down the M.67 safely, leaving Waghorn's average speed of 528·879 km/h (328·629 mph) to take the Trophy for Great Britain. Dal Molin in the M.52R, was second averaging 457·38 km/h (284·2 mph), with Grieg's S.6 third averaging 454·02 km/h (282·11 mph).

Warrant Officer Tomaso Dal Molin roars overhead in the Macchi M.52R (No. 4) leaving a smoke trail from his Fiat AS.3 engine during the 1929 contest. (*Flight*)

With two consecutive British victories, the 1931 contest would be crucial to the future of the entire Schneider Trophy series. There was little doubt that Italy was not a spent force. It was underlined at the celebratory dinner when Gen Balbo, Italy's Air Minister, said, 'We have obtained the results we expected, but we have now finished playing our part as sportsmen. Tomorrow our work as competitors will begin.' Prime Minister Ramsay MacDonald showed that Britain, too, was intending to hold the Trophy for all time when he said, 'We are going to do our level best to win again.' The stage had thus been set for two years' tremendous effort by any participating country, with the promise of great things to come at the end of them.

41

The three Supermarine aircraft which were prepared for the 1931 contest and the attempts on the world speed record. Right to left they are Boothman's Trophy-winning S.6B S1595 (No. 1), its back-up S.6A N248 (No. 4) and Stainforth's first speed record S.6B S1596 (No. 7). Their pilots are ranged in front of the aircraft seen here by the Calshot tower, a renowned landmark. (*Flight*)

# Calshot 1931

It was only three days after Great Britain's victory in the 1929 contest that Marshal of the Royal Air Force Sir Hugh Trenchard reiterated his long opposition to RAF involvement with Britain's efforts to win and to retain the Schneider Trophy. 'I am against this contest,' he wrote in a minute to the Secretary of State for Air. 'I can see nothing of value in it.' He went on to express his belief that high-speed aircraft would continue to be developed without the vast expenditure of time, money, and effort, which was required to create the Schneider Trophy aircraft. This hardly squared with his support for RAF participation in the 1927 contest, but clearly the cost of the venture was becoming too great to contemplate continuance of Service support.

Following Ramsay MacDonald's pronouncement at the celebratory dinner, it came as a great shock to the British public to read in the daily papers that the Cabinet had decided at its 25 September, 1929, meeting not to enter an RAF team in the 1931 contest, leaving private enterprise to provide the money for this venture—reckoned to be about £80,000—and to undertake the organization and running of the event.

Throughout the following year a major political battle was fought on the floor of the House where there was a paradoxical situation of the Conservative Opposition constantly taunting the Socialist Government on its reliance on private enterprise while urging State intervention and participation in the contest. The aviation and national press joined in, but the Government was adamant. The RAF had learned all that it required about high-speed flight during the 1927 and 1929 contests and further expenditure of public money could not be countenanced. A parallel battle was being waged between the Royal Aero Club and its French and Italian counterparts over the amount of the entry deposit, the closing date for entries, and the substitution of the lengthy navigability tests by a take-off and alighting test with full fuel load. In January the FAI approved Britain's proposal of a 200,000 francs deposit to discourage frivolous entries but in June changed this to only 5,000. This prompted three entries each by France and Italy, which Britain returned as unacceptable. In November the FAI confirmed the higher entry deposit and the final entry date as 31 December, a ruling acceptable to all parties.

The French and Italian entries, both Government-sponsored, prompted the Royal Aero Club to ask the British Government to reverse its earlier decision, but the answer, given on 15 January, 1931, was unchanged; except that it spelled out in some detail all the things the Government would not do to defend British title to the Schneider Trophy. One of them was that these would apply even if all the money was raised privately. Yet, on 27 January, Ramsay MacDonald received a deputation of five Members of Parliament and Sir Philip Sassoon, Royal Aero Club Chairman; he agreed to reconsider the Government decision and promised to make a statement in the House three days later. Before he could do so, any doubts over the private financing of the British entry were virtually removed by his receipt of a telegram from Lady Lucy Houston, reputed to be the richest woman in Britain following the death of her wealthy ship-owner husband, Sir Robert Houston, some five years earlier. Approached by a friend, Col the Master of Sempill, who had been President of the Royal Aeronautical Society since 1927 and a renowned practising aviator and aviation adviser, Lady Houston had agreed to provide the money to ensure that Great Britain could enter the 1931 contest. The Prime Minister's statement of 29 January, coloured no doubt by the opinion that 'Britain ought to take part in the contest' voiced by the new Chief of the Air Staff, Air Chief Marshal Sir John Salmond, confirmed the Government's antipathy to the whole idea of rival government teams locked in competitive flying. However, the Government was prepared to authorize the RAF to defend the Schneider Trophy provided that the necessary funds be made available from private sources.

Because of the series of delays by almost everyone concerned except the aircraft and engine manufacturers, there were only nine months remaining before the contest in which to develop a new aircraft and engine. The task had been under consideration for some months and informal discussions had taken place between representatives of the Vickers-Supermarine and Rolls-Royce companies. At a special conference with the Air Ministry on the last day of January 1931, Rolls-Royce managing director A. F. Sidgreaves undertook to increase the power of the R engine by not less than 400 hp, bringing it up to 2,300 hp at 3,200 rpm.

Vickers-Supermarine's task was to be limited to refining the S.6 design to use the additional engine power and to meet the new contest regulations requiring a fully loaded take-off and alighting immediately before the start. Two new aircraft were ordered, designated S.6B, and the two 1929 S.6s were to be brought up to the same standard and redesignated S.6A. The main changes were in the engine-associated oil, fuel, and coolant systems, to provide greater capacities to meet increased consumption and the need for greater heat dissipation, in the floats to provide improved water handling and reduced drag in the air, and in the control system to provide improved handling characteristics at the higher speeds envisaged. Fuselage stiffening was a structural modification embodied in the older S.6s.

Rolls-Royce was faced with a similar series of design changes to increase the power of the R engine but reduce the specific fuel and oil consumption to limit the load for the two take-offs and the near full-load alighting test. Testing went on from April until 12 August when the engine delivered the required power output for a full hour.

While Orlebar and Stainforth had remained with the Flight after the 1929 victory, the remainder had dispersed to other squadron tasks. Newcomers were Flt Lieuts F. W. Long and E. J. L. Hope, and when Stainforth moved on, Flt Lieut J. N. Boothman replaced him. The decision to enter the 1931 contest brought additional members; Stainforth rejoined the team with Flg Off L. S. Snaith, and Fleet Air Arm Lieut R. L. Brinton, plus Flt Lieut W. F. Day as Engineer Officer. When practice flying began with the first S.6A (N247), on its first flight Orlebar experienced severe rudder flutter when travelling at about 350 mph (563 km/h). He throttled back until just below 200 mph (322 km/h), the vibrations stopped and he alighted safely. N247 was returned to the factory for repair and the fitting of horn balances on the rudder and ailerons. These modifications were embodied in all four aircraft. The second S.6A with the uprated engine (N248) had several minor snags on early flights but, with these cleared, Hope got airborne in it on 3 July, only to have an engine cowling panel blow loose and he decided to alight. Unfortunately, N248 hit a bad swell from a passing ship as it alighted, was thrown into the air, the port wingtip dug into the water and the aircraft cartwheeled, remaining afloat long enough to support Hope, who was

The 1931 British Schneider team. Left to right are Flt Lieut W. Dry, Sqn Ldr A. H. Orlebar, Flt Lieuts J. N. Boothman and G. H. Stainforth, Flg Off L. S. Snaith, Lieut G. L. Brinton, RN, and Flt Lieut E. J. L. Hope.

rescued, and then sank. Three days later it was salvaged and returned to the factory for extensive rebuilding.

Swing on take-off had long been a problem with the higher-powered seaplanes and only lengthy trials and analysis of results led to the use of larger-diameter propellers.

The Flight suffered its second fatality when Brinton, who had temporarily rejoined his squadron before being posted back to Calshot, badly bounced N247 on take-off when, apparently, he eased the control column forward instead of holding it back while flying speed increased. Leaping nearly 30 ft into the air, N247 dived, nose down, to the sea bed, breaking Brinton's neck on impact with the water.

Other practice flights decided the best turning techniques to be adopted, solved various water and flying handling characteristics, and helped to iron out engine snags.

In Italy, Macchi and Fiat, the two most experienced and successful Schneider contest airframe and engine manufacturers, were working on a refinement of the Macchi M.67 but with a completely new engine concept. This was the AS.6, virtually two 1,500 hp twelve-cylinder inline water-cooled vee engines, bolted back to back, driving two counter-rotating adjustable-pitch two-blade propellers through two co-axial shafts. The new aircraft, designated Macchi-Castoldi MC.72, was all metal with the exception of the wooden tail unit, and promised to be very fast indeed with its long slender fuselage with small frontal area, and its big 2,500 hp engine and the hoped-for advantages of the counter-rotating

45

propeller installation. These were the elimination of torque problems which could allow smaller volume floats to be used and provide improved thrust from smaller-diameter propellers.

The high-speed training unit at Desenzano on Lake Garda received the pilots nominated for the contest. Led by Col M. Bernasconi, they were Capt G. Monti and Warrant Officer F. Agello, all three veterans of the 1929 meeting, with Lieuts S. Bellini, A. Neri and P. Scapinelli.

In June 1931 the first of the MC.72s (probably 177) arrived at the unit and was flown for the first time by Monti. The take-off without the usual torque problems was easy, but when the throttle was pushed open the engine began misfiring with quite violent backfiring, due to a carburettor malfunction which threatened to wreck it. In spite of this, the MC.72 was timed at speeds around 604 km/h (375 mph) showing its contest-winning potential when this fault could be cured. On 2 August, Monti made a low run across the Desenzano engineering area soon after getting airborne, so that the engineers on the ground could hear an especially bad spell of irregular firing of the AS.6 engine. Then, as they listened and watched, the nose of the MC.72 pitched up, then dropped, the aircraft spun through a quarter of a turn and dived straight into the lake. The official findings of an Italian Air Force investigating board was that the counter-rotating propellers had touched, following failure of a bearing. This tragic accident sparked off rumours of an Italian withdrawal from the contest, but, with the arrival of the second MC.72, practice flying continued and, with a third aircraft still being prepared, the rumours were denied.

While great advances had been made in the design of high-speed aircraft by Italy, the United States, and Great Britain in their efforts to win the Schneider Trophy, and their aircraft had established many new records, no French entrant had completed more than one and a half laps in a contest since 1914 at Monaco when Pierre Levasseur, in a Nieuport, completed 17 laps before retiring. Thus, when France planned an attempt to wrest the Trophy from Great Britain in 1931, there was a great gap in that country's experience of designing, building and flying high-speed seaplanes. The Bernard and Nieuport-Delage aircraft built for the 1929 contest, even had they been developed in time to compete at Calshot, were not remarkable for their good design or engineering, and were not comparable with the Supermarine, Gloster or Macchi aircraft. Neverthe-less, early in 1930, orders for new seaplanes were placed by the French Air Ministry with the Bernard and Nieuport-Delage companies and the Société Aéronautique Française. The engines to be developed for these aircraft were to be the 2,200 hp Lorraine Radium twelve-cylinder inline water-cooled inverted vee engine, and a Renault twelve-cylinder inline liquid-cooled vee unit of between 1,500 and 2,000 hp. Testing of the Hispano-Suiza engined aircraft intended for the 1929 contest would continue, and these would be used for practice flying when ready. One of them, the Nieuport-Delage ND.450, crashed when alighting on the Seine in Paris while being returned to the factory for modifications following initial flight on Lake Hourtin by Sadi Lecointe. The pilot, Fernand Lasne, was not seriously injured but the aircraft was badly damaged.

A team of French pilots assembled at Étang de Berre near Marseilles to begin practice flying. Commanded by Capt J. Amanrich, a renowned naval pilot, they were Capts M. Vernhol, and Marty, Lieut Bougault, Adjutants Doerner and Raynaud, Sgt Maj Baillet, and Sgts Dumas, Goussin and Labreveux.

Just a few of the hundreds of thousands of people who thronged the Solent coastlines to watch the 1931 contest. This picture shows a section of the beach at Southsea as Boothman banks his S.6B during a preliminary check of the course.

A more serious loss was experienced when Lieut Bougault crashed while flying a Bernard H.V.120 practice aircraft. The cause was not definitely established, opinion varying between propeller disintegration and a blown out sparking plug smashing through the windscreen and killing Bougault.

From the United States some earlier encouraging news about a private venture entry by Al Williams was short-lived when it was learned that the enterprise had failed. It seemed that the pace of development of aircraft to oppose the Vickers-Supermarine S.6As and S.6Bs at Calshot was slackening as time ran out. On 3 September, 1931, there was a request from France and Italy, made jointly to the Royal Aero Club, for at least a six months' postponement of the contest. The reply was made without hesitation. The rules allowed only for postponement on a day to day basis. When the French proposed an appeal to the FAI, the Royal Aero

Club pointed out that if it approached the Fédération, it would be tantamount to admitting that Great Britain, too, could not meet the contest date set for 12 September; while adding that the British public would be greatly disappointed if the French and Italian aircraft did not come to the starting line. The following day, in an effort to persuade the two challengers not to withdraw from the contest, the Royal Aero Club announced that even if there was no opposition, the British team would complete its planned programme and fly over the course. In a final brave gesture, the names of the French and Italian teams were handed in later on in the day; but on 5 September official confirmation was received that neither would compete at Calshot.

Tragedy left its mark on the Italian team yet again two days before the contest when, in an attempt on the world speed record, Bellini was killed in the second MC.72 after flying into rising ground at the completion of a very fast low-level run across Lake Garda near the Desenzano training base. It was, perhaps, the bitterest moment for Italy.

The course laid out for the 1931 contest reverted to the three-leg triangular pattern but with the same starting and finishing line off Ryde Pier on the Isle of Wight. The first leg ran down to a position off St Helen's Point marked with a destroyer-mounted pylon, with the second leg terminating at a pylon on West Wittering shore on the mainland. The long third leg led westward along the coast to another pylon on a destroyer anchored off East Cowes where a second acute 140 deg turn brought the aircraft onto the final run down to Ryde Pier.

While the event turned out to be a 'no contest', nevertheless, it was of considerable interest to the general public; there were, too, many plans to be discussed and tactics to be decided by the British team to ensure that it did not result in a fiasco through unopposed failure. All three aircraft were serviceable and it was announced that the first S.6B (S1595) should fly the course in an attempt to improve on the 1929 contest record and the 100 kilometre record. If it failed, then the S.6A (N248) would try, with the second S.6B (S1596) readied for a third attempt if required. Because of public interest, and a decision not to turn the contest into a race between the three British aircraft, it was agreed that if either of the first two aircraft captured the Trophy, then, as an added spectacle, S1596 would make an attempt on the world speed record.

Stainforth, as senior pilot in the team, chose to have a go at the world record, with the other three pilots allocated to the various tasks and aircraft in order of Service seniority; thus Boothman would fly S1595, Long would take N248 and Snaith S1596.

Bad weather on 12 September, the contest day, caused a 24-hr postponement, but the 13th was perfect and vast crowds packed the Hampshire coast and the Isle of Wight vantage points. S1595 was launched from its pontoon a few minutes after 1 p.m. and Boothman began his take-off in the heavily loaded aircraft. Once airborne, he checked the handling and then prepared to make the mandatory alighting and the two minutes

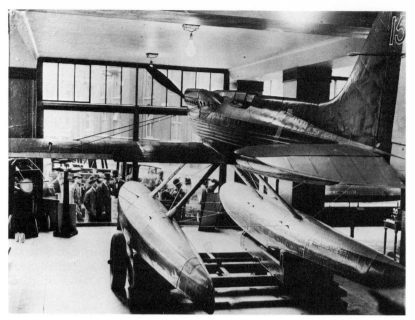

After the 1931 contest. The winning aircraft on show in Vickers House, Broadway, Westminster. This photograph shows well the aileron and rudder mass balances, and the 'well-lived in' external appearance of the aircraft after its arduous programme of high-speed flying. (*Vickers Ltd*)

period afloat before, once again, taking-off to begin the course fly-over. Everything was going well and Boothman kept the throttle wide open but watched his engine temperature gauge very carefully. The first lap speed was 553 km/h (344 mph), lower than hoped for but enough to secure the Trophy. On the second lap, as the engine temperature began to rise, Boothman throttled back and his lap speeds began to fall, the second being completed at 550 km/h (342 mph), the third at 547 km/h (340 mph) and the remaining three at a slightly slower speed. The seventh and final lap was flown at 542 km/h (337 mph) to record an overall average speed of 547·297 km/h (340·08 mph). Jacques Schneider's Coupe d'Aviation Maritime was to be held by Great Britain for all time.

At 4 p.m. Stainforth took off in S1596 and, making four perfect high-speed runs over a three-kilometre course off Lee-on-Solent, established a new world record with an average speed of 610·02 km/h (379·05 mph).

# The Participating Aircraft

## Deperdussin

The winning aircraft of the first Schneider Trophy contest appears to have had no designation other than the name of the man who—ostensibly—paid for its design and construction. It was Armand Deperdussin, a French silk broker who, in 1909 had, first, given financial support to Louis Béchereau, a young design engineer obsessed with the idea of speed, and then, a year later, acquired the company which Béchereau had helped to found and changed its name to Société pour les Appareils Deperdussin or SPAD. The address of the company, prophetically, was 19 rue des Entrepreneurs, Paris. A flying school also was established at Courey-Bétheny (Marne). This was not the SPAD company which created many outstanding First World War aircraft. Thus the aeroplane flown to victory on 16 April, 1913, at Monaco was designated simply Deperdussin.

Louis Béchereau, who designed the Deperdussin racing land monoplane in 1912, had earlier studied the designs of Louis Blériot and Edouard de Nieport. He believed that he could improve on their monoplanes which featured enclosed fuselages and cockpits and streamlined struts. His faith in his abilities was justified when his little 5·94 m (19 ft 6 in) span monoplane, powered by a 160 hp Gnome fourteen-cylinder two-row rotary engine and piloted by Jules Védrines, won the 1912 Gordon Bennett Aviation Cup in Chicago at a speed of 106·02 mph over a 200 km course; and he repeated this success the following year at Reims when Maurice Prévost flew the Deperdussin F.1 to victory with a speed of 129·79 mph.

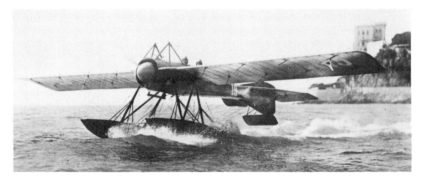

Maurice Prévost taxi-ing his Deperdussin at Monaco before the 1913 contest. Note the multiplicity of alighting gear struts, bracing wires, wing-warping control cables, and the long carburettor intake tube under the engine in the propeller slipstream. (*Musée de l'Air*)

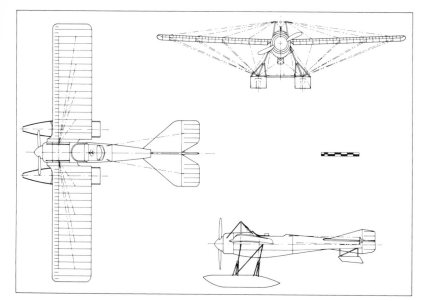

Deperdussin monoplane

A single-seater Deperdussin type B.1, powered by a 50 hp Gnome seven-cylinder rotary engine, sold for the equivalent of £960. Built entirely in wood, the first Deperdussin racing seaplane featured a fuselage of monocoque—literally 'single-shell'—construction which was of nearly oval section along its length from just behind the engine almost back to the sternpost. This load carrying 'single-shell' skin fuselage was built up from three layers of ⅛ in thick tulip wood veneers which were glued together over a mandrel or mould in the form of the fuselage shape. The outer surface then had linen fabric glued to it and the shell was removed from the mould. A second layer of linen fabric was then applied to the inner surface and several coats of varnish applied to the linen, each being carefully rubbed down after drying to produce a very fine smooth finish. This method of fuselage construction was used in the Deperdussin seaplane specially prepared for Maurice Prévost to compete in the 1913 Schneider Trophy contest. A fundamental difference between the fuselages of the earlier landplane and the seaplane variants was that the latter was almost circular in section. Of similar depth, the longer fuselage of the seaplane also had a better fineness ratio. This type of construction also provided great strength in the forward part of the fuselage where there was a large cutout for the cockpit and internal mountings for the fuel tank, the controls and the wing spar attachments. It also provided improved protection for the pilot in the event of a crash. The Gnome rotary engine, which was mounted on a wooden bulkhead, revolved inside an aluminium cowl and drove a two-blade mahogany propeller having a

51

The modified and more refined appearance of the 1914 contest Deperdussin is apparent in this view showing the neat engine cowling and installation of the broad-chord propeller.
(*Musée de l'Air*)

large bull-nosed spinner which left only a small annular gap between it and the inside diameter of the cowl for cooling airflow.

Lateral control of the aircraft was through wing-warping, and ailerons were not fitted. The spars and ribs were made of 'selected timber of great strength' according to a contemporary description, spruce for the spars and pine for the 23 ribs in each wing. The constant-chord wing had sharply backward-raked wingtips and a stepped-forward leading edge at the root. The linen covering was heavily doped to tighten and protect the material and to prevent distortion of the wooden structure beneath. The wings were each warped by three or four steel cables and had bracing wires running from the top surface to a double tripod-type structure mounted on top of the fuselage in front of the pilot; return control cables and lift wires were attached to the undersurface of the wing and to the floats. The control cables and bracing wires were reputed to be capable of withstanding loadings of up to 20 times those experienced in straight-and-level flight. Turnbuckles were fitted on all cables and wires to enable the wings to be trued-up when rigging the aircraft. It is recorded that 'a patent device was embodied in the control wires attached to the rear spar which prevented distortion of the wing in gusts but enabled the pilot to have exceedingly powerful and effective warp'. The wing had a medium-cambered section with some washout toward the tips.

The cantilever cruciform tail unit was made of spruce spars with pine ribs and leading and trailing edges, and covered with heavily doped linen fabric.

Spruce was used for the heavily stayed and wire-braced float attachment struts, which were given a streamlined section, and the float spacer bars which were varnished and rubbed down to produce a fine surface finish. The box-section wooden floats had a flat planing surface and were mounted with their leading edges canted upwards to help break the 'stiction' between the surfaces of the water and the floats. As the centre of gravity was well aft, there was a small stabilizing float under the tail.

The control system was patented by Béchereau and was the outcome of careful study and experience with the smaller landplane racer. A wheel was mounted at the top of two arms hinged at their lower ends to the wooden monocoque fuselage. Moving the wheel backwards and forwards operated the elevators, and turning the wheel warped the wings to effect lateral control. The rudder was cable-operated by means of an orthodox rudder bar.

Deperdussin landplane racing aircraft won the 1912 and 1913 Gordon Bennett Aviation Cup races. During the second race Maurice Prévost, in a short-span Deperdussin F.1, became the first man to travel more than two miles in a minute. Deperdussins also established ten world speed records, raising the speed to 203·72 km/h (126·59 mph). Sadly, Armand Deperdussin had built his achievements on the sands of money which was not his. He was arrested in his Paris flat on 5 August, 1913, and subsequently given a five-year suspended prison sentence following the discovery of his involvement with fraud totalling more than £1 million. Deperdussin ultimately shot himself in a Paris hotel on 11 June, 1924.

When Deperdussin's empire had crumbled, Louis Blériot took over ownership and changed the company name to Société Anonyme pour l'Aviation et ses Dérives. The acronym of the name remained Spad and it was for this organization that Louis Béchereau created designs for the renowned Spad fighters of the First World War.

Single-seat twin-float racing monoplane. All-wood construction with monocoque fuselage and fabric-covered wings and tail unit. Pilot in open unfaired cockpit.

1913—one 160 hp Gnome fourteen-cylinder twin-row air-cooled rotary engine driving a 2·8 m (9 ft 3 in) diameter two-blade fixed-pitch mahogany propeller; 1914—one 200 hp Gnome eighteen-cylinder twin-row air-cooled rotary engine. Fuel: 136 litres (30 gal) in a fuselage tank.

Span 8·95 m (29 ft 4¼ in); length 5·75 m (18 ft 10¼ in); wing area 9 sq m (96·87 sq ft). Dimensions for 1913 version.

Empty weight 290 kg (639 lb); loaded weight 400 kg (882 lb); wing loading 44·4 kg/sq m (9·1 lb/sq ft).

Maximum recorded speed 104·6 km/h (65 mph).

Production—one long-span aircraft built during 1913.

Colour—Prévost's Deperdussin for the 1913 contest was blue overall with the contest number 19 in large white figures on each side of the fuselage just forward of the tailplane.

A Morane-Saulnier Hydro-monoplane with tail well up. (*Courtesy The Royal Aeronautical Society*)

# Morane-Saulnier Hydro-monoplane

Roland Garros' Morane-Saulnier floatplane racer in the 1913 contest was a diminutive monoplane developed from a proven type with a wheeled undercarriage. Its design was as simple as possible. The fuselage was a wooden frame structure of rectangular section, which tapered sharply in side elevation to a chisel edge at the rear and was fabric covered. The 50 hp Gnome seven-cylinder air-cooled rotary engine, driving a two-blade wooden propeller, was housed in a circular cowling and was mounted on a similarly-shaped bulkhead attached to the four main fuselage longerons. There was no fixed fin, or tailplane, only a small, almost square, rudder and an elevator.

The fabric-covered wooden-structure mainplane had two main spars and was shoulder-mounted on the fuselage. Three pairs of warping control cables ran from the top of an inverted V structure mounted on top of the fuselage, and returned to a control yoke under the fuselage. The mainplane was markedly curved in section.

The small square-section main floats were carried on long forward-raked struts, and a tail float was mounted below the rear fuselage.

Single-seat twin-float racing monoplane. Wooden construction with fabric covering. Pilot in open cockpit.

One 80 hp Gnome seven-cylinder air-cooled normally-aspirated rotary engine driving a two-blade fixed-pitch wooden propeller.

Span 9·2 m (30 ft 2 in); length 6·38 m (20 ft 11 in); wing area 14 sq m (150·69 sq ft).

Loaded weight 290 kg (639 lb); wing loading 20·71 kg/sq m (4·24 lb/sq ft).

Maximum speed 120 km/h (74·56 mph).

Production—believed to be only one racing floatplane built during 1913.

Colour—unknown, possibly natural linen fuselage, wings and tail unit; metal engine cowling; natural varnished wood alighting gear, struts and floats.

# Nieuport

During the First World War Nieuport fighters were widely used by the Allies in France and even more widely known elsewhere. Yet the name, Nieuport, cloaked the identity—if rather thinly—of a young man who had moved to France from Algeria and who, in 1908, had designed and built a handsome 20 hp Darracq-engined monoplane in which he had achieved a measure of streamlining by covering the wooden girder structure of the fuselage with fabric. In addition to the airframe, this accomplished engineer built the engine, a number of its components and the propeller.

During the next three years he became well known in French aviation circles and it was this fame, which his family regarded as notoriety, which caused him to change his name from Edouard de Nieport to Nieuport. Such was the regard which his family had for the new field of aviation.

When Nieuport and his brother Charles were killed in air accidents —Edouard on 6 September, 1911, and Charles two years later—that great industrialist and patron and benefactor of French aviation, Henri Deutsch de la Meurthe, acquired and continued the Nieuports' business interests, creating a limited company named Société des Établissements Nieuport. This new company was based at Issy-les-Moulineaux, near Paris. Following a subsequent merger and managerial changes in 1921, the company achieved continuing fame with racing aircraft under the name Nieuport-Delage.

Two years before the first Schneider Trophy contest and with some three years' experience of Nieuport's designing, building and flying his own aeroplanes, a Nieuport monoplane, powered by a 100 hp Gnome

A fast taxi-ing Nieuport seen with a large amount of starboard mainplane warp applied. (*Musée de l'Air*)

seven-cylinder air-cooled rotary engine, and claimed to have an 80 mph top speed, had won the third Gordon Bennett Aviation Cup race at Eastchurch, Isle of Sheppey. With a United States pilot, Charles Weymann, at the controls, the 8·38 m (27 ft 6 in) span racer completed the 25-lap 93¼ mile race at an average speed of 78 mph. Nieuports also took third and fifth places in this race.

For the 1913 Schneider contest the Nieuport company produced a sleek monoplane with a marked resemblance to the Gordon Bennett winner but about half as big again and twice the weight. The rectangular-section rear fuselage was built up from spruce longerons with spruce frames which were all wire-braced with piano wire. Control cables to the tail unit passed through wood-framed apertures in the flat sides of the fuselage. The top and sides of the Gnome engine were enclosed in an aluminium cowl, and the curved top decking in front of the open cockpit and the floor were of plywood. Varnished fabric covered the remainder of the fuselage. A raised lip around the cockpit was leather bound. The two spars of the markedly cambered aerofoil section wing were of spruce, with spruce leading- and trailing-edge strips, and ash ribs. Fabric covering was also applied to the wings. Control and bracing wires passed from a four-leg wooden cabane to the front and rear spars and down to the two main floats. The large curved butterfly-shaped tailplane and elevator unit was mounted on top of the rear fuselage. The tailplane was a cantilever all-wood fabric-covered structure, as were the dorsal and ventral fins. The elevators and the rudder were of similar all-wood fabric-covered construction. The alighting gear comprised four main float-mounting struts of wood with special wire-braced shock-resisting struts attached to the underside of the fuselage and to the forward of the pair of float spreader bars. Duralumin tips were fitted to the flat-sided hard chine wooden floats which initially had slightly rounded top surfaces, a single step half-way along their length and a deep vertical transom. Before the contest, in order to improve the take-off characteristics, floats with a three-step 31·75 cm (12½ in) wide keel, giving a saw-tooth effect, were fitted to Weymann's Nieuport. A circular-section 'tear-drop' shaped stabilizing float was mounted on unbraced struts under the rear fuselage.

Single/two-seat twin-float racing monoplane. Wooden construction with fabric covering. Pilot and one crew in tandem in open unfaired cockpit.

1913—one 100 hp Gnome seven-cylinder air-cooled rotary engine driving a two-blade fixed-pitch wooden propeller; 1914—one 160 hp Gnome fourteen-cylinder twin-row air-cooled rotary engine driving a 2·3 m (7 ft 6 in) diameter two-blade fixed-pitch wooden propeller.

Span 11·88 m (38 ft 11½ in); length 8·7 m (28 ft 7 in); height 2·8 m (9 ft 3 in); float length 3·58 m (11 ft 9 in); maximum wing chord 1·88 m (6 ft 2 in).

Empty weight 600 kg (1,323 lb); loaded weight 850 kg (1,874 lb).

Maximum speed 115·87 km/h (72 mph).

Production—about six seaplane racers built during 1912–14.

Colour—1913 contest. Believed overall yellow with black contest number.

The little Sopwith Tabloid which was converted into a floatplane in 1914 to give Great Britain its first Schneider Trophy victory. (*British Aerospace – Kingston*)

# Sopwith Tabloid

Great Britain's first Schneider Trophy aspirant was the Sopwith Tabloid, a small biplane which was designed by T. O. M. Sopwith and Fred Sigrist. The side-by-side two-seat Tabloid prototype, which was first flown in November 1913 by Harry Hawker, the Sopwith Aviation test pilot, was later to be energetically developed into an effective little single-seat scout for use by the Royal Flying Corps and the Royal Naval Air Service during the First World War.

Powered by an 80 hp Gnome nine-cylinder air-cooled rotary engine driving a two-blade wooden propeller, the Tabloid was of wire-braced fabric-covered all-wood construction. It featured slightly staggered biplane wings of constant 5 ft (1·52 m) chord; and with only a single pair of interplane struts in the 4 ft 3 in (1·29 m) gap, and two centre-section struts each side, it was one of the few single-bay biplanes of that period. Ailerons were not fitted and lateral control was achieved by wing-warping. A large bull-nosed metal cowling enclosed the engine and metal panels extended aft to clad the fuselage sides back to the cockpit. A 'comma' shaped rudder—which shape typified many subsequent Sopwith aeroplanes—without a fin was used with a large-area tailplane and elevators. These flying surfaces were cable operated. A twin wheel-and-skid main undercarriage and a tailskid were conventional features.

On 29 November at the Royal Aircraft Factory, Farnborough, the Tabloid achieved a maximum speed of 92 mph with a 36·9 mph stalling speed during official trials, and later the same day was displayed by Hawker at a Hendon flying meeting before some 50,000 people. From his own experience of air racing, Sopwith knew its value in terms of publicity and as a stimulus to engineering and aerodynamic development of aircraft. Accordingly, he decided to modify an early production Tabloid as a seaplane for the 1914 Schneider contest due to take place at Monaco on 20 April, and engaged C. Howard Pixton, an experienced Australian pilot, to undertake the development testing and to fly the Tabloid in the contest. More power was a prime need and Sopwith chose a new 100 hp Monosoupape Gnome rotary which differed from other Gnome engines by dispensing with inlet valves, having only single exhaust valves in each cylinder, hence its Monosoupape—'single-valve'—name. A single central-float alighting gear with wingtip stabilizing floats was designed and fitted very rapidly—perhaps too rapidly—and at the end of March 1914 the Tabloid was moved from Sopwith's Kingston-upon-Thames factory to a site on the Hamble river for water and air tests. These began on 1 April but when Pixton opened the throttle to taxi away from a jetty, the nose of the main float dug into the water and the aircraft turned over and sank. Fortunately Pixton was thrown out and managed to swim back to the jetty. In their haste to ready the Tabloid for Monaco, Sopwith, Sigrist and Sydney Burgoine, a boatbuilder, had rigged the float too far aft and it could not balance the increased power of the engine. The following

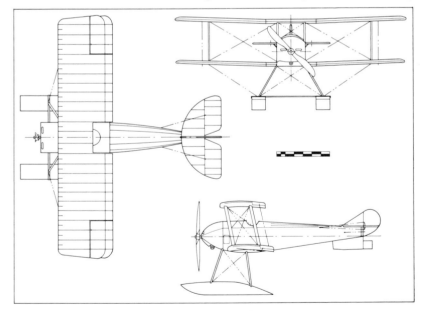

Sopwith Tabloid

Scarcely visible, Howard Pixton lounges nonchalantly in the shadow of the port upper mainplane of the Sopwith Tabloid at Monaco in 1914. The rear part of the floats and support struts are under water, as is the elevator trailing edge. (*British Aerospace – Kingston*)

morning the soaked and partially wrecked Tabloid was recovered from the mud, dismantled and returned to Kingston, where a new twin-float alighting gear was sketched out. Burgoine simply sawed through the single main float to produce a pair of smaller units which were completed by boxing in their now open inboard sides. Two spreader bars connected them and they were attached to the fuselage by two pairs of struts, the whole gear being wire braced. The underwing floats were removed, a small tail float was fitted, and a small triangular shaped fin was mounted in front of the rudder to balance the increased keel surface of the new floats. As there was insufficient time to return to the Hamble, some furtive early morning trials took place on 7 April on the Thames, initially just below Kingston Bridge, but when Thames Conservancy Board officials objected the Tabloid was moved to Ham below Teddington Lock where the Port of London Authority assumed control of the water, Teddington's ancient name 'Tide-end town' being indicative of the significance of this point on the river. The water trials showed that the new floats performed very well, running smoothly on the surface during the take-off runs.

At Monaco a preliminary flight-trial two days before the contest was scheduled to take place showed that several modifications needed to be made. Pixton found that the engine was over-speeding and the Gnome engine company representatives recommended that, as the large diameter moderate-pitch propeller allowed the engine to run at 1,350 rpm, which was too fast for the contest (expected to last some two hours), a smaller-diameter propeller of coarser pitch should be fitted. An extra six-gallon fuel tank was fitted to increase the flight duration and stronger float bracing wires replaced the original wires which had stretched during the flight trial.

59

The successful development and modification of the Tabloid as a seaplane not only bore fruit in the contest but also led to the production of the Sopwith Schneider, a single-seat scout seaplane, for the RNAS. Powered by a 100 hp Monosoupape Gnome engine, the Schneider differed very little from Pixton's Tabloid, the major changes being an extra pair of struts in the alighting gear, a water rudder on the tail float, an increased area fin, the use of ailerons on all four wings in place of wing-warping, and the angled mounting of a Lewis gun firing through an aperture in the upper centre section. The Sopwith Baby was a further aerodynamically refined development which made a valuable contribution to coastal air defence of the United Kingdom during 1915–16. Whatever else justified the creation and development of the Tabloid, it occupies a unique position as the progenitor of an apparently endless line of scouts, fighters and attack aircraft to emanate from Kingston.

Single-seat twin-float racing biplane. Wooden construction with fabric covering. Pilot in open cockpit.

One 100 hp Gnome Monosoupape nine-cylinder air-cooled rotary engine with a 7 ft 6 in (2·28 m) diameter two-blade fixed-pitch carved mahogany propeller.

Span 25 ft 6 in (7·77 m); length 20 ft (6 m); height 10 ft (3 m); wing area 240 sq ft (22·29 sq m).

Empty weight 992 lb (450 kg); loaded weight 1,433 lb (650 kg); wing loading 6 lb/sq ft (29·29 kg/sq m).

Maximum speed at sea level 92 mph (148 km/h); stalling speed 38 mph (61 km/h).

Production—one Tabloid floatplane racer built by Sopwith at Kingston-upon-Thames in 1914.

Colour—pale golden yellow overall with black markings—SOPWITH on fuselage sides, contest number 3 on rudder—polished aluminium engine cowling and cockpit decking; and varnished natural wood floats and interplane struts.

# FBA Flying-boat

Franco-British Aviation Co was founded at Vernon, Eure, in France, during 1913 by Lieut de Conneau (who is better known as André Beaumont, winner of the Paris–Rome race, and the Circuits of Europe and Britain) and a M Shreck, formerly of the French Wright Co. FBA took up patents covering the French Donnet-Levêque flying-boats, which were described as 'classic' aeroplanes and the first of their type having the tail unit mounted directly on the hull rather than carried on struts as in the Curtiss flying-boats. The aircraft entered for the 1914 Schneider contest, and the only flying-boat in the list, was developed from the earlier 1912 13·7 m (45 ft) span two-seat patrol bomber, serialled 18, which was the first military flying-boat type in British Royal Navy service.

The very graceful slender hull, with pointed stem and curved-up tail, was of all-wood construction with spruce stringers mounted on formers

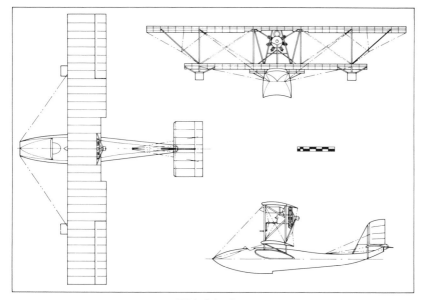

FBA flying-boat

and covered with sheeting. The planing bottom was concave, like the later Italian Conflenti hulls, with the chines forming vertical 'fins' toward the rear. A small triangular tail fin was carried, clear of the rear hull section, on a steel-tube frame, to which the wire-braced wood and fabric tailplane also was attached. A rectangular rudder and the large-area elevators also were of fabric-covered wooden construction.

The open cockpit was immediately in front of the lower mainplane which was raised clear of the hull on short struts. Control cables emerged from the hull about half way along its length and stretched externally up to the tail unit.

The markedly cambered two-bay mainplanes were constructed around two spruce or ash spars with wooden ribs with steel compression tubes and wire braced, and all fabric covered. The upper mainplane had a large overhang which was braced by two diagonal struts from the base of the outboard interplane struts. Small wooden stabilizing floats were mounted on struts under the tips of the lower mainplane. The entire structure was wire braced, including two wires from the hull stem-head to the top of the outboard interplane struts. Broad-chord ailerons were carried on the top mainplane only. The 100 hp Gnome rotary engine, driving a two-blade propeller, was mounted high between the mainplanes on four raked-back struts with four more struts connecting it to the upper mainplane. This Gnome was reputed to have a better power/weight ratio than other previous rotary engines. A teardrop-shaped metal fuel tank was fixed below the upper mainplane on the centre line.

61

A contemporary comment on the FBA flying-boats was that 'these boats, though very lightly built, have done good work. Being so light they climb well and fly fast'.

The pilot of the FBA aircraft in the contest was Ernest Burri. It was not known whether he flew it to Monaco or whether it travelled overland.

Single-seat racing biplane flying-boat. Wood and metal construction. Pilot in open cockpit.

One 100 hp Gnome seven-cylinder air-cooled rotary engine driving a two-blade fixed-pitch wooden pusher propeller.

Span 12·15 m (39 ft 10¼ in); length 7·72 m (25 ft 3¾ in); wing area 26 sq m (279·86 sq ft). Loaded weight 470 kg (1,036 lb); wing loading 18 kg/sq m (3·7 lb/sq ft).

Maximum speed 109 km/h (68 mph); initial rate of climb 83 m/sec (164 ft/min).

Production—total production unknown; however the nose markings on the aircraft flown in the 1914 Schneider contest could indicate that either it was the 26th aircraft to be built by FBA or was the 26th of its type. It is believed that the former indication is the more likely.

Colour—unknown although some contemporary photographs show the aircraft in an all-over finish which could have been silver.

# Savoia S.13

As a maritime nation it was only natural that Italy would become a very active participant in the Schneider Trophy contests. Its first entrant was the S.13, a modified version of a fast little two-seat bombing and recon-naissance two-bay biplane flying-boat. In only two weeks it was converted to a single-seater, the mainplanes were clipped for racing and converted to single-bay configuration, and the Isotta-Fraschini engine was tuned to produce some ten additional horse power.

A standard Savoia S.13 two-seat flying-boat of the type which was rapidly converted into a single-seat racing aircraft with single-bay mainplanes for the 1919 contest. (*SIAI Marchetti*)

Guido Jannello's Savoia S.13 in S. E. Saunders' hangars at Cowes in 1919. In the group at the left are (*left to right*) Guido Jannello in dark uniform, Lorenzo Santoni, Savoia's founder and president, pointing to the aircraft across the chest of Raphael Conflenti, Savoia's designer. (*Flight*)

The single-step hull was built up from wooden formers and stringers clad with marine plywood. The strut-braced tailplane was mounted on the fin which was an integral part of the hull structure. The wooden elevators and rudder were fabric covered. The straight mainplanes were of conventional two-spar wooden construction with fabricated wooden ribs and fabric covered; the ailerons, fitted only on the upper mainplane,

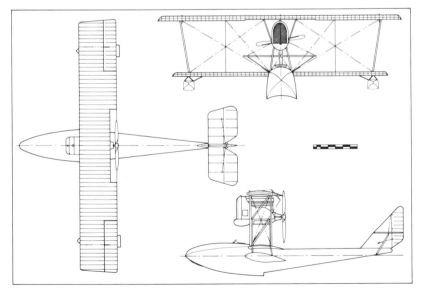

Savoia S.13

were of similar construction; two small stabilizing floats were strut-mounted under the lower mainplane; and the whole structure was wire-braced. The engine was mounted above the hull on two N-struts, and two other N-struts supported the upper mainplane. The radiator was carried forward of the engine with an oil cooler below it. All flying-control surfaces were cable-operated. The front and lower portion of the engine was cowled with aluminium panels leaving the rear top section uncowled. The engine drove a four-blade wooden pusher propeller in place of the two-blade unit of the military S.13.

When the modifications were completed, the aircraft was dismantled, crated and transported overland by rail and by ship to Britain. Only a few practice flights were possible before the contest in which the S.13, flown by Sgt Guido Jannello, was the only aircraft to complete the required number of laps, but was flown on an incorrect course.

Single-engine racing biplane flying-boat. All-wood construction with wood and fabric covering. Pilot in open cockpit.

One 250 hp Isotta-Fraschini Asso 200 six-cylinder water-cooled, direct-drive normally aspirated inline engine driving a 2·1 m (6 ft 11 in) diameter four-blade fixed-pitch wooden propeller.

Span 8·1 m (26 ft 7 in) (upper), 7·28 m (23 ft 11 in) (lower); length 8·3 m (27 ft 3 in); height 3·05 m (10 ft); wing area 19·6 sq m (210·97 sq ft).

Empty weight 730 kg (1,609 lb); loaded weight 940 kg (2,072 lb); wing loading 47·96 kg/sq m (9·82 lb/sq ft).

Maximum speed 243 km/h (151 mph).

Production—one S.13 converted to single-seat racing configuration by Società Idro-volanti Alta Italia in 1919.

Colour—overall red with white bottom to hull and stabilizing floats; natural metal engine cowling; green, white and red national stripes on fin and rudder; white-edged black contest number 7 on rudder; blue and white pennant with name Savoia on hull nose.

# Supermarine Sea Lion I

The old Pemberton Billing Co. and its Supermarine Works at Woolston, near Southampton, were bought by Hubert Scott-Paine in 1916 when Noel Pemberton Billing became a Member of Parliament. It was re-named Supermarine Aviation Works and in 1918 designed and built the Baby, to Air Board specification N.1B, which was one of the very few single-seat fighter flying-boats to be produced during the First World War. The Baby was a biplane with a wing span of 30 ft 6 in (9·29 m) and, powered by a 200 hp Hispano-Suiza engine, had a maximum speed of 116 mph (186·6 km/h). Two prototypes, N59—60, were built and flown, but the Baby did not go into quantity production because military requirements changed.

When the Schneider Trophy contests were re-established in 1919 and the first postwar venue was to be Bournemouth, Scott-Paine decided that because of its proximity to the Supermarine factory his company would enter the lists. Since time was short, he obtained one of the Babies, whose forward hull had been modified to reduce spray while on the water as part of a programme to produce a civil Baby to be known as the Sea King. The Hispano-Suiza engine was replaced by a 450 hp Napier Lion twelve-cylinder broad-arrow engine driving a two-blade wooden pusher propeller. Although the redesign of this aircraft was to produce a purely racing machine, it was fully equipped with a bilge pump, sea anchor and mooring equipment. The hull, of Linton Hope design, was of similar construction to that used in the Blackburn Pellet. The single-bay mainplanes and centre section were built up around two spruce spars and wooden ribs which were fabric covered. The four mainplanes were built separately and were rigged without stagger but with dihedral from the flat centre section. Large balanced ailerons were carried on all four mainplanes. The interplane struts were sloped out toward the tops to support the longer-span upper mainplane. Deep, narrow, stabilizing floats were carried beneath the lower mainplanes. The tailplane was mounted on top of the fin and was braced on each side by a pair of steel-tube struts to the hull. A horn-balanced rudder, extended downward to act as a water rudder, was carried on the fin which was covered with wood sheeting. The remainder of the tail unit was of wood and fabric construction. The engine was mounted on four steel-tube struts carrying two ash engine-

The Supermarine launch *Tiddlywinks* takes in tow the Sea Lion I, G-EALP, as it is launched from the company's slipway at Woolston. The uncowled Napier Lion engine, laminated mahogany propeller, and spray dams at the base of the inboard interplane struts, are seen clearly. (*Flight*)

The Supermarine Sea Lion I is taxied down Southampton Water by Sqn Ldr Basil Hobbs.
(*Vickers Ltd*)

bearers and supported the upper centre section on four more struts. An oval-shaped radiator was mounted in front of the engine and was enclosed in an aluminium nacelle. The redesign work was entrusted to the young Reginald J. Mitchell, who in later years was to become renowned as the designer of a series of Supermarine racing floatplanes for the Schneider contests and of the Spitfire.

The use of the Lion engine prompted the name Sea Lion for this little racer which received the civil registration G-EALP. The eliminating trials to select the British team were scheduled for 3 September, and while the Sopwith, Fairey, and Avro companies had flown their aircraft by the day before the trial, the Sea Lion's first flight was delayed by the non-delivery of the propeller—due to a strike at the manufacturers. However, it arrived in time for engine running to begin at 8 p.m. in the evening before the trials; but torrential rain prevented these taking place. On 5 September Sqn Ldr Basil Hobbs, the Supermarine pilot, made the initial flight. Flight trials continued with all four British aircraft, the final decision to include the Sea Lion in place of the Avro entrant being delayed until 9 September when a new propeller gave the Sea Lion an additional five or six miles per hour.

The events of the contest day are recorded elsewhere in this book, but afterwards the Sea Lion was dismantled and its hull was loaned to the Science Museum in London for an exhibition in 1921. Sadly it was broken up some years later when the Museum no longer required it.

Single-seat racing biplane flying-boat. Wood and metal construction. Pilot in open cockpit.

One 450 hp Napier Lion IA twelve-cylinder water-cooled normally-aspirated geared broad-arrow engine driving a 7 ft 10 in (2·38 m) diameter two-blade fixed-pitch wooden propeller.

Span 35 ft (10·66 m); length 26 ft 4 in (8·02 m); height 11 ft 8 in (3·55 m); wing area 380 sq ft (35·3 sq m).

Empty weight 2,000 lb (907 kg); loaded weight 2,900 lb (1,315 kg); wing loading 7·63 lb/sq ft (37·22 kg/sq m).

Maximum speed 147 mph (236·57 km/h).

Production—one Sea Lion I built by conversion of Baby by Supermarine Aviation Works, Woolston, Southampton, in 1919.

Colour—believed to have been dark blue hull and tailplane support struts, with remainder pale blue, grey or silver; engine nacelle natural aluminium; Supermarine in large white capital letters on hull sides forward of mainplanes with small Sea Lion above, white civil registration letters G-EALP on hull sides aft of mainplanes; white contest number 5 on fin.

# Fairey III

The Fairey III G-EALQ, sometimes known as the N.10 or by its construction number F.128, was the sole prototype of a carrier-based floatplane built to Admiralty specification N.2 (a) during the summer of 1917. It made its first flight from the Isle of Grain on 14 September, piloted by Lieut-Cmdr Vincent Nicholl, just two weeks after delivery from the Hamble factory to the RNAS.

Powered initially by a 260 hp Sunbeam Maori II twelve-cylinder liquid-cooled vee engine, the Fairey III was of wooden construction, with spruce and ash being used for the mainplane and fuselage structure, the whole being fabric covered. In its original form the aircraft had equal-span two-bay folding mainplanes having full-span variable-camber gear

The Fairey III in Schneider contest single-bay configuration.

67

The Fairey III, or N10, G-EALQ which was entered for the 1919 contest as a single-bay floatplane is seen here after conversion to a two-bay amphibian for the 1920 Air Ministry amphibian competition in which it was placed third. (*The Fairey Aviation Co*)

on the lower unit and with ailerons only on the upper unit. There were square-section single-step main floats, and a large tail float.

It was extensively modified at the Isle of Grain experimental establishment for test flying as a floatplane and as a landplane during 1917–19; it was then bought back by the Fairey company for competition and communications flying.

For its 1919 Schneider Trophy outing at Bournemouth, G-EALQ was modified yet again to a single-bay configuration and was powered by a 450 hp Napier Lion twelve-cylinder liquid-cooled broad-arrow engine. After the contest, in which the Fairey III, flown by Vincent Nicholl, retired in the first lap due to complete lack of visibility in the fog which enshrouded the course, this aircraft reappeared in August 1920 with a combined wheel/float undercarriage for an Air Ministry competition for commercial aircraft. It was placed third—and last—in the amphibian section, but won a £2,000 prize. This aeroplane was scrapped in 1922 but was the forerunner of the long line of Fairey III variants and sub-variants which, with one exception, were produced in greater numbers than any other British military type between 1918 and the era of the Royal Air Force expansion scheme in the mid-1930s.

Two-seat twin-float biplane. Wooden construction with fabric covering. Pilot in open rear cockpit, front cockpit faired over.

450 hp Napier Lion twelve-cylinder liquid-cooled broad-arrow engine driving a two-blade fixed-pitch wooden propeller of about 9 ft (2·74 m) diameter.

Span 28 ft (8·53 m); length 36 ft (10·97 m); height 10 ft 6 in (3·2 m).

Maximum speed at sea level 108 mph (173·8 km/h).

Production—one prototype Fairey III built by Fairey Aviation Co Ltd, Hayes and Hamble, in 1917.

Colour—believed white upper wing, rear fuselage sides and rudder, with blue lower wing, forward fuselage sides and top decking, fin, tailplane, elevators, main and tail floats.

# Sopwith Schneider

For the first postwar Schneider Trophy contest Tom Sopwith decided to build a new floatplane, using all of his company's wartime experience of making fast, manoeuvrable fighter-type aircraft. In addition, he abandoned the well-established rotary and inline engines and chose instead the new 450 hp Jupiter nine-cylinder air-cooled direct-drive radial engine, designed by Roy Fedden of Cosmos Engineering Ltd. The circular shape of the Jupiter dictated the cross-sectional shape of the new floatplane's fuselage, and Sopwith's designer, W. George Carter, produced a business-like aircraft with good lines. The fuselage was built up from ash longerons with spruce struts and ply formers carrying stringers to give a curved shape to the sides. Fuel was carried in tanks mounted in front of the pilot's cockpit and immediately aft of a large circular steel-faced multi-ply wooden engine-mounting bulkhead. The single-bay biplane wings had ash spars with spruce struts and ribs. Ailerons were fitted to the upper and lower wings and were interconnected with single streamlined wires. An unusual feature was that the upper wings were staggered $2\frac{1}{2}$ in

The first Cosmos Jupiter engine being installed in the Sopwith Schneider fuselage at Sopwith's Canbury Park Road factory at Kingston. The main fuel and oil tanks are in the uncovered front fuselage section. (*British Aerospace – Kingston*)

The completed Sopwith Schneider, with the polished aluminium engine cowling, cylinder fairings and front fuselage panels, the sturdy interplane struts and broad-chord mainplanes, and the design of the twin floats, well displayed in this view. (*Rolls-Royce*)

behind the lower wings. The wire-braced tail unit was a wooden structure and, like the remainder of the rear fuselage and the wings, was fabric covered. All the flying control cable runs were inside the main structure and bestowed a very clean external appearance to the Schneider. Aluminium panels enclosed the forward part of the fuselage, and the engine cowling, through which protruded the heavily finned cylinders, was also of aluminium. A large spinner closed the aperture through which the splined propeller shaft passed to drive a two-blade fixed-pitch wooden propeller. The four wooden struts of the alighting gear carried two flat-sided stepless, almost symmetrical, aerofoil-section wooden floats. A small windscreen and faired headrest were provided for the pilot who sat in an open cockpit positioned beneath the trailing edge of the upper wing. Registered G-EAKI and flown by Harry Hawker in the 1919 contest in fog at Bournemouth, the Schneider was a potentially fast entrant which had little opportunity to show its paces in the poor conditions.

After the contest the floats were removed and a wheeled undercarriage fitted. Renamed Rainbow, G-EAKI had 3 ft clipped from its wing-span and was re-engined with an ABC Dragonfly air-cooled radial engine for the 1920 Aerial Derby, from which it was disqualified due to an incorrect finish. It was later entered for the Gordon Bennett race but was lacking a good engine, and when, in September 1920, the Sopwith Engineering Co closed through financial troubles, the Rainbow was withdrawn— although a private enterprise effort by a group of racing enthusiasts and sportsmen almost got it flying again. With the formation of H. G. Hawker

Engineering Co Ltd in the same month, the aircraft was again equipped with a Jupiter engine, renamed the Sopwith Hawker and flew in the 1923 Aerial Derby, in which it finished in second place.

Plans to convert G-EAKI back to a floatplane for that year's Schneider Trophy contest never came to fruition and the aircraft was completely written off in a forced landing on 5 October, 1923.

Single-seat twin-float racing biplane. All-wood construction with fabric and metal covering. Pilot in open cockpit.

One 450 hp Cosmos Jupiter nine-cylinder air-cooled direct-drive normally-aspirated radial engine driving an 8 ft 4 in (2·54 m) two-blade fixed-pitch wooden propeller.

Span 24 ft (7·31 m); length 21 ft 6 in (6·55 m); height 10 ft 6 in (3·2 m); wing area 222 sq ft (20·62 sq m).

Empty weight 1,750 lb (794 kg); loaded weight 2,200 lb (998 kg); wing loading 9·92 lb/sq ft (48·43 kg/sq m)—approximate figures.

Maximum speed at sea level 170 mph (273·58 km/h); stalling speed 55 mph (88·51 km/h) —estimated figures.

Production—one Schneider built by Sopwith Engineering Co Ltd at Kingston-upon-Thames in 1919.

Colour—believed all-over blue with white interplane and alighting gear struts; white panel on fuselage sides carrying black registration letters G-EAKI and white panel on rudder carrying black national identity prefix letter G; Sopwith in white letters on fin. The allocated contest number 3 was not carried.

# Savoia S.12bis

Perhaps the S.12 came nearer to Jacques Schneider's ideals than any other aircraft which participated in the contests. His aim had been to promote the creation of seaworthy long-distance load-carrying maritime aircraft, and the S.12, basically, was all of these, being developed from a two-seat bomber type which had good range and load-carrying character-istics. As the only entry in the 1920 contest to attempt the navigability trials in appalling weather, through which it came with flying colours, this sturdy flying-boat proved its seaworthiness.

In appearance, it was almost identical to the standard S.13 before its conversion to a racing aircraft. The long slender hull was of all-wood construction with a tall curved-back fin and rudder carrying a strut-braced tailplane. A full-width windscreen protected the open cockpit in front of the mainplane. On the standard S.12 the tailplane span was about 4·8 m (16 ft) but this was reduced to 2·9 m (9 ft 6 in) on the S.12bis racing variant.

The 15·07 m (49 ft 5 in) span mainplanes of the military original also had been reduced, by more than 3 m. A wire-braced two-bay structure, the two-spar mainplanes had plywood ribs giving a markedly curved aerofoil section. Ailerons were fitted only on the upper mainplane and, like the elevators and rudder, were fabric covered. The inboard inter-

The Savoia S.12bis was generally similar to the S.13bis seen here (*SIAI Marchetti*)

plane struts were vertical but the outboard struts were canted outward to their upper ends. Two square-section stabilizing floats were strut mounted beneath the lower mainplanes. The 550 hp Ansaldo-San Giorgio twelve-cylinder water-cooled pusher engine was mounted on a pair of N-struts between the mainplanes. A large radiator and integral oil cooler was fitted in front of the engine, the lower portion of which was cowled leaving the top exposed. A second, lighter, pair of N-struts supported the upper mainplane.

Mechanical troubles, transport difficulties and bad weather eliminated all but the S.12 from the list of entries for the 1920 contest at Venice. Having completed the pre-contest trials, Lieut Luigi Bologna had only to fly it over the course to win, which he did at an average of 172·561 km/h (107·224 mph) and secured the Trophy for Italy.

Single-engined racing biplane flying-boat. All-wood construction with wood and fabric covering. Pilot in open cockpit.

One 550 hp Ansaldo-San Giorgio 4E-29 twelve-cylinder water-cooled direct-drive normally-aspirated vee engine driving an Ansaldo four-blade fixed-pitch wooden pusher propeller of about 1·98 m (6 ft 6 in) diameter. Fuel: about 270 litres (60 gal).

Span 11·72 m (38 ft 5½ in) (upper); length 10 m (32 ft 10 in); height 3·8 m (12 ft 5½ in); wing area 46·52 sq m (500·74 sq ft).

Empty weight 1,560 kg (3,438 lb); loaded weight 2,360 kg (5,202 lb); wing loading 50·73 kg/sq m (10·38 lb/sq ft).

Maximum speed 222 km/h (138 mph).

Production—believed to be only one S.12bis produced (serialled 3011) by Società Idrovolanti Alta Italia at Sesto Calende, Italy, in 1920.

Colour—unknown. Carried contest number 7 on side of hull nose and on rudder, S.12 on hull nose and Savoia in large script letters down length of hull.

# Macchi M.7

The Società Anonima Nieuport-Macchi, formed by Giulio Macchi in 1912 at Varese, a small Italian town near the Swiss border, undertook the manufacture of Nieuport designs until 1919 when its own designs of landplanes began to enter production. The Macchi flying-boat and seaplane tradition began in a curious manner during hostilities between Italy and Austria in 1915. When the Austrian Lohner L.1 flying-boat L.40 was forced down, virtually undamaged, on the water near Porto Corsini seaplane base at Rimini, it was immediately taken to Varese, and Macchi was instructed to build a copy. The Macchi L.1 was in the air for the first time only a little over a month later, and it formed the basis of a number of successful Macchi flying-boats, among them the M.5 single-seat fighter design of Felice Buzio.

An experimental single-seater, the M.6, led on to the M.7, which was the first design of Alessandro Tonini, the Macchi company's chief engineer. Powered by a 260 hp Isotta-Fraschini six-cylinder water-cooled inline engine, it had a maximum speed of about 210 km/h (130 mph). While the earlier Macchi fighter flying-boat designs had incorporated vee interplane struts, inherited from the classic Nieuport biplane fighters, the M.7 had the more conventional paired interplane struts and a wingspan reduced to 11·88 m (39 ft).

The slim, single-step, rectangular-section hull was built up from an ash framework with a spruce skin, the fin being built integral with the hull. The slightly swept unequal-span, single-bay, unstaggered biplane mainplanes of markedly curved aerofoil section had ash spars with spruce ribs, all fabric covered. The upper centre section above the engine was supported on wooden N-struts. Ailerons were carried only on the upper mainplane and were mounted at the extreme tips. The pairs of interplane struts were splayed out at the top when viewed both from front and sides, and the whole structure was braced by the conventional wires. The engine was carried above the hull on a pair of N-struts which also supported the upper centre-section struts. It was uncowled, with a large radiator mounted directly in front of the two banks of cylinders, and a smaller oil cooler was in a bulged fairing beneath the radiator. The tail unit consisted of a fabric-covered wooden-structured tailplane which was carried half-way up the quite tall and narrow-chord fin and was strut-braced to the hull. The rudder was only a little more than half the height of the fin and extended very little below the tailplane. Two square-section stabilizing floats were carried on struts under the lower wing. The open cockpit was directly below the water radiator, was protected by a small curved windscreen, and had a faired headrest for the pilot.

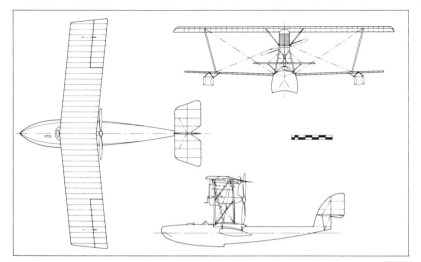

Macchi M.7

Determined to win the 1921 Schneider Trophy contest in Venice, and to take another step toward permanent possession of it, Italy gathered sixteen flying-boats for a series of national elimination trials to select a team. Among them were five M.7s flown variously by de Briganti, Buonsembiante, Corgnolino, Falaschi and de Sio, and with varying fortunes. De Briganti and Corgnolino won places in the Italian team, the M.7s of Buonsembiante and de Sio were withdrawn from the trials, and Falaschi crashed before they got under way.

Having won the 1921 contest, largely through the failure of the other entries either before or during the event, an M.7bis, I-BAFV, was entered for the 1922 contest when one of the selected team aircraft, the Savoia S.50, crashed. It took fourth, and last, place at an average speed of 199·607 km/h (124·029 mph).

Production of later versions of this tough little flying-boat fighter continued almost throughout the 1920s. One variant, the M.7ter, equipped all of the Italian squadriglie di caccia marittima (seaplane fighter squadrons) until 1929, with 163 Squadriglia retaining its M.7s for a further year.

Single-seat racing biplane flying-boat. Wood construction with wood skinning and fabric covering. Pilot in open cockpit.

One 260 hp Isotta-Fraschini Semi-Asso six-cylinder water-cooled inline engine driving a 2·2 m (7 ft 3 in) diameter two-blade wooden pusher propeller. The 1922 variant had a four-blade propeller.

Span 9·95 m (32 ft 8 in); length 8·13 m (26 ft 6½ in); height 2·97 m (9 ft 9 in); wing area 23·8 sq m (256·18 sq ft).

Empty weight 780 kg (1,719 lb); loaded weight 1,080 kg (2,381 lb); wing loading 45·37 kg/sq m (9·29 lb/sq ft).

Maximum speed 209 km/h (130 mph); stalling speed 100 km/h (62 mph).

Production—five refined versions of the Macchi M.7 military flying-boat were prepared for the 1921 Schneider Trophy contest by Società Anonima Macchi at Varese. At least one, the M.7bis, had its wings clipped by approximately 2·2 m (7 ft 3 in). It is not certain whether any more M.7s were prepared for racing, but one aircraft, registered I-BAFV, flew in the 1922 contest.

Colour—few details of colour schemes can be found but it is believed that I-BAFV had a pale green hull and silver mainplanes and tail unit. The registration letters were black, carried on a white rectangle on the hull sides aft of the mainplanes, and the contest number 10 was similarly carried on a white rectangle on the hull sides just forward of the cockpit. The name Macchi M.7 was carried on both sides of the hull nose. It is recorded that in common with all the other aircraft participating in the 1921 Italian team selection trials, the M.7s carried on the hull sides forward, a variety of coloured identity 'patches' of different shape, including yellow and red rectangles and a green circle or star.

# Macchi M.19

Throughout the Schneider contest series Italy left little to chance in its efforts to win. It sought and won rule changes, adopted every legitimate strategem and tactical ruse, and backed them all with sound planning and, generally, a high standard of engineering.

To meet the 1920 rule regarding the carriage of 300 kg of non-disposable load, Tonini produced designs for a big 15·86 m (52 ft) span flying-boat specifically to meet this rule. Although described as a single-seater in at least one of Macchi's records, the M.19, serialled 3098, was unique in that it was the only two-seat aircraft specially designed for the Schneider contests.

Although the M.19 has been described in official records as being developed directly from the M.7, this big flying-boat was an almost completely new design. Of conventional construction, the hull featured a prominent keel, with the chine lines sweeping up gently from the single step to the stemhead, and a flared bottom. The wire-braced tailplane was mounted on a tall graceful fin which carried a large narrow-chord rudder.

The rectangular-plan mainplanes, which were strut-braced to the hull, were two-spar structures and fabic covered. Stabilizing floats were strut-mounted below the lower mainplanes. Warren girder interplane struts were used, and the huge 650 hp Fiat A.14 twelve-cylinder engine was supported on a pair of N-struts and positioned on the upper centre section. The radiator and oil-cooler were fitted in front of the engine, and the power unit drove a 3·27 m (10 ft 9 in)* four-blade tractor propeller.

Possibly because the Italians believed their '300 kg load' rule was to be a permanent requirement, the production of two M.19s was planned but only one was built. Piloted by Arturo Zanetti, it first flew in August 1920, only a few days before the original dates chosen for that year's Schneider contest at Venice. Unfortunately, the enormous torque reaction from the

*This diameter and that shown in the data both appear in the records of the M.19.

This view of the sole Macchi M.19 shows well the Warren girder mainplane struts and the large Fiat A.14 engine. (*Aeronautica Macchi*)

57,250 cc engine had been badly underestimated and the Macchi design team decided that the rear hull section should be lengthened and a larger horn-balanced rudder fitted. Clearly this work ruled out the M.19 as a contest entry and it was withdrawn. While these and other modifications were embodied and M.19 3098 was prepared for the 1921 contest selection trials, the '300 kg load'—the M.19's raison d'être—was abandoned; nevertheless, having been placed first in these trials, it was included in the list of Italian entrants.

The 1921 contest was a fly-over for Italy as the only competition for the M.19 was two aging M.7s, but on the 12th lap the big Fiat engine's crankshaft broke, fractured a fuel pipe, causing fire to break out in the engine bay and upper mainplane. Zanetti made an emergency alighting out on the circuit, and, with his mechanic Pedetti, was picked up by a rescue launch, while the M.19 burnt itself out.

Two-seat racing biplane flying-boat. Wood and metal construction. Pilot and mechanic in open cockpit.

One 650 hp Fiat A.14 twelve-cylinder water-cooled direct-drive normally-aspirated vee engine driving a 3·29 m (10 ft 9¾ in) diameter four-blade fixed-pitch wooden propeller.

Span 15·86 m (52 ft 0½ in) (upper), 11·72 m (37 ft) (lower); length 11·4 m (37 ft 5 in); height 3·7 m (12 ft 2 in); wing area 45 sq m (484·4 sq ft).

Empty weight 2,160 kg (4,762 lb); loaded weight 2,660 kg (5,864 lb); wing loading 59·1 kg/sq m (12·1 lb/sq ft).

Maximum speed 240 km/h (149 mph).

Production—one M.19 (3098) was built by Aeronautica Macchi at Varese in 1920–21.

Colour—unknown. Believed to have had red mainplanes, red-topped hull and tail unit, white lower hull, and red floats. Contest number 4 allocated but photographs do not show where and whether it was carried on the aircraft.

# Supermarine Sea Lion II

Expedience and economy were ever the watchwords of British aircraft manufacturers in the years between the wars and, clearly, were observed by Hubert Scott-Paine at Supermarine when producing aeroplanes for the Schneider contests. Following the use of the N.1B Baby hull in the Sea Lion I, when the decision was made to build an entrant for the 1922 contest the company used an existing airframe on which to base it. During 1919 two civil sporting amphibian versions of the Baby, named Sea King I, had been built but neither had been sold. One of these became the Sea Lion I; in 1921 the second was developed as the Sea King II, an amphibian fighting scout with a single ·303-in Lewis machine-gun and provision for light bombs, but when it, too, failed to win orders it was modified to become the Sea Lion II G-EBAH.

This view of the Supermarine Sea Lion II in which Henri Biard won the contest in 1922 shows clearly the hull form.

The Sea King hull, constructed of circular-section wooden frames with wood skinning, was retained. The bow was modified, which shortened the Sea King hull to 24 ft 9 in (7·54 m) in its Sea Lion II form. A built-on wooden planing bottom and steps, which were divided into watertight compartments, were added. The upper surface was single-skin planking and the whole structure was covered with fabric and doped. The manually-operated wheeled undercarriage and all military equipment and fittings were removed. The Sea King's mainplanes structure was retained, with four vertical interplane struts replacing the splayed-out struts of the Sea Lion I. The Sea King's wing area was reduced by introducing a narrower chord in the mainplanes, and their span is believed to have been increased by 1 ft 6 in (45 cm) to reach 32 ft (9·75 m). The mainplanes, built as four separate sections, were attached to the upper and lower centre sections. They were built up around two spruce spars with wooden ribs, all wire braced and fabric covered. In place of the earlier 300 hp Hispano-Suiza engine, a 450 hp Lion II, loaned by Napier, was installed, which drove a four-blade wooden pusher propeller of about 8 ft 6 in (2·59 m) diameter. To offset the increased torque and maintain stability, the fin area above the tailplane was enlarged by forward curvature of the leading edge. Because the engine was mounted high between the wings and produced a high thrust-line resulting in a pitching moment, the tailplane had a reverse camber to counteract this. Fuel was supplied to the engine by a high-pressure air system with all fuel lines being kept short and run as clear of the hull as possible.

The earlier Sea King II had not only proved itself capable of aerobatics—Henri Biard, Supermarine's test pilot had rolled and spun the aircraft—but it had also been very stable at all speeds. These characteristics were inherited by the Sea Lion II which was a very tractable aeroplane.

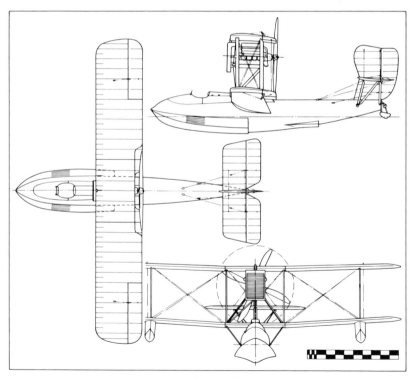

Supermarine Sea Lion II

78

This painting by Leslie Carr shows the Supermarine Sea Lion II passing a balloon marking the 1922 course. (*Vickers Ltd*)

The 1922 Schneider contest was scheduled to take place in Naples during the latter part of August, but the Italians decided to advance the date by some ten days. Unfortunately, the Sea Lion II was still incomplete when news of the change was received by the Royal Aero Club, and so the work was pressed ahead with all speed. When the day came for preliminary engine running the Lion started almost immediately and it was decided to make a preliminary test flight. With Biard aboard, the Sea Lion II got airborne very easily after a short take-off run—but suddenly, when it was some 200 ft over rows of luffing cranes and the masts of ships in Southampton Docks, the Lion engine stopped. Biard managed to pick out a stretch of clear water and glided down to alight safely. The Sea Lion was towed back to Woolston where a fault in the fuel system was diagnosed and corrected. But a precious day was used up.

The following evening Biard again flew the Sea Lion and, finding all was going well, opened the throttle wide to achieve a speed in excess of 150 mph, faster than any British flying-boat had then flown. There followed several days while final modifications were made to the airframe and flying time was built up, then the Sea Lion was dismantled and crated for its journey by sea to Naples.

With the Sea Lion re-assembled, Biard and the Supermarine team launched a cloak-and-dagger operation, first to find out the strength of the French and Italian opposition, and then to conceal from their prying eyes and stop watches the capabilities of the British flying-boat. Accordingly, Biard confined his full-throttle runs to an area well clear of Naples Bay, and made sure that his practice circuits always included some cautious turns around the pylons. This plan worked so well that the Italians publicly proclaimed the inferiority of the Sea Lion when compared with the Macchi M.17 and Savoia S.51. But there was almost disaster, when he flew too close to Vesuvius in an attempt to look down into its crater, and a strong thermal suddenly lifted the Sea Lion some 2,000 ft above its original flight path.

In the contest Biard's tactical flying, plus the Sea Lion's speed, brought the Trophy to Britain; additionally they established world closed-circuit speed, duration and distance records, the first to be recognized for seaplanes.

Soon after its return to the Supermarine factory, the Sea Lion II G-EBAH was bought by the Air Ministry for development flying work, but it has not been established whether it was moved to Felixstowe; it was not, however, removed from the Civil Aircraft Register.

There was also a plan to fly G-EBAH in the 1922 King's Cup air race. That a flying-boat should take part in a race flown entirely over land was a tribute to the reliability of the Lion engine. A report in *Flight* of 7 September records that 'at the moment of going to press we learn this machine will not start'. There were no other references to the Sea Lion in reports of the race.

Single-seat racing biplane flying-boat. Wood and metal construction. Pilot in open cockpit.

One 450 hp Napier Lion II twelve-cylinder water-cooled normally-aspirated geared broad-arrow engine driving an 8 ft 6 in (2·59 m) diameter four-blade fixed-pitch wooden pusher propeller. Fuel: 55 gal (250 litres).

Span 32 ft (9·75 m); length 24 ft 9 in (7·54 m); height 12 ft (3·65 m) approx; wing area 384 sq ft (35·67 sq m).

Empty weight 2,115 lb (959 kg); loaded weight 2,850 lb (1,292 kg); wing loading 7·42 lb/sq ft (36·22 kg/sq m).

Maximum speed 160 mph (257·49 km/h).

Production—one Sea Lion II (G-EBAH) converted from Sea King II by Supermarine Aviation Works, Southampton, in 1922.

Colour—believed to have been overall blue hull, interplane and tailplane support struts; cream or white mainplanes and tailplane; white registration G-EBAH on rear hull sides and national letter G on rudder, black contest number 14 on white panel on hull sides aft of cockpit.

# Savoia S.51

With victories in the 1920 and 1921 contests, Italy was determined to win in 1922 and keep the Schneider Trophy permanently. Accordingly, preparations were made to enter five aircraft in elimination trials. Alessandro Marchetti's S.51 I-BAIU was the most aesthetically appealing flying-boat then built; it was also the fastest of the trials' aircraft. Again Marchetti used the sesquiplane configuration with a tiny lower mainplane half the span of the upper unit and less than 20 per cent of its area. The wooden single-step high-fineness ratio hull had an integral fin with a very

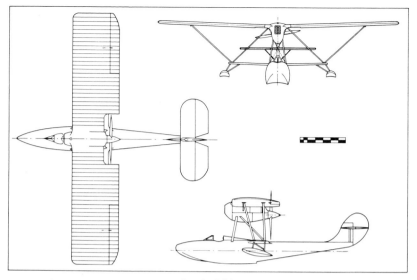

Savoia S.51

large area horn-balanced rudder. A single strut each side supported the fin-mounted tailplane. The open cockpit had a vee windscreen and a long rear head fairing.

The small rectangular lower mainplane was mounted on the hull and was positioned at about mid-chord below the upper unit. Warren girder type interplane struts supported the upper mainplanes. Stabilizing floats were carried on N-struts beyond the tips of the lower mainplane to increase their 'track', and like the hull they had concave undersurfaces.

The 300 hp Hispano-Suiza Itala eight-cylinder water-cooled engine and radiator were mounted in a well-streamlined nacelle forming part of the

I-BAIU, the Savoia S.51 sesquiplane flying-boat, on the tranquil waters of Lake Maggiore. (*SIAI Marchetti*)

upper centre section, and were supported on a pair of N-struts. The two-blade pusher propeller had a long pointed spinner. An unusual feature was the way in which the exhaust gases vented through the top of the nacelle above the mainplane.

Marchetti had designed the S.51 to have minimum drag and the completed aircraft was proof of his achievement.

Alessandro Passaleva was selected to fly the S.51 in the contest at Naples, and during the practice flying the aircraft proved very fast and handled well in the air. Unfortunately, during the mooring-out trials it capsized, and this, while it did not result in disqualification, caused the S.51 to lose the contest when the propeller laminations began to part after their soaking. With a new propeller fitted, the S.51 later showed its speed capabilities—but too late.

The bitter pill of failure in the contest was sweetened a little when, on 28 December, 1922, Passaleva flew I-BAIU and established a new world speed record for seaplanes with an average of 280·15 km/h (174·07 mph) over the one kilometre course.

During 1923 the S.51 was flown in a desultory fashion while plans were made to enter it in that year's Schneider contest and to fit a more powerful new engine. However, neither Hispano-Suiza nor Fiat was able to supply a suitable engine and so I-BAIU was withdrawn.

Single-seat racing biplane flying-boat. Wood and metal construction. Pilot in open cockpit.

One 300 hp Hispano-Suiza Itala eight-cylinder water-cooled normally-aspirated direct-drive vee engine driving a two-blade fixed-pitch wooden propeller.

Span 4 m (13 ft 1¼ in) (lower), 10 m (32 ft 9½ in) (upper); length 8 m (26 ft 3 in); height 2·5 m (8 ft 2½ in); wing area 23 sq m (247·57 sq ft).

Empty weight 780 kg (1,719 lb); loaded weight 1,080 kg (2,381 lb); wing loading 46·9 kg/sq m (9·6 lb/sq ft).

Maximum speed in excess of 280 km/h (174 mph).

Production—one S.51 (I-BAIU) built by Società Idrovolanti Alta Italia in 1922.

Colour—believed all-over red with white rudder. S.51 and stylized blue and white pennant on hull nose, Savoia Marchetti and contest number 8 below cockpit, civil registration I-BAIU on sides of rear hull.

# Macchi M.17

When Alessandro Tonini, Macchi's technical director, designed his first racing seaplane, the M.17, in 1919, he drew heavily on the design of the earlier M.7. Two M.17s were built, the first, powered by a 260 hp Isotta-Fraschini six-cylinder water-cooled inline engine, won the Grand Prix at the 1920 seaplane Rallye at Monaco carrying the number 36. Unfortunately, on alighting it was written off, injuring its pilot, Arturo Zanetti.

It was intended to have flown this aeroplane in the Schneider contest in the following September as a replacement for the still unfinished M.19; however, construction of a second M.17 (I-BAHG) was put in hand but this aeroplane was not completed in time to compete. Italy had pushed through a change in the contest rules, making it obligatory for all entrant aircraft to carry 300 kg of unusable ballast as a commercial load, which favoured the flying-boats then being built by Italian companies. Had the M.17 taken part in the 1920 contest Italy would have been hoist with its own petard for it was underpowered, compared with the M.19, and would not have shown up well against the potential opposition. By 1921 this load rule was abandoned, but the M.17 was not entered in that year's Schneider contest.

Arturo Zanetti's Macchi M.17bis I-BAHG on its launching trolley. Note the unusual single interplane struts and the comparative bulk of the Isotta-Fraschini V.6 engine. (*Aeronautica Macchi*)

The aircraft as prepared for the 1922 contest bore a strong resemblance to the M.7 except that the wing gap was markedly reduced as the upper mainplane was below, rather than above, the pusher engine, the thrust-line of which remained almost unchanged. The upper mainplane had marked dihedral but there was very little on the lower unit. The hull shape was also changed, with the forward section appearing deeper and with a vee-bottom. The structure of the hull and tail unit was almost identical to the M.7 but it is possible that the mainplanes were built up around a single spar with multiple ribs instead of the more conventional two-spar structure.

The engine was mounted on two transversely wire-braced N-struts, with the forward units being of massive broad-chord construction. Only the front was cowled, the rear portion being exposed. A large radiator was carried in front of the engine above the mainplane and the oil-cooler was mounted below it. The engine drove a two-blade pusher propeller.

Single narrow interplane struts were used, with small V-struts top and bottom supporting and attaching them to the mainplanes. The entire structure was wire-braced. Ailerons were carried only on the upper mainplanes, and boxy stabilizing floats were strut-mounted below the lower mainplanes.

During pre-contest practice flying the M.17, flown by Arturo Zanetti, showed a useful turn of speed and promised to pose a real threat to the Sea Lion II but, on the day, managed only third place.

The M.17 was used as a trainer aircraft during 1923 but it was soon recognized by the Macchi design team, now led by Mario Castoldi, that neither the M.17 nor the M.19 could be developed and it is believed that I-BAHG was broken up.

Single-seat racing biplane flying-boat. Wood and fabric construction. Pilot in open cockpit.

One 260 hp Isotta-Fraschini six-cylinder water-cooled direct-drive normally-aspirated inline engine driving a 3·09 m (10 ft 2 in) diameter two-blade fixed-pitch wooden pusher propeller.

Span 8·8 m (28 ft 10½ in) (upper), 7·84 m (25 ft 9 in) (lower); length 7·81 m (25 ft 7½ in); height 2·7 m (8 ft 10½ in); wing area 17 sq m (182·9 sq ft).

Empty weight 750 kg (1,653 lb); loaded weight 950 kg (2,094 lb); wing loading 55·88 kg/sq m (11·44 lb/sq ft).

Maximum speed 240 km/h (149 mph).

Production—official Aeronautica Macchi records show that two M.17s were built during 1920. Some doubts about this have been recorded elsewhere and the view expressed that possibly the first M.17, which was wrecked at Monaco, was rebuilt to become I-BAHG but this is considered to be unlikely.

Colour—initially red hull with white top to forward section, white mainplanes, red floats, white interplane and engine support struts. Black MACCHI-17 on hull nose and I-BAHG on white panel on rear hull sides. Letter I on rudder. Later believed to have been all-over red with white tail unit and engine cowling panels and black contest number 9 on white panel on hull sides below cockpit.

This fine view of Curtiss CR-3 A6081, with David Rittenhouse in the cockpit, shows well the main design features. They include the metal-bladed propeller, the twelve exhaust stubs and the very long float struts. (*Courtesy Royal Aeronautical Society*)

# Curtiss CR-3

When the two Curtiss CR-3 floatplanes, A6081 and A6080, took first and second places respectively, in the 1923 Schneider contest, their design had a long pedigree and the aircraft themselves a history of racing success.

The Curtiss Aeroplane Company and Glenn H. Curtiss, its founder, were no strangers to the world of air racing; flying a biplane of his own design and construction, he had won the first Gordon Bennett Aviation Cup race in 1909, and the company was aware of the importance of racing as a method, even a subterfuge, for advancing the design, performance and reliability both of airframes and engines.

During early 1921 the US Navy carried out a 60-hour test programme on a new direct-drive variant of the very successful Curtiss C-12 engine, redesignated CD-12, and subsequently ordered two engines, with the idea of using them for racing. In May of that year the US Navy, still smarting over the US Army victory in the 1920 Pulitzer Trophy race in which the Navy's best placed entrant was fifth, decided to contest the 1921 race with an 'experimental pursuit' type aeroplane. Accordingly, on 16 June, 1921, the Navy gave a contract to the Curtiss company for the design and construction of two such aircraft. Their design was crystallized early in June, the aircraft initially being designated Curtiss Racer 1 and 2 and later taking the Navy designation CR-1 and CR-2. Construction was completed by 1 August when the CR-2 A6081 was rolled out. It was a sleek single-bay biplane with a closely-cowled engine, the only incongruous note being struck by the two Lamblin 'lobsterpot' radiators on the undercarriage struts. A6080 joined it a week later.

Of predominantly wooden construction, the fuselage, which was made in two halves and joined longitudinally, was a monocoque structure of three layers of Curtiss-ply two-inch wide strips of two-ply spruce, each being glued and copper pinned to bulkheads, and laid diagonally to each other around a hardwood form. Rather appropriately perhaps, for a Navy aircraft, the fuselage was 'clinker-built' in that the copper pins were driven through the three spruce layers and clinched over inside when the monocoque was removed from the form. Ash bearers supported the small frontal area CD-12 engine. The mainplanes were of the spruce multi-spar and multi-rib type with a ply load-bearing skin. The upper was a one-piece unit; the lower ones were built as separate items and carried the full-span ailerons which, like the other control surfaces, were steel frames with fabric covering. The pair of streamlined section N interplane struts were produced in one piece from cross-laminated wood. The one-piece upper mainplane was supported on a thin sharply-swept pylon mounted ahead of the pilot and this, plus the use of streamlined flying wires, provided a very robust assembly. Long conventional wooden V-struts carried the wheeled main undercarriage, which used bungee for shock absorption, and a multi-leafed spring was used for the tailskid. A very large cockpit opening was provided, but once the pilot was aboard a fairing was fitted to enclose him more closely.

The first flight of A6081 was made on 1 August, 1921, by Bert Acosta, Curtiss' chief test pilot, who soon proved the aircraft's excellent handling characteristics, but after landing the wheels ran into small hollows in the ground and the aircraft gently tipped onto its nose. Nevertheless, Acosta and William Wait, the racer's designer, were startled to find that the two halves of the fuselage monocoque had parted company around the cockpit due to the lack of any local reinforcing. A modification was introduced to prevent a recurrence. Flight testing continued through the autumn of 1921 and when the Navy and Army withdrew their entries from that year's Pulitzer Trophy race, Curtiss borrowed A6081 for Acosta to fly in the race—which he won at an average speed of 149·71 mph, in spite of two broken flying wires. An earlier Curtiss racer, the Cactus Kitten triplane, came second. Then, on 22 November, Acosta flew CR-2 A6081 to a new United States absolute speed record of 184·86 mph.

During 1922 both aircraft were modified in readiness for the 1922 Pulitzer race. A6081's Lamblin radiators were replaced with brass wing-surface radiators, the wheels and tyre side-walls were faired over with aluminium discs, and control surface gaps were sealed with strip rubber. Most important was the fitting of a new Curtiss D-12 engine which, during subsequent flight trials, improved the maximum speed by some 17 mph. To provide greater strength to the upper wing at these increased speeds, struts replaced the rear inboard flying wires on A6081 and the forward wires on A6080. Both aircraft subsequently were modified to this standard, A6080 being redesignated CR-2.

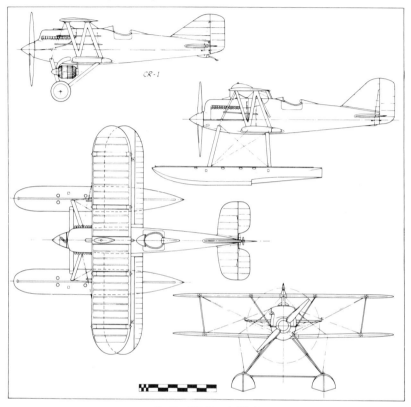

Curtiss CR-3 and CR-1

In the race USN Lieut H. J. Brow came third in CR-2 A6081. First and second were two new Curtiss R-6 racing aircraft entered by the Army. After the race the two Curtiss CR-2s were placed in storage to await—who knew what? As no foreign entrant had ever managed to get to the Pulitzer race starting line it was apparent that this purely fratricidal battle was not presenting the flying challenge nor the technical stimulus which the United States was seeking. Inevitably, it looked to Europe for fresh fields to conquer. In its twin search for prestige to promote commercial interests, and a means of meeting high-speed military aircraft requirements coupled with research into piloting techniques, the US Government and particularly the Navy, believed that they would find both in a Schneider Trophy contest victory. Thus in February 1923 the Navy decided to prepare four aircraft and the necessary team of pilots, engineers and support services, for that year's contest at Cowes.

The aircraft included the two CR-2s, to be converted to floatplanes, a new Navy racer built by Wright Aeronautical Co plus a spare lower-powered aircraft for practice flying. Conversion of the CR-2s began almost at once with removal of the wheeled undercarriages and their replacement by twin-floats. An interesting design feature was the manner in which the four streamlined wooden mounting struts and two spreader-bars were an integral part of the float structure, which, like the Curtiss-ply skin, was all wood. An eight-gallon auxiliary fuel tank was carried in each of the nearly 18 ft (5·48 m) long floats which had a shallow vee-bottom and a single step. The gear assembly was braced by streamlined wires.

The D-12 engines were tuned to deliver 465 hp running on a 50 per cent benzole mixture, and drove Curtiss-Reed two-blade metal propellers produced by machining and twisting a single slab of duralumin to obtain the correct blade section and profile. Cowling panels recontoured to a more streamlined shape enclosed the engine. The extensive area of surface radiators on the upper mainplane was increased and occupied all of the wing with the exception of about the outer 16 inches of the tips. Struts replaced both pairs of inboard flying wires and the swept wing-support pylon was reduced in chord.

Because of the increased keel surface forward following the installation of the floats, the fin area was increased and remained wire braced. Great attention was paid to creating a glassy-smooth high-speed finish on the entire aircraft, with control surface gaps being reduced to the bare

Curtiss CR-3, A6081, on S. E. Saunders' slipway at Cowes. The neat engine and propeller installation and the overall cleanliness of the CR-3 design are apparent in this view.

David Rittenhouse's Curtiss CR-3, A6081 (No. 4), takes-off at the start of the 1923 contest at Cowes. Just visible behind A6081's spinner is Rutledge Irvine's CR-3, A6080 (No. 3), as it climbs away just ahead. This photograph shows the rocked-back 'heels-down' attitude of these Curtiss floatplanes during the take-off run.

minimum and fuel tank fillers and access doors being patched over and varnished to provide a smooth external surface.

With these modifications embodied the two floatplane racers were again redesignated, to become Curtiss CR-3s. The work was completed by early July and the aircraft were removed some eight miles from the Curtiss factory, near Garden City, Long Island, to the company's hangars at Port Washington. Here Lieuts Rutledge Irvine and David Rittenhouse, the two pilots selected to fly in the Schneider contest, began flight trials. Curtiss had a convenient 4·26 miles 'speed course' of its own over Long Island Sound between easily identifiable Execution Rock and Stepping Stone Light. This stretch of open water was well covered by Irvine and Rittenhouse in their preparations for the forthcoming battle above the waters of the Solent in Britain. No aircraft or team could have been better prepared. After Rittenhouse's Schneider contest victory both aircraft were overhauled and prepared to defend the Trophy at Baltimore in 1924. To strengthen their now well-taxed fuselage monocoques, two narrow longitudinal duralumin strips were screwed along the flanks. A6081, the older of the two aircraft, was selected as a contest entrant while A6080 was the team reserve aircraft. When the expected opposition from Europe failed to materialize, the United States sportingly cancelled the contest on 4 September, 1924, rather than stage a fly-over. Instead, on 25 October, USN Lieuts George T. Cuddihy and Ralph A. Ofstie, the pilots who had been chosen to fly them in the cancelled contest, put on a public demonstration of speed flying—with a purpose. Cuddihy in A6081 established a new world speed record for floatplanes at 188·13 mph, and

Ofstie, flying over the prepared Schneider contest course, set closed-circuit records over 100 km, 200 km and 500 km; the first two distances at 178·24 mph and the latter distance at 161·13 mph.

Then, sadly, A6080's work in the air completed, its airframe was used in test-to-destruction structural research tests in the Naval Aircraft Factory, Philadelphia. A6081 is believed to have survived as a practice aircraft for the 1925 and 1926 Schneider contest teams.

Single-seat twin-float racing biplane. Predominantly wooden construction with some metal components. Pilot in an open cockpit.

One 465 hp Curtiss D-12 twelve-cylinder water-cooled direct-drive normally-aspirated vee engine driving an 8 ft 9 in (2·6 m) diameter Curtiss-Reed two-blade fixed-pitch metal propeller. Fuel: 67½ US gal (365·76 litres); oil 4 gal (15 litres).

Span 22 ft 8 in (6·9 m); length 25 ft 0⅜ in (7·62 m); height 10 ft 9 in (3·27 m); wing area 168 sq ft (15·6 sq m); float length 17 ft 11 in (5·46 m).

Empty weight 2,119 lb (961 kg); loaded weight 2,746 lb (1,245 kg); wing loading 16·35 lb/sq ft (79·82 kg/sq m).

Maximum speed 194 mph (312·2 km/h); stalling speed 76 mph (122·3 km/h).

Production—two CR-3s were produced by conversion of CR-2 airframes by Curtiss Aeroplane Co, Long Island, in 1923.

Colour—US Navy grey overall, except for yellow fin, white rudder, and natural brass radiators. Black stripe down leading edge of rudder. Black serial number carried on rudder with black letters USN edged in white on fuselage sides. Black contest number 4 edged in white carried on fuselage side forward of letters, and on rudder without white edging. US Navy seal on side of fuselage below cockpit. For 1924 world speed-record runs black number 8 without white edging was carried (A6081). The same colour scheme was applied to the other CR-3, which carried the contest number 3. The scheme used for 1924 closed-circuit speed-record runs is not known for certain, but it is believed that the aircraft was finished the same way with the same style of markings, except that a number 9 was carried on the fuselage sides and rudder (A6080).

# Supermarine Sea Lion III

For the 1923 Schneider contest the Air Ministry decided that the old Sea Lion II G-EBAH should participate again. Reginald Mitchell at Supermarine rapidly produced drawings to initiate a general modification programme aimed at cleaning up the hull and increasing its fineness ratio. As a result the hull length was increased by 2 ft 9 in (83 cm). A new planing bottom was attached to the hull and the bow section refined; in addition the wing span was reduced by 4 ft (1·21 m), and the area of the fin and rudder was increased by making them taller.

During the flight-test programme the shoe-shaped floats were removed and oval-section stabilizing floats, with pairs of small hydrovanes at their forward end, were mounted on short struts and wire braced to the underside of the lower mainplanes near the tips. For the first time on a Sea Lion, a small glass windscreen was mounted in front of the open cockpit.

Henri Biard taxies the Supermarine Sea Lion III G-EBAH past the moored Blackburn Pellet during practice flying. A feature of this Sea Lion variant was the large fin and rudder area above the tailplane.

This close-up view of the Sea Lion III G-EBAH shows details of the long radiator air intake, the engine mounting struts, and fixed starting handle. What appears to be an additional 'lash-up' pitot head is carried on the starboard outer interplane struts.

Power for the Sea Lion III came from a 525 hp Napier Lion III which drove a four-blade wooden pusher propeller. The engine, in its aluminium nacelle with a circular-section radiator housed in a long-chord tubular cowling, was supported on a pair of N-struts; the fuel lines were carried up inside a streamlined radiator support strut from the hull fuel tank to the engine.

A strange feature of this cleaning-up process was that the engine starting handle was permanently fixed to the power unit and protruded from the port side of the nacelle; moreover, the tailplane had no less than eight wire-braced support struts, and the original combined water-rudder/tailskid was retained.

In the contest, although Biard and the Sea Lion III returned a speed some 12 mph faster than that at which they had won the previous year's event, they were outclassed by the Curtiss CR-3s and could only take third place.

During the first few weeks following the contest, Biard flew the Sea Lion III on some further flight trials; then during the first week of December it was taken on RAF charge, serialled N170 and moved to Felixstowe.

Single-seat racing biplane flying-boat. Wood and metal construction. Pilot in open cockpit.

One 525 hp Napier Lion III twelve-cylinder water-cooled normally-aspirated geared broad-arrow engine driving an 8 ft 8 in (2·64 m) diameter four-blade fixed-pitch wooden pusher propeller. Fuel: 60 gal (272 litres).

Span 28 ft (8·53 m); length 28 ft (8·53 m); wing area 360 sq ft (33·44 sq m).

Empty weight 2,400 lb (1,088 kg); loaded weight 3,275 lb (1,485 kg); wing loading 9·09 lb/sq ft (44·4 kg/sq m).

Maximum speed 175 mph (281·61 km/h); alighting speed 55 mph (88·51 km/h).

Production—one Sea Lion III (G-EBAH) converted from Sea Lion II by Supermarine Aviation Works, Woolston, Southampton, in 1923.

Colour—believed overall blue hull, silver mainplanes and tail unit, natural aluminium engine nacelle. Black registration letters G-EBAH on white panel on hull sides, and contest number 7 on white panel on nose aft of cockpit and on rudder. A sealion's 'face' was painted in white on the noses of the hull and the two stabilizing floats as was the name *Sea Lion III* on the hull sides beneath the cockpit.

# CAMS 38

A further refinement of the CAMS 36 flying-boat, Conflenti's CAMS 38 (F-ESFD) was built for the 1923 Schneider contest. Its basic structure was almost identical to that of the earlier aircraft and used a hull with a concave bottom surface. The major changes were the physical reversing of the engine installation to produce a pusher-type unit and the positioning of the pilot forward of the mainplanes.

Detail alterations to the engine installation included the repositioning of the oil coolers, which were located in an arc under the engine nacelle, and the use of a more efficient low-drag radiator. While this type of installation allowed the mainplanes to enjoy a fairly undisturbed airflow, the propeller operated in an airstream which had been disturbed by its passage through a radiator, around the quite bulbous nose of the engine nacelle and its mounting struts. It did, however, keep the propeller well clear of spray or green water and enabled the pilot to be located in a position where he had an unimpeded view forward and upward.

Maurice Hurel in the CAMS 38 F-ESFD takes-off for the contest past the uss *Pittsburgh* anchored off Cowes.

The CAMS 38 F-ESFD at Cowes. The aircraft carries military markings on the upper wing as well as its civil test registration. (*Courtesy Jacques Gambu*)

The CAMS 38 travelled with the CAMS 36bis from France to Cowes for the Schneider contest in a French naval vessel. All of the CAMS flying-boats sat low in the water, with little freeboard, and their pilots all

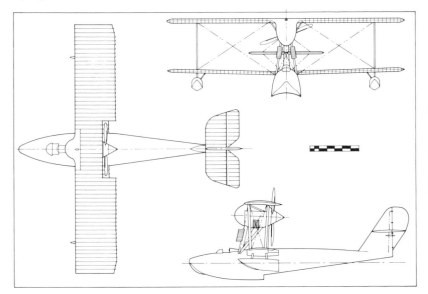

CAMS 38

preferred calm conditions when flying. Nevertheless, even though the waters of the Solent were rough for the navigability trials, the CAMS 38 handled well, and its pilot, Lieut de Vaisseau Maurice Hurel, completed them satisfactorily. During the CAMS 38's take-off run in the contest on 28 September, the starboard tailplane and elevator were damaged by rough water; however, Hurel safely got airborne and, with the control column held back to maintain height, he bravely set out on his first lap of the course. This was completed in a very slow time and, when the Hispano-Suiza engine began to vibrate and lose power on the second lap, Hurel alighted with some difficulty out on the course near to the first turning point at Selsey Bill. After the contest the CAMS 38 returned to the manufacturer's test site at St Raphaël where it was used for general flight-trials work.

Single-seat racing biplane flying-boat. Wood and fabric construction. Pilot in open cockpit.

One 360 hp Hispano-Suiza modèle 42 eight-cylinder water-cooled direct-drive normally-aspirated vee engine driving a 2·05 m (6 ft 9 in) (approx) four-blade fixed-pitch wooden propeller. Fuel: 295 litres* (65 gal).

Span 8·6 m (28 ft 2½ in); length 8·32 m (27 ft 3½ in); height 2·79 m (9 ft 2 in); wing area 18·8 sq m (202·36 sq ft).

Empty weight 941 kg (2,075 lb); loaded weight 1,255 kg (2,766 lb); wing loading 66·75 kg/sq m (13·66 lb/sq ft).

Maximum speed 270 km/h (167·76 mph).

Production—one CAMS 38 (F-ESFD) built by Chantiers Aéro-Maritimes de la Seine at St Denis and St Raphaël, France, during 1922–23.

Colour—believed to have been mainly white; black registration letters on hull sides and below lower mainplane; contest number 9 on sides of nose and on rudder.

*Estimated figure.

# Curtiss R2C-2

In a leap-frogging sequence with the US Navy, the US Army won the 1922 Pulitzer Trophy race at Selfridge Field, Michigan, when First Lieut Russell L. Mangham flew the Curtiss R-6 (AS.68564) into first place at an average of 205·85 mph (331·27 km/h), followed in second place by First Lieut Lester J. Maitland in another R-6 (AS.68563) at 198·85 mph (320·01 km/h). The Navy came third and fourth; Lieut Harold J. Brow in the Curtiss CR-2 (A6081) led in Lieut Alford J. Williams in the slightly older CR-2 (A6080).

The two R-6s were a quantum jump forward in racing aircraft design with their single broad-chord interplane struts and wire-braced single-strut landing gear, an updated wing and control surface structure plus the latest Curtiss D-12 engine.

The Curtiss R2C-2, A6692, built for the 1924 contest at Baltimore which was cancelled. It was the reserve US Navy aircraft for the following year's contest but was not required to participate. (*Flight*)

Their victory and the manner in which they achieved it stimulated the Navy to seek an instrument by which they could redress the situation. Using air racing as a means to an end, the Navy was developing two new engines for use in its Service aircraft; one of the engines intended to be a 500 hp unit for Navy fighters, was a developed Curtiss D-12, designated D-12A.

A method of creating a high-speed racing aircraft, capable of winning the Pulitzer Trophy, and of advancing the D-12 development programme at once became apparent. Accordingly, early in 1923 the Navy ordered two new landplane racers from Curtiss which, in March of that year, took the designation R2C-1.

These aeroplanes (A6691 and A6692) were closely related to, but were different in a number of important aspects from, the R-6s. Like earlier Curtiss racers designed by Bill Wait, the R2C-1 had a monocoque fuselage built up from layers of Curtiss-ply. The wing structure was of the multi-spar-and-rib type, in which the spar webs had been reduced in weight by routering, all clad with a Curtiss-ply skin. Brass wing-surface radiators overlaid this wood skinning, with the integral header tank forming part of the leading edge. The upper mainplane was mounted directly to the top of the fuselage and the lower was of shorter span and chord. Ailerons were fitted on upper and lower mainplanes. The fin and tailplane were cantilever structures and all the control surfaces were fabric-covered duralumin structures, which were operated through a differentially geared control system. Redesign of the D-12 engine's oil system produced a power unit with a smaller frontal area, an improved

96

carburetion system enabled a high rpm and power output to be obtained, and the whole engine was some 40 lb (18 kg) lighter than its predecessor. The new D-12A was carried on high-tensile steel-tube bearers which were attached to the front of the fireproof engine bulkhead.

In the Pulitzer Trophy race held, after a three-day weather delay, on 6 October, 1923, at Lambert Field, Missouri, Al Williams came home first in A6692 at an average 243·67 mph (392·14 km/h) and Harold Brow was in second place in A6691 at 241·77 mph (389·08 km/h). During the following month Williams and Brow took turns in their respective aircraft to raise the world speed record and finally, on 4 November, Williams' average of 266·59 mph (429·02 km/h) was allowed to stand and was ratified as a record.

During the following winter both aircraft remained in store until, in April 1924, A6691 was 'sold' to the Army for $1 and redesignated R-8. A6692 was overhauled, solid laminated wood interplane struts replaced the partially hollow struts used earlier; and twin-floats, mounted on raked forward inverted V-struts with streamlined spreader-bars and heavily wire-braced, were fitted. In this form the new Curtiss racing floatplane was designated R2C-2 and prepared for entry in the Schneider Trophy contest at Baltimore.

Although the contest was cancelled, Lieut David Rittenhouse flew, downwind, over Curtiss' unofficial measured course in Long Island Sound at an average 226·99 mph (365·31 km/h). In 1925 A6692 was listed as an entrant in the contest with Lieut Frank H. Conant as pilot, but later it was relegated to the reserve slot and did not participate. Its flying life ended on 13 September, 1926, when Marine Corps First Lieut Harmon J. Norton formated on two Army aircraft over the Potomac River near the Anacostia Naval Air Station. Having finished some low-level practice runs in the R2C-2 he pulled up behind the two military aeroplanes, then stalled and dived inverted into the water. A6692 was written-off and Norton was killed.

Single-seat twin-float racing biplane. Wood and metal construction with wood and fabric covering. Pilot in open cockpit.

One 507 hp Curtiss D-12A twelve-cylinder water-cooled direct-drive normally-aspirated vee engine driving an 8 ft 4 in (2·53 m) diameter Curtiss-Reed two-blade fixed-pitch metal propeller. Fuel: 60 US gal (227 litres); oil 5 US gal (19 litres).

Span 22 ft 8 in (6·9 m) (upper), 19 ft 3 in (5·86 m) (lower); length 27 ft 8 in (8·43 m); height 10 ft 6 in (3·2 m); wing area 144·25 sq ft (13·4 sq m).

Empty weight 2,036 lb (923 kg); loaded weight 2,540 lb (1,152 kg); wing loading 17·6 lb/sq ft (85·97 kg/sq m).

Maximum speed 227 mph (365·31 km/h); stalling speed 80 mph (128·74 km/h).

Production—one R2C-2 was produced by conversion of an R2C-1 airframe by Curtiss Aeroplane Co, Long Island, in 1924.

Colour—US Navy grey overall with regulation USN red, white and blue rudder stripes, black serial number on white stripe, white number 6 carried on fuselage sides, regulation USN marking carried on top surface of upper wing.

One of the Curtiss R3C-1s which were converted to R3C-2 floatplanes for the 1925 contest. The event was won by Lieut James Doolittle flying the R3C-2 A7054. (*Courtesy RAF Museum*)

# Curtiss R3C-2, -3 and -4

With the advance of aircraft design and production technologies and the growing cost of producing technically complex racing machines, early in 1925 the US Army and Navy decided to contribute jointly to the costs involved in creating four examples of a new Curtiss racer, one airframe to be used for structural strength tests. In the event, in April when Curtiss was given authority to proceed with this work, the US Navy paid the lion's share.

Designated R3C, the 'new' racers were modified airframes of the earlier R2Cs and thus, dimensionally, were very similar. Two major differences were in the powerplant and the wing section chosen. Power for these latest Curtiss racers came from the new Curtiss V-1400, which was a development of the D-12A but which had a far superior power-to-weight ratio. It drove a new Curtiss-Reed propeller having drop-forged, rather than the earlier twisted, duralumin blades. An improved oil cooler also was fitted. The Curtiss C-80 aerofoil section had an almost incredible six per cent thickness/chord ratio and a shape producing maximum lift with minimum drag. Because of its thin section two of the spruce spars were doubled for two-thirds span to provide additional strength inboard.

The first R3C (A6978) was pushed out of the factory on 11 September and was flown for the first time by Navy Lieut Alford Williams. Almost immediately he began having problems; first, the aluminium fairings over the wheels and tyre walls fell off in the air. When Lieut James H. Doolittle got airborne and put in a particularly high-speed run, he felt the lateral control changing; sensing disaster he did a quick visual check on the R3C's ailerons, only to find that the port upper mainplane was showing signs of structural failure. Doolittle throttled back and landed safely, thus saving himself—and A6978, which was repaired. On a later flight the propeller spinner also split, one half being thrown back by the propeller, damaging the wing surface radiators and tail unit. About ten days after its roll-out this aircraft was fitted with floats.

Doolittle, as an Army test pilot at McCook Field, spent many hours perfecting high-speed turning techniques both for military landplanes and for the Schneider Trophy floatplanes. For the 1925, and last, Pulitzer Trophy race, Al Williams flew the second R3C-1, A6979, in which he was placed second to Army First Lieut Cyrus Bettis in another R3C-1. After this race the remaining R3C-1s were mounted on floats and took the designation R3C-2.

The USN pilots selected as team members with Doolittle for the 1925 Schneider Trophy contest were Lieuts G. Cuddihy and Ralph Ofstie, but in the contest itself, on 26 October, Doolittle's greater experience of high-speed flying plus his immaculate cornering paid off and he won conclusively. He was almost assured of being the first US pilot home because both of the Navy aircraft experienced engine failure out on the course, one with a broken magneto quill shaft and the other with over-heating and fire.

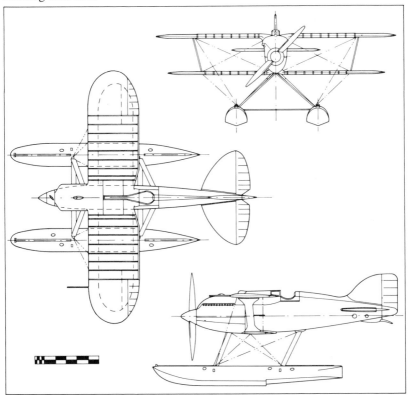

Curtiss R3C-2

On the day after the contest both aircraft were repaired, check flown, and then returned to Philadelphia's Naval Aircraft Factory for the traditional winter storage. Doolittle, however, flying the Pulitzer-winning R3C, set a world speed record for floatplanes at 245·7 mph (395·4 km/h).

With two Schneider Trophy victories plus a number of absolute and closed-circuit records to its credit, the United States was confident, perhaps over confident, that a third consecutive win in the 1926 contest was merely a formality. This confidence was clearly illustrated by the decision to equip each of the Curtiss racers with a different engine. Thus the contest was to be a function of various engine development programmes and not solely a means of winning the Trophy outright. It also was to be a vindication of the Navy's policy of promoting the Packard company to compete with Curtiss in the creation of high-performance aero engines.

With hindsight, the wisdom of this decision can be called into question. How much more would have been gained by concentrating on the development of one engine and airframe combination is open to conjecture, but such a step could have led to total victory and an earlier end to the contest series.

The new Curtiss engine, yet another development along the D-12 line, was designated V-1550 and produced some 685 hp at about 2,600 rpm. It was built within the same scantlings as the V-1400 yet with an even smaller frontal area. Curtiss had toyed with the idea of fitting a reduction gear, but the engine emerged as a direct-drive unit. The Packard engine, like the V-1550, was the latest in a development line which stretched back some four years. A twelve-cylinder liquid-cooled normally-aspirated geared vee engine, it was known as the 2A-1500 and produced some 650 hp at 2,700 rpm. The third engine was the older, but well proven Curtiss V-1400 which powered the R3C-2 in which Doolittle had won the 1925 contest and which, later, had been taken on charge by the US Navy serialled A7054.

Ofstie's R3C-2, A6978, was converted to have the Packard 2A-1500 at the Naval Aircraft Factory; also it was fitted with Curtiss floats of a new design and there were some detail changes around the cockpit. In addition the windscreen was redesigned and surface radiators were fitted on the forward float struts. In this form it was redesignated R3C-3. While the symmetrical lines which the geared Packard gave to the nose and engine bay of the R3C-3 were unique, unfortunately, Jesse Vincent, the engine's designer, had flouted United States naval aircraft convention and design by making the 2A-1500 turn the big Standard steel propeller in the opposite direction to the direct-driven Curtiss propellers. Not unexpectedly, pilots, used to correcting for a yaw to port when that float dug into the water in response to the Curtiss' torque reaction, suddenly found the yaw was to starboard. It was an additional hazard which the Schneider Trophy team pilots could have done without.

Curtiss' new V-1550 was fitted in A6979, which also had floats of the

A6978, the first Curtiss R3C after conversion from R3C-2 and being fitted with a 650 hp Packard 2A-1500 engine to become the R3C-3. (*Courtesy Peter M. Bowers*)

new Curtiss design plus surface radiators on the forward float struts, like those on the R3C-3. In this form the aircraft became the R3C-4. Sadly, the Navy pilot assigned to fly it, Lieut H. Conant, was killed. He was succeeded by Lieut Carleton C. Champion who had his own ideas about the precise ingredients of the fuel 'cocktail' necessary to keep the V-1550 running efficiently. His insistence on using the wrong mix caused severe

The 1925 Curtiss R3C-2 A6979 after conversion to R3C-4 with 685 hp Curtiss V-1550 engine. The aircraft had earlier been an R3C-1. (*Courtesy Peter M. Bowers*)

detonation which wrecked the engine and the cooling system. However, when a new V-1550 was fitted and the radiators repaired, Cuddihy took it up on an air test; it proved to be a very potent entrant for the Schneider Trophy contest. The engine performed so well at slightly higher rpm that a larger propeller was fitted.

Before the mandatory navigability tests the R3C-4 had some minor snags cured in the V-1550's lubrication system, the hand pump to raise fuel from the float tanks was replaced, and a propeller blade, a little bent from smashing through some heavy float spray, was straightened.

On 12 November, when the weather finally allowed the navigability and flying trials to continue, the pilots allocated to the R3C-3 and -4 were Lieut William G. Tomlinson and the experienced Cuddihy respectively. Although Cuddihy had few problems, Tomlinson had difficulty coping with the opposite-handed torque reaction of the R3C-3's propeller. He got airborne with some difficulty and, although he handled the aircraft well enough in the air, he dropped it heavily while alighting, cartwheeled and sank in an inverted position. Happily, Tomlinson was rescued unhurt and flew an ageing Curtiss Hawk in the contest.

Single-seat twin-float racing biplane. Wood and metal construction with wood and fabric covering. Pilot in open cockpit.

One 650 hp Packard 2A-1500 twelve-cylinder water-cooled geared normally-aspirated vee engine driving a Standard two-blade fixed-pitch metal propeller (R3C-3, A6978).

One 685 Curtiss V-1550 twelve-cylinder water-cooled direct-drive normally-aspirated vee engine driving a 9 ft 4 in (2·84 m) diameter Curtiss-Reed two-blade fixed-pitch metal propeller (R3C-4, A6979).

One 565 hp Curtiss V-1400 twelve-cylinder water-cooled direct-drive normally-aspirated vee engine driving an 8 ft 4 in (2·53 m) diameter Curtiss-Reed two-blade fixed-pitch metal propeller (R3C-2, A7054).

Fuel: 60 US gal (227 litres); oil 4 US gal (15 litres).

Span 22 ft (6·7 m) (upper), 20 ft (6·09 m) (lower); length 22 ft (6·7 m); height 10 ft 4 in (3·14 m); wing area 144 sq ft (13·37 sq m).

Empty weight 2,144 lb (927 kg); loaded weight 2,738 lb (1,242 kg); wing loading 19 lb/sq ft (32·89 kg/sq m)—R3C-2. Empty weight 2,350 lb (1,066 kg); loaded weight 2,800 lb (1,270 kg); wing loading 19·44 lb/sq ft (34·98 kg/sq m)—R3C-3 estimated. Empty weight 2,250 lb (1,020 kg); loaded weight 2,800 lb (1,270 kg); wing loading 19·44 lb/sq ft (34·98 kg/sq m) R3C-4 estimated.

Maximum speed 258 mph (415·2 km/h) R3C-3 A6978; 256 mph (411·98 km/h) R3C-4 A6979; 238 mph (383·01 km/h) R3C-2 A7054.

Production—three R3C variants produced by conversion of previous year's aircraft. R3C-2 was modified aircraft which won 1925 Schneider Trophy contest; R3C-3 was 1925 R3C-2 airframe with Packard 2A-1500 engine; R3C-4 was 1925 R3C-2 airframe with Curtiss V-1550 engine. A fourth airframe was reputed to have been used for structural test programme by Curtiss.

Colour—fuselage, tail unit and alighting gear overall blue-black; chrome-yellow wings; natural brass surface radiators. Standard US rudder stripes and wing markings carried. White contest numbers carried on fuselage sides for 1925 contest were: 1/A6978, 2/A6979, 3/later A7054; for 1926 contest: ?/A6978, 4/A6979, 6/A7054.

The Gloster IIIA N195 at Baltimore, showing the increased chord on the dorsal and ventral fins to improve the longitudinal stability which was embodied after preliminary flight trials at Felixstowe. (*US Air Force*)

# Gloster III

The United States Navy's victory in the 1923 Schneider Trophy contest at Cowes acted as a great stimulus to both the British and Italian Air Ministries, and when the 1924 contest was postponed for a year, the Gloster and Supermarine companies redoubled their efforts to produce new designs for high-speed floatplanes. In February 1925 the Air Ministry placed orders with these two companies, the one for Gloster being worth £16,000 and covering the design and production of two aircraft.

Like its predecessors, the Gloster III was a single-strut biplane powered by a 700 hp Napier Lion VII twelve-cylinder engine, which made it the smallest aircraft for its power ever built in Great Britain to that time. Almost inevitably it was a biplane and it needed all of Folland's ingenuity to produce an aerodynamically clean airframe. The result was a small frontal-area fuselage of wooden monocoque construction built up from a framework of light ash formers with three-ply skinning. The wire-braced dorsal and ventral fins had wood skinning with fabric-covered rudder and elevators. The traditional Folland S.E.5-style fin and rudder was used initially. The three banks of cylinders were carefully cowled with long duralumin 'helmets'. The mainplanes had spruce spars with ash ribs and were fabric covered and the patent Gloster method of attaching fabric to the ribs was retained. Ailerons were fitted only on the lower wings which continued the earlier squared-off tip design while the full-rounded tips were retained on the upper wings. Folland had designed

103

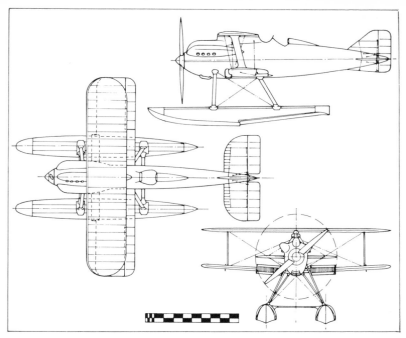

Gloster IIIA

surface radiators for the Gloster III but unfortunately they were not completed in time to be fitted for flight trials, and so long Lamblin radiators were mounted on the leading edges of the lower mainplanes. Duralumin floats, built by Shorts and weighing some 368 lb (167 kg), were fitted on four streamlined wire-braced struts with two streamlined spreader-bars. These floats were first fitted and tested on the Gloster I before equipping the Gloster III.

At Felixstowe, 12-day taxi-ing trials of the prototype (N194) began on 16 August, 1925, and were completed with some success even though there was very rough water and bad weather throughout the period of the trials. On 29 August Hubert Broad made the first flight of the Gloster III and subsequently reported that, apart from some directional instability, handling characteristics and performance were satisfactory. It was proposed that dihedral should be introduced in the upper mainplanes to match that of the lower ones; however, there was insufficient time for this fundamental modification to be embodied and it was decided only to increase the chord of the dorsal and ventral fins. With these fin changes the aircraft were designated Gloster IIIAs, and N194 made only four flights with the new tail configuration before it was crated for despatch to Baltimore. Bert Hinkler flew the second aircraft, G-EBLJ, on 3 June, 1925, still hampered by poor weather and water conditions, before it was serialled N195 for the contest; but this was his only flight before the aircraft were crated for shipment. The Gloster contingent of the British team arrived at Bay Shore Park on Chesapeake Bay, near Baltimore, on 6 October, 1925, to find weather conditions were even worse than at Felixstowe. No hangars were available for the two Gloster IIIs and the Gloster I—which had been taken over as a spare aircraft—nor accommodation for the crews. Ultimately a leaky canvas hangar was arranged for the Gloster team's use but, largely because of continuing bad weather, the aircraft remained unassembled for several days. On 13 October Hubert Broad managed a 15-min flight in N194 and, when Henri Biard crashed during preliminary flying with the Supermarine S.4—Broad being the first to reach Biard as he taxied in after the Gloster III's navigability tests—Hinkler's aircraft, N195, was hastily prepared for the contest as a replacement.

Twice Hinkler attempted to complete navigability tests but each time the weather defeated him. Finally, after a 48-hr postponement of the contest date, he set off yet again early in the morning of 26 October, but the waves were so strong that they broke two of his float struts and bracing wires. The nose dropped and the propeller chopped into the floats, putting rapid repair beyond possibility. Thus, with hopes of a British victory finally pinned on Broad's Gloster IIIA, the little biplane fought a losing battle with the faster and winning Curtiss R3C-2, and did well to take second place with an average speed of 199·167 mph

Hubert Broad's Gloster IIIA N195 after it had been fitted with surface radiators, revised fin and cantilever tail unit.

105

(320·53 km/h). Had the Royal Aero Club entered three aircraft in the contest instead of only two, the second Gloster III would have been in competition trim when the S.4 crashed. Had Folland's surface radiators been fitted and the two aircraft completed earlier to give Broad and Hinkler more flying experience at Felixstowe, then the whole pattern of events there and at Baltimore would have been different and Gloster's name could have been in the 1925 contest winner's slot.

After the contest the two Gloster IIIs and the Gloster I were returned to Cheltenham where further modifications were embodied in N195. They included the fitting of the surface radiators on all four mainplanes, a streamlined expansion header tank on the upper centre section, a revised and enlarged windscreen, a fully cantilevered tail unit from which all external control levers were removed and with a curved leading edge to the fin, and the use of streamlined bracing wires in place of the earlier round wires used in N194. With these modifications embodied, N195 was redesignated Gloster IIIB. N194 was re-delivered to Felixstowe in June 1926 and N195 followed it there in November, when both aircraft were used as trainers for the pilots of the RAF High Speed Flight preparing for the 1927 Schneider contest. It is reported that during December 1926 and into April 1927 a number of propellers were flown on development trials on N194, powered with a 700 hp Lion VII engine. They included Fairey Reed and Hele-Shaw Beacham adjustable-pitch units of different diameters.

The ultimate fate of the two Gloster IIIs cannot be established.

Single-seat twin-float racing biplane. Wooden construction with plywood and fabric covering. Pilot in open cockpit.

One 700 hp Napier Lion VII twelve-cylinder liquid-cooled broad-arrow engine, driving a Fairey Reed two-blade fixed-pitch metal propeller. Fuel: 54¾ gal (249 litres); oil 4¼ gal (19 litres).

Span 20 ft (6·09 m); length 26 ft 10 in (8·1 m); height 9 ft 8 in (2·94 m); wing area 152 sq ft (14·12 sq m).

IIIA Empty weight 2,028 lb (920 kg); loaded weight 2,687 lb (1,218 kg); wing loading 17·68 lb/sq ft (86·32 kg/sq m).

IIIB Empty weight 2,278 lb (1,033 kg); loaded weight 2,952 lb (1,343 kg); wing loading 19·4 lb/sq ft (94·71 kg/sq m).

Maximum speed at sea level 225 mph (362 km/h) Gloster IIIA; 252 mph (405 km/h) Gloster IIIB; alighting speed 80 mph (128 km/h).

Production—two Gloster IIIs built by Gloucestershire Aircraft Co Ltd, Cheltenham and Hucclecote, in 1925.

Colour—Cambridge blue fuselage, remainder ivory with dark blue contest number 5 on fuselage sides. After the contest an overall silver finish was applied with regulation RAF roundels and rudder stripes, black serial number N194 on fuselage sides and rudder (Broad's aircraft). Cambridge blue fuselage, remainder ivory, initially with dark blue contest number 5 on fuselage sides. This was roughly obscured and a crude number 4 substituted when this Gloster III took the S.4's contest number after it had crashed. Contest number 5 was re-allocated to Broad's aircraft. After the contest an overall silver finish was applied, with regulation RAF roundels and rudder stripes, black serial number N195 on fuselage sides and rudder (Hinkler's aircraft).

Giovanni de Briganti's Macchi M.33 (MM.49) which took third place in the 1925 contest. This was the first cantilever monoplane to complete a Schneider contest. (*Aeronautica Macchi*)

# Macchi M.33

Sadly, political influences in sport were apparent in Italy's Schneider contest endeavours during 1925. Then, Mussolini's Government, professing to be sponsoring Italian participation, limited its support to providing two Curtiss D-12A engines, purchased from the United States in the previous year. Even these had spent many hours on Fiat's testbeds and were unable to produce their full rated power output. Thus the Macchi company bore the cost and responsibility for Italy's attendance at the Baltimore contest.

To match the potential performance of the new Curtiss racers, Mario Castoldi, Macchi's chief designer, conceived the design of a sleek cantilever monoplane flying-boat, his first racer for his company. While at first sight it appeared much like earlier Macchi biplane racers with the upper mainplane removed, it was more than that. The slim hull had a very flat planing bottom, a single step well forward with a long rear section terminating in a graceful swept-up fin and rudder. Initially the rudder was unbalanced but later was modified to embody a balancing surface forward of the hinge line. The open cockpit had a streamlined headrest and was located above the mainplane. The two-spar wooden mainplane had a relatively thick 16 per cent thickness/chord ratio of bi-convex symmetrical section. It was built in three sections: a centre section built integral with the hull, and two long outer panels. Small teardrop stabilizing floats

107

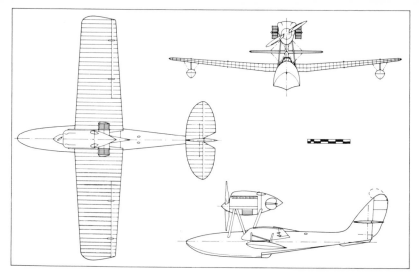

Macchi M.33

were strut mounted and wire braced below the mainplane. Long-span narrow-chord ailerons occupied two-thirds of the trailing edge. The alleged 500 hp D-12A engine was mounted high above the hull on a pair of N-struts and was enclosed in a neat streamlined nacelle, the lines of which were spoiled by two large plate-type radiators mounted at the rear of the nacelle. An oil-cooler was fitted flush with the nacelle undersurface. It drove a 2·28 m (7 ft 6 in) diameter two-blade propeller.

Three M.33s were built at Varese; two were flying examples (MM. 48—49) and the third was for structural test work. Flight testing took place on Lake Maggiore where a 50 km race circuit was set out. Riccardo Morselli and Giovanni de Briganti, the Macchi test pilots, achieved speeds of nearly 320 km/h (199 mph) in the M.33s but they had some misgivings about the cantilever mainplane and found that the tired engines misfired and needed careful handling.

At Baltimore these engine problems again proved almost insurmountable during practice flying and the navigability trials. Some dedicated work by the engineers got both aircraft serviceable for the contest day but a faulty ignition system prevented Morselli from starting MM.48's engine and this aircraft was withdrawn. De Briganti was placed third in the contest.

Both aircraft were later used for training at Italy's school for high-speed flying.

▶

The drawing opposite shows Curtiss D-12A installation, hull-housed fuel tank, and cockpit of the Macchi M.33. (*Aeronautica Macchi*)

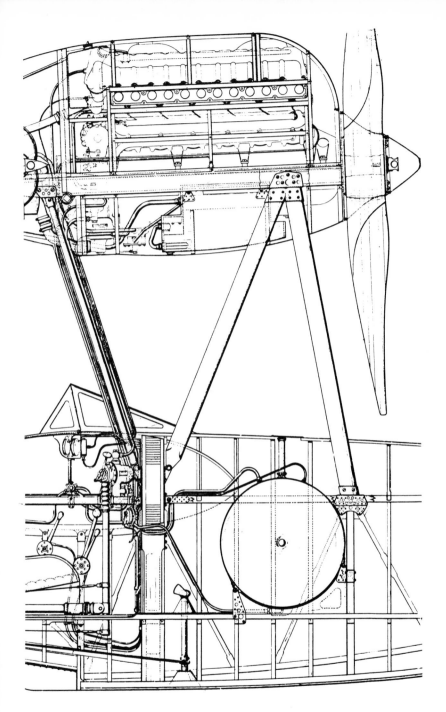

Single-seat racing monoplane flying-boat. Wooden construction with wood and fabric covering. Pilot in open cockpit.

One 500 hp Curtiss D-12A twelve-cylinder water-cooled direct-drive normally-aspirated vee engine driving a 2·28 m (7 ft 6 in) diameter two-blade fixed-pitch wooden propeller.

Span 10 m (32 ft 10 in); length 8·28 m (27 ft 2 in); height 2·68 m (8 ft 9 in); wing area 15 sq m (161·46 sq ft).

Empty weight 975 kg (2,149 lb); loaded weight 1,255 kg (2,766 lb); wing loading 83·66 kg/sq m (17·13 lb/sq ft).

Maximum speed 320 km/h (198·83 mph).

Production—two M.33s (MM.48—49) for flying and one for structural testing built by Aeronautica Macchi at Varese in 1924–25.

Colour—overall white. Italian fasces motif on sides of nose, and stripes in national red, white and green colours on fin and rudder.

# Macchi M.39

Mario Castoldi, technical manager and designer of Aeronautica Macchi in 1925, was nothing if not thorough in his design thoughts and preparations for each of his new aircraft. Typical of the man was the time and effort he devoted to examining and recording all the 'go faster' design features and details of the winning Curtiss aircraft during his visit to the 1925 Schneider contest at Baltimore. He took photographs, made drawings, asked questions and observed, to augment his knowledge for use when designing future racing floatplanes for Italy's Schneider Cup team. Even the failure of the S.4 provided vital information by persuading him to eschew the cantilever monoplane configuration. He believed that Italy was lagging behind other countries in the development of specialized high-speed floatplanes, and he was determined to bridge the technology gap as quickly as possible.

All this information was to prove of particular value when the Italian Air Ministry failed to get United States approval for the purchase of six Curtiss V-1400 565 hp twelve-cylinder water-cooled inline vee engines of the type which had powered the Curtiss R3C-2 to victory at Baltimore. On 4 February, 1926, the Macchi company received a request for proposed designs to meet the needs of the Italian team. Fiat had earlier assured the Air Ministry that it could develop the A.24 twelve-cylinder water-cooled vee engine to produce some 800 hp, by increasing the compression ratio and rpm. Zerbi and his team set to work with such despatch and enthusiasm that by the middle of March the first of the new engines was running on the test bench.

About the same time Castoldi had submitted to the Air Ministry his designs for a high-speed low-wing monoplane floatplane and had had them almost immediately accepted. The resulting contract covered three aircraft finished to contest standard, two more for training and practice flying, and an additional airframe for structural test work. The produc-

Ferrarin's Macchi M.39, MM.75, in which he was forced to retire while on the fourth lap of the 1926 contest. (*Courtesy Richard Ward*)

tion of a number of models for testing in the Varese wind-tunnel and in the float development tanks was also included in the contract. Completion of the first of the two trainer airframes (MM.72 and 73) was scheduled for April.

Meanwhile, Fiat was meeting with innumerable problems with the development of the engine, particularly with the carburetion system, but eventually managed to produce a little over 880 hp at 2,500 rpm with the test-bench engine. The AS.2 engine destined for the trainers proved very satisfactory and units were delivered for these airframes during June in time for the launch of the first contest M.39 (MM.74) only five months from the receipt of offers to quote. The following day, 6 July, Romeo Sartori, Macchi's chief test pilot, climbed into the M.39's cockpit, the windscreen was swung down and locked into position and he was soon getting Castoldi's latest floatplane airborne for the first time at Varese. The fuselage of the M.39 was built in two major sub-sections: a monocoque rear section and a forward section of steel-tube carrying the engine. The rear structure was composed of four spruce longerons with 17 oval formers all covered with wooden skinning. The dorsal and ventral fins were built integral with this rear fuselage section by extending upwards and downwards the last three or four sets of formers. They, too, were covered with wood. The tailplane was attached to doubled fuselage frames and was built entirely of wood with multiple spar and rib structure. The rudder and elevators were of wooden construction with fabric covering. The front part of the fuselage consisted of a tubular-steel engine mounting attached to the front face of the first wooden bulkhead. It cradled the engine and was supported by diagonal tube-struts on each side. A finned oil cooler occupied the whole of the underside of the nose from the wing leading edge forward to the propeller spinner. Aluminium cowling panels, shaped closely to the engine, enclosed the nose and led

111

into a central longitudinal fairing which ran back to the forward edge of the hinged windscreen. A dorsal fairing ran back from the pilot's headrest along the top of the rear fuselage to the fin. In side view the fuselage had almost an aerofoil section outline and a very small frontal area of less than 0·55 sq m (6 sq ft).

The one-piece wing was built up around wooden spars and ribs and was attached to reinforced strong points on the fuselage frames. It was rigged without dihedral and had three degrees of sweepback. More than 60 per cent of the wing surface was covered with brass engine coolant radiators. They conformed exactly to the sharp-edged bi-convex symmetrical 10 per cent thickness/chord ratio wing section to create minimum drag with high-efficiency heat dissipation. The remainder of the wing structure was wood skinned, and the wooden ailerons were fabric covered.

The single-step aluminium floats were carried on four streamlined tubular-steel struts and had two streamlined spreader-bars. The central portion of the floats contained tinned-steel fuel tanks divided into separate sealed compartments and fitted with anti-g valves. Carrying fuel in the floats enabled a smaller fuselage to be used but created problems of transferring fuel to the engine in high-g turns. In the M.39, high-pressure air forced the fuel up to a header tank in the fuselage from whence it fed the engine. This alighting gear and the wings were braced by streamlined steel bracing wires attached to the forward fuselage bulkhead, the main spars and the base of the float struts. Two weeks after Sartori had first flown the trainer variant of the M.39, which had a wing span of nearly a metre more than the M.39s to be used in the contest, Maj M. de Bernardi arrived at the Schirana training base on Lake Varese and began practice flying as a member of the Italian Schneider contest team.

In the middle of August the first racing M.39 was delivered to Schirana and Sartori made the first flight in it on 30 August, to be followed soon after by a second flight by de Bernardi. These short flights gave the team pilots the opportunity to check the AS.2 engines in the air and get the general feel of the aircraft. Both reported favourably on the new engine but found that the aircraft tended to 'dutch roll' when they were attempting straight and level flight. By the middle of September most problems, except the ever-present carburetion difficulties, appeared to have been solved and, on the 17th, de Bernardi took off in one of the contest entrants to check maximum speeds. Everyone was delighted to find that the M.39 had achieved 414 km/h (257·24 mph), much in excess of the world seaplane speed record.

This elation changed almost to despair, and certainly to great sadness, when, on 21 September, Comandante Marchese Vittorio Centurione, the Italian team captain, stalled in a steep turn while flying an M.39 trainer, crashed into Lake Varese and was killed. Centurione was a most capable pilot who, like the other team pilots, had logged a number of hours' practice flying in the M.33 and the earlier M.18 before flying the new M.39, and his death was a severe blow.

While the pilots continued their practice flying, at Fiat's Turin factory and at Schirana, Zerbi and his engine experts tried to solve the carburetion problems of the AS.2. On one flight in MM.76 Bernardi's engine suddenly burst into flames and only prompt action with extinguishers by ground engineers saved the situation. Bernardi proposed a modification to limit the size of the carburettor air intakes and as this appeared to overcome the carburetion snags the other racing aircraft were similarly modified.

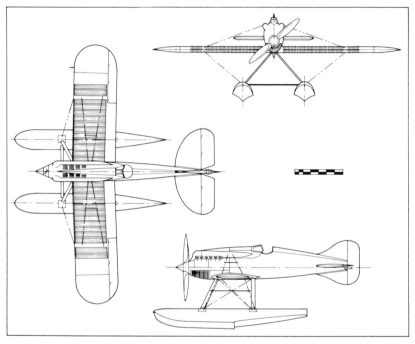

Macchi M.39

In spite of the speed with which the aircraft had been built and prepared for the contest, by the end of September only de Bernardi, now team captain, and Sartori had flown them, and the remaining pilots, Capt A. Ferrarin and Lieuts A. Bacula and G. Guasconi, had only just arrived at Varese. When they had completed their conversion to the M.39 and had experienced its longitudinal instability they recommended different remedies, but it was overcome by increasing the ventral fin area, something which should have been embodied very much earlier.

Italy appealed to the organizers of the 1926 Schneider contest for a delay to enable training to be completed. This was agreed, much to the chagrin of Great Britain which had pulled out of the contest believing there was insufficient time to prepare an entry; now time was being made available.

113

The Italian team and its aircraft arrived at Chesapeake Bay on 25 October. Here, after some preliminary engine running and carburettor adjustments, de Bernardi had the unnerving experience of an engine fire in the air. He alighted and put out the flames with an extinguisher given to him by the crew of a US Navy floatplane. Clearly, the carburetion problems had returned and it was not until 9 November that Ferrarin managed a practice flight during which, out on the circuit, he got caught in a heavy storm but returned to base safely. Other problems which beset the Italian pilots included a holed float, a badly vibrating engine which forced Ferrarin to alight in the dusk with a cracked crankcase, which needed 18 hr nonstop work to rebuild a new engine for his aircraft, and high oil temperatures which prompted the enlarging of the oil cooler on de Bernardi's aircraft. Ultimately all three contest aircraft were brought to a satisfactorily serviceable condition and completed their navigability tests.

In spite of problems in the air, de Bernardi, in MM.76, won the contest at an average speed of 396·698 km/h (246·496 mph), Bacula was third in MM.74 averaging 350·845 km/h (218 mph). A burst oil pipe in MM.75 forced Ferrarin to retire in the fourth lap.

Four days after the contest, on 17 November, a big crowd again gathered at Hampton Roads to see whether the Italians could add a world seaplane speed record to their Schneider contest victory. Mario de Bernardi in MM.76 did not disappoint them or his compatriots, since he achieved an average speed of 416·618 km/h (258·873 mph) over the 3 km course, another world record. This Macchi 39 is the sole survivor of the six aircraft built and is on show in a Turin museum.

Single-seat twin-float racing monoplane. Wood and metal construction with wood and fabric covering. Pilot in open cockpit.
One 600 hp Fiat AS.2 twelve-cylinder water-cooled direct-drive normally-aspirated inline vee engine driving a 2·08 m (6 ft 10 in) diameter two-blade fixed-pitch wooden propeller (M.39 trainer).
One 800 hp Fiat AS.2 twelve-cylinder water-cooled direct-drive normally-aspirated inline vee engine driving a 2·13 m (7 ft) diameter two-blade fixed-pitch wooden propeller (M.39 contest aircraft).
Both groups of aircraft were later fitted with Fairey Reed two-blade fixed-pitch metal propellers. Fuel: 272 litres (60 gal); oil: 68 litres (15 gal) approx.
Span 10·23 m (33 ft 7 in) trainers, 9·26 m (30 ft 4½ in) contest aircraft; length 6·73 m (22 ft 1 in); height 2·97 m (9 ft 9 in); wing area 14·29 sq m (153·9 sq ft) contest aircraft, 15·49 sq m (166·8 sq ft) trainers.
Empty weight 1,257 kg (2,772 lb); loaded weight 1,572 kg (3,465 lb); wing loading 110 kg/sq m (22·5 lb/sq ft). Figures for contest aircraft.
Maximum speed 439·44 km/h (272·13 mph)—achieved during world seaplane speed record flight; alighting speed 152 km/h (94·44 mph) estimated.

Production—two M.39 trainers (MM.72—73) and three M.39 contest aircraft (MM.74—76) built by Aeronautica Macchi (1926). One additional airframe built for structural testing.

Colour—overall scarlet gloss. Black M.39 and serial numbers MM.72—76 on each side of rear fuselage close to tailplane. White contest numbers 1 (MM.74), 3 (MM.75), and 5 (MM.76) on fuselage sides. Three vertical stripes in the Italian national colours of green, white and red, and the insignia of the House of Savoy have been added on the rudder and the number 11 to the flanks of the sole surviving M.39, de Bernardi's MM.76, now in the Centro Storico Scientifico de Volo in Turin.

The author has now been able to establish, without doubt, the half span of the M.39 contest aircraft. From the aircraft centreline to the port wingtip the span was 4·7 m and to the starboard wingtip 4·56 m. This was to improve the handling characteristics of the M.39 in the many steep high-g turns of the Schneider contest's left-handed circuits. The floats were modified to be of unequal buoyancy to help overcome the propeller torque reaction.

## Curtiss F6C-3 Hawk

Just as the long line of Hawker biplanes epitomize British military fighters during the 1930s, so are the Curtiss Hawks evocative of US Army and Navy fighter operations—albeit in peace—during the same period of aviation history.

The prototype of the whole Hawk line was the Army's XPW-8B of 1924: the last variant, the BF2C-1, was phased out of US Navy service in 1937. In between lay a great variety of sub-types, among them the F6C-3, and it was the first of a production batch of 35, serialled A7128, which, mounted on floats, took part in the 1926 Schneider contest at Hampton Roads. Not that it was the first-choice aircraft for the US team; it was a reserve, pressed into service in the contest when the Curtiss R3C-3 was wrecked in an alighting accident during practice flying. However, this

A United States Navy Curtiss F6C-3 Hawk on floats. One example took part in the 1926 contest. (*Courtesy Peter M. Bowers*)

standard squadron service aeroplane took fourth place, at an average speed of 220·406 km/h (136·953 mph), flown by US Navy Lieut William Tomlinson.

The Hawk could trace its origins back to the Curtiss racers built for the US Army and Navy during the early 1920 era. With differing operational requirements, the Hawks developed for these two Services differed to a marked degree in power unit, and in detail design and equipment, but their basic structural details remained almost unchanged.

The fuselage was a welded steel-tube frame with wooden formers to provide shape and fabric covered. The engine bay was covered with aluminium panels which extended aft to the cockpit. The wire-braced tail unit was a fabric-covered metal frame structure, as were the control surfaces. Two spruce spars with plywood ribs reinforced with capping strips formed the basic wing structure. The leading edges of both upper and lower mainplanes were plywood covered while the remainder was fabric covered. Metal and fabric ailerons were carried only on the upper mainplane and were operated by a push rod from the lower mainplane. The undercarriage was of streamlined steel-tube carrying the wheels on a cross-axle. Wooden N-interplane struts were used. Power in the Service F6C-3 was provided by a 400 hp Curtiss D-12 engine and the radiator generally was housed in a cowling under the nose.

In the floatplane variant the floats were carried on four long streamlined steel tubes and were wire-braced to the fuselage.

F6C-3s were also extensively modified for racing; one, A7147, being converted to a braced high-wing monoplane with a heavily spatted undercarriage.

Single-seat fighter (land and floatplane). Fabric-covered metal and wood construction. Pilot in open cockpit.

One 507 hp Curtiss D-12A twelve-cylinder water-cooled direct-drive normally-aspirated vee engine driving a two-blade fixed-pitch metal propeller was used on A7128. Fuel: 100 US gal (378 litres); oil: 6·6 US gal (25 litres).

Span 31 ft 6 in (9·6 m) (upper), 26 ft (7·92 m) (lower); length 25 ft 5 in (7·74 m); height 10 ft 8½ in (3·26 m); wing area 250 sq ft (23·22 sq m).

Empty weight 2,519 lb (1,142 kg); loaded weight 3,263 lb (1,480 kg).

Maximum speed 159 mph (255·88 km/h); alighting speed 65·4 mph (105·24 km/h).

Production—thirty-five F6C-3 Hawks (A7128 to A7162) built by Curtiss Aeroplane Co, Long Island, during 1926–27.

Colour—during the 1926 period the metal portions of US Navy aircraft were painted grey and the fabric silver. National markings were carried on the upper and lower surfaces of the respective mainplanes. The whole tail unit was also painted in another colour as a unit identification, beginning in 1926, and it is not known whether A7128 had this feature or retained the red, white and blue vertical rudder stripes carried by US Navy aircraft prior to that year. The aircraft serial number was usually in black and carried on the white vertical rudder stripe. It is most likely that A7128 flew in standard Service colours with the addition of the contest number 2 on the fuselage.

This view of the Supermarine S.5 at Woolston shows well the scoop-shaped engine mounting, the Lion engine installation, and the forward hingeing windscreen. (*RAF Museum*)

# Supermarine S.5

No one could describe R. J. Mitchell as anything but a sound practical engineer and designer; yet his S.4 had been an enormous leap forward to an ideal which he firmly believed would meet the practical requirements of a Schneider contest entrant. Its apparent failure to do so provided him with many valuable lessons which he was quick to learn, and, in his determination to produce a safe but effective monoplane racer, Mitchell and the Supermarine company carried through a wide-ranging research programme. In addition to the work inspired by the company, in March 1926 the Air Ministry asked that a series of three-quarter scale models be tested in wind-tunnels at the Royal Aircraft Establishment and the National Physical Laboratory. The Air Ministry had produced specifications for three types of racing floatplane; they called for high speed at low altitude, setting a 265 mph (426 km/h) minimum at 1,000 ft (305 m), an alighting speed not to exceed 90 mph (144·83 km/h), plus good handling characteristics at both these speeds and seaworthiness. The wind-tunnel work would prove whether the manufacturers selected—Supermarine, Gloster and Short—could meet these criteria with their designs.

Using the S.4 as a basis Supermarine produced three main models having a common fuselage, tail unit and alighting gear. Because of uncertainty about the cantilevered wing of the S.4, the major differences between the models was in the wing and its bracing. Two low-wing models were tested; the first had W struts bracing the wing and floats with a spreader-bar between the floats, in the second model the outer struts and spreader-bar were replaced by bracing wires, while in the third model the high wing was blended into the fairings over the cylinder banks and had the W strut bracing.

117

By 1926 the RAE, NPL and Supermarine experts were well acquainted with Reynolds number, or scale, effects when evaluating tunnel performance of models; thus their estimates of S.5 performance proved to be accurate to one per cent when compared with that achieved by the full-scale aircraft. Further, the low wing, wire-braced to the fuselage and alighting gear, was found to be the most effective configuration and was adopted for the S.5. It reduced the frontal area, produced a lighter wing structure and gave the pilot a much better view when compared with the S.4. Other improvements were the use of flush wing-surface radiators and a more powerful Napier Lion engine geared to a more efficient propeller. All these measures were effected to provide a 70 mph (112·65 km/h) increase in speed over the S.4, making the S.5 a 300 mph (482 km/h) aircraft.

In addition to the aerodynamic and structural research programmes, a good deal of work was done on solving hydrodynamic problems. One of the measures proposed and adopted was the use of a longer starboard float,* to provide additional buoyancy for the fuel carried in it, which was mounted eight inches further from the aircraft centreline than the port float.

With the design established, manufacture of these S.5s began at Woolston. Mitchell had advanced cautiously, using a mixed metal and wood construction, the fuselage being mainly duralumin and of a semi-monocoque type. It was built up around 32 closely-spaced broad top-hat section formers with wide flanges to which the duralumin skin was riveted. The fin was built integral with the rear fuselage, with thicker frames being used for the tailplane spar mounting and for the rudder post. On the forward end of the monocoque a heavy main frame carried the main and rear spar attachment brackets, the forward alighting gear

*About 1 ft longer than the standard 18 ft 6 in, and fitted only to N219.

The fuselage of a Supermarine S.5 under construction. (*Supermarine Aviation Works*)

Flt Lieut O. E. Worsley under tow in the Supermarine S.5 N219. (*Flight*)

strut mountings and strong points for the bracing wires. A fireproof bulkhead also was fitted to this frame, forward of which the fuselage consisted of a scoop-shaped engine bay containing the cross-braced front and rear engine bearers. The cockpit was positioned over the wing trailing edge and was a very snug fit, the pilot sitting almost on the bottom of the fuselage.

The mainplanes were of wood and were built separately. Two spruce spars and three-ply spruce ribs, with wide top and bottom flanges to take the radiator attachment screws, formed the basic structure. To prevent the mainplane twisting and inducing flutter, a wooden stiffening member ran diagonally outboard from the wing bracing wire attachment-point on the rear spar to the front spar. The turnbuckles and fork ends on the bracing wires were all carried internally.

The radiators were fabricated from two layers of copper sheet, the outer surface was smooth and the inner surface nearer to the skin being corrugated to form transverse channels for the water. The radiators were made in $8\frac{1}{2}$-in wide sections so that any damage could be contained and repaired with the minimum disruption of the cooling system. Water troughs were attached to the leading and trailing edges of the radiators to carry the main flow and return water. The radiator sections were laid on the wing skin and secured by screws passing through sealed holes in the radiator and the skin into the rib flanges. Heated water from the cylinder blocks passed into a header tank behind the engine, then was piped to the troughs at the rear edges of the radiator. It then flowed across the mainplanes to the leading edges from where it was piped back to the engine.

Oil cooling was provided by 11-ft (3·35 m) long corrugated steel coolers on the fuselage sides, the oil passing from the engine back through one cooler and a filter into a tank behind the pilot and then returning to the

The S.5 N219 which took second place in the 1927 contest. (*The Aeroplane*)

engine through the second cooler. The Lion engine was closely cowled with duralumin panels, and the two outer cylinder blocks were similarly cowled with very broad chord fairings nearly 8 ft (2·43 m) in length. The propeller was a 7-ft (2·13 m) diameter two-blade metal unit. The single-step floats were of duralumin, the starboard unit containing a tinned steel fuel tank. They were built up around a central longitudinal keel member with transverse frames supporting the chine members and stiffened by stringers, and covered with a duralumin skin. The alighting gear struts were built rigidly into the float structure, being reinforced where they passed through the float skin to take the enormous bending loads at those points.

The Supermarine S.5 N220 which won the 1927 contest, seen here at Calshot. (*The Aeroplane*)

During the latter part of 1926, while this construction work was in hand, the Royal Air Force's first High Speed Flight pilots began practice flying with the two Gloster IIIBs and the Gloster I at the Marine Aircraft Experimental Establishment at Felixstowe. A number of the pilots had been posted from the MAEE to the Flight which was activated on 1 October.

Bad weather delayed this flying programme, as did the non-appearance of any of the seven special high-speed aircraft being built for the 1927 Schneider contest. At last, in May 1927 the first of them, the Short Crusader, was delivered and it was soon followed by the Gloster IV. Early in June the first S.5, serialled N219, was delivered to Calshot, and Flt Lieut O. E. Worsley was detached there to fly it. During early July the entire Flight moved from Felixstowe to Calshot and during the next two weeks Flt Lieut S. N. Webster and Flg Off H. J. Schofield also got in

Flt Lieut S. M. Kinkead about to make his first flight in the Supermarine S.5 N221. This was the third S.5 and Kinkead was killed in it during an attempt on the World Absolute Air Speed Record on 12 March, 1928.

practice flights in N219. All three pilots commented on the fore-and-aft trim, and the tailplane incidence was changed to correct the nose-heaviness; after which it was regarded as viceless and a delight to fly, having very positive handling characteristics particularly during high-speed low-level runs.

One problem which was encountered and overcome was that of exhaust fumes entering the cockpit. The cure was the introduction of ducts carrying ventilating air from the wings.

As with so many floatplanes, getting airborne was a difficult task, for immediately the throttle was opened the torque reaction from the propeller caused the port float to dig into the water, in spite of the weight of some 50 gal (227 litres) of fuel housed in the starboard float in an effort to counter-balance the torque. As a result the aircraft yawed to the left and the bow wave was blasted back over the cockpit, completely obscuring the view forward. However, continued practice enabled the pilots to develop a technique of applying right rudder and of keeping their heads well tucked down into the cockpit until the floats got up onto the step; then the spray problem disappeared and the view was restored. Porpoising, which would grow in amplitude if the pilots kept the throttle open, could only be overcome by closing the throttle, waiting for the aircraft to stop pitching, and then starting the take-off again. Alighting needed equal skill and required the aircraft to touchdown on the heels of the floats after a long flat approach until flying speed was lost.

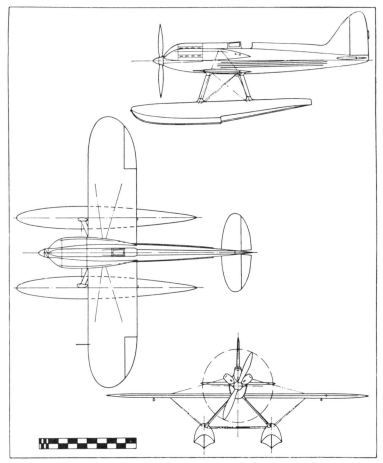

Supermarine S.5

Flt Lieut S. N. Webster's S.5, N220, with a geared Lion engine, at Calshot before being shipped to Venice for the 1927 contest. (*Flight*)

Bad weather continued to hinder practice flying with N219, and as the other two S.5s (N220 and N221) were still undergoing some preparatory work on the ground, what flying could be got in was in the Gloster aeroplanes. On 17 August, N219, the Crusader and the Gloster IVA were shipped to Venice, the location for the contest, with the other two S.5s and the Gloster IVB following them ten days later. During the second week of September the engines were removed from N219 and N220 and were replaced with new ones; a geared Lion VIIB with a more robust crankshaft was fitted in N220, and N219 had a new direct-drive Lion VIIA installed. These were the two contest aircraft in which only a minimum of flying experience had been gained. They were flown in the contest by Webster and Worsley respectively.

After the contest, when the British aircraft were returned to the United Kingdom, the High Speed Flight was disbanded; it was, however, re-formed in February 1928, and Flt Lieut S. M. Kinkead, who had flown the Gloster IVB in Venice, prepared to establish a new world speed record at Calshot in S.5 N221. Sadly, he was killed in the attempt when the aircraft failed to pull out of its approach dive to the measured course and plunged into the sea. His replacement in the Flight, Flt Lieut D. D'Arcy A. Greig, also made an attempt in N220 on 4 November but the speed achieved was not a sufficiently great improvement on the existing record to be recognized.

Both N219 and N220 were used as practice aircraft by pilots of the Flight preparing for the 1929 Schneider contest. When the composition of the team for that contest was revealed it included the S.5 N219 and the two new S.6s.

123

A rare photograph of the S.5 N220 at 'full-chat' with Webster up. (*Courtesy Ron Brown*)

Although the failure of the two Gloster VIs left no alternative to that of flying the S.5, it resulted in a good mix of new and untried aircraft with one which had performed reliably and with some distinction in a previous contest. The major change in N219 was the installation of a Lion VIIB geared engine in place of the earlier direct-drive Lion VIIA. In this form it was flown on pre-contest trials by D'Arcy Greig who had the most experience on the type.

Single-seat twin-float racing monoplane. Metal and wood construction. Pilot in open cockpit.

One 900 hp Napier Lion VIIA twelve-cylinder water-cooled direct-drive normally-aspirated broad-arrow engine driving a 7 ft (2·13 m) diameter Fairey Reed two-blade fixed-pitch metal propeller (N219).

One 875 hp Napier Lion VIIB twelve-cylinder water-cooled geared normally-aspirated broad-arrow engine driving a 7 ft 7 in (2·31 m) diameter Fairey Reed two-blade fixed-pitch metal propeller (N220 and, possibly, N221). Later N219.

Fuel: 50 gal (227 litres); oil: 5 gal (22·7 litres); water 15 gal (68 litres).

Span 26 ft 9 in (8·15 m); length 24 ft 3½ in (7·4 m); height 11 ft 1 in (3·38 m); standard float length 18 ft 6 in (5·63 m); wing area 115 sq ft (10·68 sq m).

Empty weight 2,680 lb (1,215 kg); loaded weight 3,242 lb (1,470 kg); wing loading 28 lb/sq ft (136·7 kg/sq m).

Maximum speed 319·57 mph (514·29 km/h); alighting speed 85 mph (136·79 km/h).

Production—three S.5s built by Supermarine Aviation Works Ltd, Southampton, 1926–27.

Colour—overall blue fuselage and fin and float bottoms; silver wings, tailplane, engine cylinder cowling, alighting gear struts and float tops. RAF stripes on rudder with black serial numbers. White disc and contest number 4 on fuselage side (N220); white contest number 6 only (N219).

# Macchi M.52

If the 1923 contest, with the arrival of the United States team and the Curtiss racing aeroplanes, marked the end of the beginning of the Schneider series, then 1927, without doubt, was the beginning of its end. It was in that year that Italy and Great Britain began their duel which was to bring ultimate victory and the Trophy for one of the contestants.

As always, Italy was determined to win and its team prepared for the contest in its customary professional manner, confident that in its own Venetian skies victory was almost certainly assured.

With the earlier success of the M.39 in mind, during December 1926 it was decided to develop this aeroplane rather than create a radically new design. This plan had the twin benefits of limiting the cost and speeding the production programme. Following joint consultation, Tranquillo Zerbi, Fiat's chief engineer, believed that he could develop the AS.2 engine to produce a 1,000 hp power unit while Mario Castoldi agreed to restyle the M.39 to accept the new AS.2 and its additional power. Thus, with the principal participants in the creation phase in complete accord, the Italian Air Ministry placed contracts with Macchi for three aircraft—which would be designated M.52—and with Fiat for five AS.3 engines. A clause in the Macchi contract stipulated that the aircraft should be capable of attaining a flying speed of at least 470 km/h (292 mph). This was a measure of the respect with which the Italians regarded the British opposition.

Mario de Bernardi's Macchi M.52 well up on the step on the waters of the Lido at Venice.
(*Flight*)

Zerbi rapidly completed his redesign work on the AS.2 and his general arrangement drawings were received at Macchi's Varese factory at the end of February 1927, enabling Castoldi immediately to begin scheming a redesign of the M.39 to accept the AS.3.

Understandably, the M.52 was of similar construction and layout to its predecessor but with a slimmer rear fuselage, wing sweep back increased to 10 degrees, and with fins, rudder and elevators of slightly reduced area. The windscreen was revised to reduce its frontal area and was hinged at its front edge to provide easier access to the tiny cockpit. This new shape did little to improve the very poor forward view however. The M.52 wing span was 28 cm ($11\frac{1}{2}$ in) less than the M.39, the wing area was reduced by a little over 1 sq m (10 sq ft) and the loaded weight was cut by some 60 kg

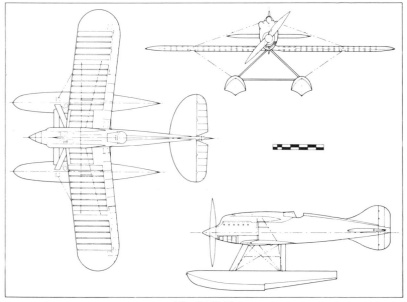

Macchi M.52

(132 lb). The 10 per cent thickness/chord ratio wing, with the exception of the tip section, was covered with coolant radiators. A change in the design of the floats produced less drag but provided almost 50 per cent more buoyancy than the loaded weight of the aircraft.

The new engine was regarded as a design triumph for Zerbi, developing 1,020 hp on a 94 octane fuel consisting of equal quantities of petrol and benzine with other alcohol additives. Compared with the earlier AS.2, the bore, stroke, capacity and compression ratio were all increased, but the additional 220 hp was achieved with a power unit of reduced frontal area but of the same length. This enabled Castoldi to design tight-fitting cowling panels to create finer lines around the engine bay. The 2·33 m (7 ft 8 in) diameter two-blade metal propeller was based

A beautiful portrait of a Macchi M.52—probably the first example. (*Aeronautica Macchi*)

127

The Macchi M.52s of Ferrarin (No.7), Guazetti (No.5) and de Bernardi (No.2), with Webster's and Worsley's Supermarine S.5s (Nos. 4 and 6) moored out during navigability tests at Venice in 1927. (*Flight*)

on the US Reed propeller and provided improved propulsive efficiency.

Although there may have been few difficulties in the design and engineering phases of the engine development they began to be encountered on the testbed. However, they were tackled promptly, if not always effectively, while the five engines were being built and test run. Many of the problems stemmed from the higher compression ratio and the design of the piston head and combustion chamber.

While design and construction of the first three M.52s proceeded at Varese, two M.33s and the four M.39s remaining from the previous contest were returned to the Macchi factory for overhaul prior to their use by the Italian team for practice flying.

The Italian team, led by Maj Mario de Bernardi, which consisted of Capts A. Ferrarin, G. Guasconi and F. Guazetti and Lieut Salvatore Borra, assembled at Varese on 16 May and, before the completion of the M.52s, began flying on the older aircraft. Just a month later Borra, who was still not used to handling even these aeroplanes, crashed and was killed when making his first flight in a long-span M.39 trainer. Through lack of experience he failed to make allowance for the drag of the floats when cornering, the aircraft stalled, rolled to the inverted position and Borra had insufficient height to regain control before hitting the water.

The first M.52 was flown during the first week of August by de Bernardi, with the second and third aircraft getting airborne some ten days later. Almost at once the same carburetion and running problems which had plagued the AS.3 on the testbed began to appear during the early taxi-ing and flying trials. De Bernardi, no mean engineer, played a major role in the flight development of the AS.3 and the efforts to improve its reliability. As in the AS.2, Zerbi decided to use magnesium pistons of new design, but due to lack of time they had not been fully bench-tested before the AS.3s were installed in the airframes.

With initial flying completed at Varese, the pilots, aircraft and ground support crews moved to Venice where practice flying resumed on 9 September. It seemed, however, to observers among the British team that the M.52s were not being flown with the usual Italian panache. It is not clear whether this resulted from the loss of Salvatore Borra or from a deliberate policy of nursing the AS.3 engines in readiness for the contest itself. Nevertheless, the Italian pilots spent a good deal of time practicing a new cornering technique involving a climbing turn followed by a dive onto the new leg of the course to regain flying speed.

In the contest the AS.3 engines in two of the aircraft failed after completing less than three laps between them, and it was left to the third M.52 to salvage any prestige for Italy by completing six laps before it, too, retired.

The disappointment of failure in the contest was sweetened somewhat on 22 October when de Bernardi, with eight runs over a 3 km course at Venice, set a new world speed record of 470·46 km/h (292·33 mph) during some spectacular flying at low level. A few hours later he increased this to 484·304 km/h (300·931 mph) with another eight runs. De Bernardi was upset that a modified propeller used during the record attempts had not been fitted for the Schneider contest and was unwilling to try and push the record any higher.

Meanwhile Castoldi was busy re-styling the M.52, reducing the wing span, tailplane area and float frontal area, and generally cleaning up the entire aircraft. Production of this new variant, designated M.52R or M.52bis, went on during the winter of 1927/28 and it is believed that a first flight took place during February 1928. De Bernardi made one or two familiarization flights and soon was being urged to attack his own speed

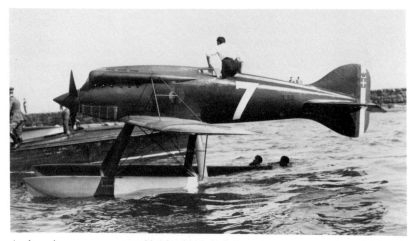

As the swimmers manoeuvre this Macchi M. 52 (MM. 82), Ferrarin obligingly leans out of the cockpit to reveal the small exhaust deflectors added to the rear of the windscreen. The port float appears to be painted in several colours. (*Courtesy Richard Ward*)

The Macchi M.52R afloat at Schirana on Lake Varese. (*Aeronautica Macchi*)

record. Initially he was reluctant, but Mussolini's insistence that he should make an attempt and the fact that Great Britain also was preparing to establish a new record spurred him on. On 30 March at Venice Lido, with six runs over the 3 km course, he averaged 512·776 km/h (318·623 mph).

During the ensuing 19 months the M.52R was used with three M.52s for high-speed practice flying at Desenzano on Lake Garda. When one of the new M.67s intended for use in the 1929 Schneider contest, crashed, killing Capt G. Motta, the M.52R flown by Warrant Officer Dal Molin was pressed into service as the third-string contestant. In the contest it plugged steadily around the course while the newer aircraft faltered, and it took second place.

Single-seat twin-float racing monoplane. All-metal construction. Pilot in open cockpit.

One 1,000 hp Fiat AS.3 twelve-cylinder liquid-cooled direct-drive normally-aspirated vee engine driving a 2·33 m (7 ft 8 in) diameter two-blade fixed-pitch metal propeller. Fuel: 272 litres (60 Imp gal).

Span 8·98 m (29 ft 5½ in); length 7·13 m (23 ft 5 in); height 3 m (9 ft 8½ in); wing area 13·3 sq m (143·2 sq ft) M.52.

Span 7·85 m (25 ft 9 in); length 7·12 m (23 ft 4 in); height 3·01 m (9 ft 11 in); wing area 10·2 sq m (109·8 sq ft) M.52R.

Empty weight 1,190 kg (2,623 lb); loaded weight 1,515 kg (3,340 lb) M.52.

Empty weight 1,170 kg (2,579 lb); loaded weight 1,480 kg (3,263 lb) M.52R.

Maximum speed 505 km/h (313·79 mph) M.52; 561 km/h (348·58 mph) M.52R.

Production—three M.52s and one M.52R built by Aeronautica Macchi at Varese in 1927–28.

Colour—overall red with natural aluminium spinner. Undersurface of floats may have been white on some aircraft. Italian national colours in rudder stripes, and insignia on fuselage sides forward of cockpit. White 2, 5 and 7 (M.52) and 4 (M.52R) contest numbers on fuselage sides aft of cockpit. Guazetti's M.52 No. 5 also had large white discs on the fuselage sides aft of the contest number.

130

# Gloster IV

During the early weeks of 1926 Folland began work on the design of a new high-speed floatplane to be built in readiness for the following year's Schneider contest in Venice. It was, again, a biplane in spite of the fact that the 1926 contest-winning Macchi M.39 and the S.5, then being created by Supermarine, were monoplanes. Folland remained unconvinced that in the tough Schneider contest conditions the sleeker monoplanes had any edge over the more robust biplane. His view was strengthened by the continued development of the Curtiss biplane racers in the United States. Using the Gloster III design as a starting point, Folland and H. E. Preston, Gloster's assistant chief engineer and designer, gradually refined and redrew the fuselage lines and, by careful attention to the points where the various components joined, a 40 per cent reduction in head resistance was achieved. The blending of the mainplane roots into the fuselage improved the drag characteristics and provided 15 per cent more lift. These aerodynamic refinements plus an increase in engine power made the Gloster IV some 70 mph (112·66 km/h) faster than its predecessor.

Three Gloster IVs were ordered at a total cost of £24,750. They were built almost entirely in wood. A monocoque fuselage was constructed from light formers and ash longerons with two layers of spruce strips, about three inches wide, laid diagonally in opposing directions to form a

The very small frontal area of the Gloster IV is apparent in this view.

stressed skin. A third spruce layer was used forward of the wings and at load-carrying points. Duralumin tube was used for the engine mounting. The broad-chord cantilever fins were integral with the fuselage. The unstaggered mainplanes were built around a multiple spar and rib structure with two layers of spruce skinning, and the single thin interplane struts were machined from solid duralumin. The roots of the upper mainplanes swept down into a fairing behind the Lion's lateral cylinder banks, and the lower mainplane roots curved up to join the fuselage at 90 deg. The main fuel tank was in the fuselage, with a smaller gravity tank and the engine cooling system header tank in a fairing aft of the centre cylinder block. The alighting gear embodied Gloster-designed and built floats carried on tubular-steel V-struts with wooden fairings.

An important feature of the flying control system was the Gloster variable control gear which provided a 2:3 gear ratio for the small control movements used at high speed and a 3:2 ratio for the larger control movements at lower speeds. This was desired when pilots found the controls became over-sensitive at high speeds.

Surface radiators were, at last, used and were of $\frac{3}{16}$ in corrugated copper with brass leading and trailing edges. They were in the form of a shaped sleeve, were slid over the mainplanes from the tip end and were secured with stainless-steel rods and brass ferrules. Additional surface radiators on the float tops gave 125 sq ft (11·6 sq m) of cooling area. After inflight problems with bursting oil tanks, a combined cooler and tank was fitted to form part of the undersurface of the nose. Later, additional corrugated-type coolers were carried on the fuselage flanks.

The Gloster IVA N222 at Gloster's Sunningend factory at Cheltenham. The completely suppressed windscreen severely limited the pilot's forward view. Note the very thin mainplanes and the smooth overall finish to the entire aircraft.

The Gloster IVB N223, probably at Calshot before going to Venice for the 1927 contest. In this view the serial appears in large characters on the blue, white and red rudder stripes. The flying-boat in the background is a Supermarine Southampton.

The three aircraft, designated Gloster IV, IVA and IVB and serialled N224, N222 and N223 respectively, were each slightly different. Because of the high efficiency of N224's mainplane, the other two aircraft had 4 ft (1·21 m) cropped from their span, effectively reducing the area by some 16 per cent. The tail unit of N222 was redesigned to a cruciform shape with fin and rudder area above and below the tailplane. N224 and N222 had direct-drive 900 hp Napier Lion VIIA engines, initially driving Gloster metal propellers of which the blades were detachable and which were machined to the correct profile from a solid duralumin forging. N223, the Gloster IVB, had a geared Lion VIIB of about 885 hp driving a similar type of propeller. All three aircraft were delivered to the High Speed Flight based at Calshot during July—August 1927 for preliminary flying which, once again, was of surprisingly short duration. N222 arrived on 29 July and was flown for only 40 min before being shipped with N223 to Venice on 16 August. In Venice further practice flying by Flt Lieut S. M. Kinkead added only 72 min to N222's log book and barely 35 min to that of N223—which was chosen to fly in the contest. During a flight on 21 September the spinner came off N223's propeller as it was alighting and damaged a blade, but the aircraft was quickly made serviceable.

In the contest Kinkead lapped steadily at around 275 mph (442 km/h), but retired in the sixth lap after the Lion appeared to falter. Back in the hangar the propeller was removed, when it was discovered that the engine's splined propeller shaft was cracked three-quarters around its diameter.

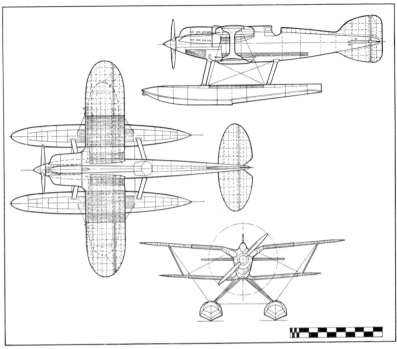

Gloster IVB

This was the last appearance of a biplane in the Schneider Trophy series, but Gloster had the satisfaction of N223's third lap of 277·1 mph (445·94 km/h) which set an all-time record for biplane types.

On 4 October both aircraft were shipped to Felixstowe where they remained on test flying duties until 21 February, 1928, when they returned to Gloster's factory for modification and conversion to trainers. To improve the pilot's forward view the upper mainplane was raised to fair directly into the top cylinder bank, and upper centre-section struts and an external header tank were fitted. N222 went back to Felixstowe in July and with N223 was flown by the 1929 Schneider team. In the following March both aircraft were back at the factory for changes in the tail unit to cure high-speed yaw. Although area was added to the dorsal fin it did not effect a cure, and a tail unit was fitted of the pattern used on N224—which had never experienced this yawing—and longitudinal stability was recovered.

N224 was sold, in 1930, to Amherst Villiers who intended to convert it into a landplane, with a normally aspirated geared Lion engine, for an attempt on Bonnet's world speed record of 278·5 mph (448·19 km/h), but the plan did not mature. The other two aircraft were used regularly at Calshot and Felixstowe until on 19 December, 1930, Flt Lieut J. Boothman crashed N223 while alighting in fog. N222 subsequently made

147 flights, a large number of them in developing the best technique for rounding pylons. It is reported that Kinkead also looped and rolled this aircraft.

Single-seat twin-float racing biplane. Wood and metal construction with plywood covering. Pilot in open cockpit.

900 hp Napier Lion VIIA twelve-cylinder liquid-cooled direct-drive supercharged broad-arrow engine driving a 6 ft 9 in (2·05 m) diameter Gloster two-blade fixed-pitch metal propeller (Gloster IV).

900 hp Napier Lion VIIA twelve-cylinder liquid-cooled direct-drive supercharged broad-arrow engine driving a 7 ft (2·13 m) diameter Gloster two-blade fixed-pitch metal propeller (Gloster IVA).

885 hp Napier Lion VIIB twelve-cylinder liquid-cooled geared supercharged broad-arrow engine driving a 7 ft 8½ in (2·34 m) diameter Gloster two-blade fixed-pitch metal propeller (Gloster IVB).

Gloster IV

Span 26 ft 7½ in (8·11 m); length 26 ft 4 in (8·02 m); height 9 ft 2 in (2·79 m); wing area 164 sq ft (15·23 sq m).

Empty weight 2,072 lb (940 kg); loaded weight 2,780 lb (1,261 kg); wing loading 16·9 lb/sq ft (82·51 kg/sq m).

Maximum speed* 265 mph (426·46 km/h); stalling speed 76 mph (122·3 km/h); duration 1·1 hr.

*Maximum speed at sea level.

The Gloster IVB N223 (contest No. 1) at Venice in 1927. N223 appeared in very small characters at the top of the rudder.

N223 (nearest) and N224, the Gloster IVB and IV at Calshot where they were used for practice flying by the 1929 British team pilots. Note that the upper mainplane roots have been raised and strut braced, a coolant header tank mounted on the upper centre section, and the fin and rudder shape have been modified. (*Flight*)

### Gloster IVA

Span 22 ft 7½ in (6·89 m); length 26 ft 4 in (8·02 m); height 9 ft 2 in (2·79 m); wing area 139 sq ft (12·91 sq m).

Empty weight 2,447 lb (1,110 kg); loaded weight 3,130 lb (1,420 kg); wing loading 22·5 lb/sq ft (109·85 kg/sq m).

Maximum speed* 289 mph (465·09 km/h); stalling speed 91 mph (146·44 km/h); duration 1·1 hr.

### Gloster IVB

Dimensions as Gloster IVA.

Empty weight 2,613 lb (1,185 kg); loaded weight 3,305 lb (1,499 kg); wing loading 23·7 lb/sq ft (115·71 kg/sq m).

Maximum speed* 295 mph (474·74 km/h); stalling speed 97 mph (156·1 km/h); duration 1·1 hr.

Production—one Gloster IV (N224), one Gloster IVA (N222) and one Gloster IVB (N223), built by Gloster Aircraft Co Ltd, Cheltenham and Hucclecote, in 1926–27.

Colour—bronze wings, cylinder block fairings and tail unit, Cambridge blue fuselage, ivory floats. White contest number 1 on fuselage sides (N223).

*Maximum speed at sea level.

136

# Supermarine S.6

With hindsight, while the success of the British floatplanes in the two final Schneider contests of 1929 and 1931 was due in great measure to the Rolls-Royce design team and the R engine, it is apparent that R.J. Mitchell's steady evolution of a basic airframe configuration from the S.4 through the successful S.5, eventually paid the ultimate dividend in the Schneider series. What is not always appreciated is the undeniable fact that Mitchell knew not only how to benefit from every possible scrap of aerodynamic refinement but also how to make the best use of every ounce of power made available to him by the wizards of Derby.

Yet there was another element in the pattern of events which was to decide the permanent holders of the Trophy; this was the attempt by General Balbo of Italy, which was feeling the strain of preparing entries for a Schneider contest every year, to coerce Britain, the host nation for the next contest in the series, to opt for a biennial contest in the future. Sir Samuel Hoare, Air Minister, however was equal to this pressure by a competitor and, though secretly agreeing with the proposal, was enough of a diplomat to get Balbo to admit openly that he would prefer to put up contenders for the Trophy only once every two years. At the January 1928 annual meeting of the FAI in Paris, the frequency of future contests was an item on the agenda. The outcome of the discussion by the FAI

N247, the first Supermarine S.6. This aircraft won the 1929 contest.

delegates, in the light of Italy's and Britain's preferred biennial contest, was a decision to stage the contest every two years; moreover, any country achieving three victories in five successive contests would be adjudged the outright winner and permanent holder of the Trophy. This two-year lead time thus enabled Mitchell, and all the other competing designers, an invaluable extra year in which to create new designs.

Although Mitchell had clung to the well-tried Napier Lion engine for the S.4 and S.5, this engine was nearing the peak of its development, and he was thus looking for a replacement engine of equal reliability but with much greater power output. He needed to look no further than Derby where Sir Henry Royce was ready to offer the R engine, eventually guaranteed to deliver a minimum of 1,500 hp.

It was around this still 'on-paper' engine that Mitchell began his design of the new Supermarine S.6 racing floatplane. This was his first all-metal design, which was evolved from his S.5 aircraft, while the R engine was a geared and faster running development of the renowned Rolls-Royce 36-litre Buzzard, equipped with special racing superchargers producing a higher compression ratio of 6:1. It was the supercharging which was the key to the plan for producing greatly increased power from an engine of small frontal area and comparatively low weight. Much of the credit for the high performance of the R engine must go to James Ellor, a super-charging expert, and to F.R. Banks (later Air Commodore Rodwell Banks) of the Associated Ethyl company, whose unique mixtures of exotic fuels, which he termed 'fuel cocktails', enabled Rolls-Royce to produce engines capable of great power output. In the 1929 R engine this was 1,900 hp for a weight of 1,530 lb (694 kg), a remarkable power/weight ratio. Although this weight was some 60 per cent more than that of the Lion VIIB which had powered the S.5 to victory in the 1927 contest, nevertheless, it produced more than twice the power.

It was these increases in weight and power which were the principal reasons for the differences, not all readily apparent to the eye of the casual observer, between the S.5 and the S.6. Fundamentally, the general concept of the two designs was the same, but every external dimension of the S.6, with the exception of the float track, was greater than the earlier aircraft. The loaded weight of the S.6 at 5,771 lb (2,617 kg) was some 75 per cent more than the S.5's 3,242 lb (1,470 kg), yet the S.6's power/ weight ratio showed a 14 per cent improvement. There were some penalties to be paid, of course; the wing loading increased by nearly 50 per cent to 40 lb/sq ft (195·29 kg/sq m) and the take-off and alighting speeds rose about 25 mph (40 km/h) and 10 mph (16 km/h) respectively.

The S.6 fuselage was a semi-monocoque structure, with 46 internal 'top hat' section frames each spaced at about six-inch centres, and with an integral fin structure formed by the three rearmost frames. The R engine was carried on, and bolted to, the only longitudinal members in the fuselage. These bearers were made from 14-gauge duralumin angle section, and were attached to the forward fireproof bulkhead. They were shaped to conform to the forward fuselage lines. Unlike the cantilever engine mountings of the S.5, the front float struts of the S.6 were moved forward to provide support to the engine. This design feature enabled a considerable saving in weight of the engine bearers to be achieved.

The whole of the fuselage was covered with duralumin skinning, and removable duralumin panels were provided around the engine bay. An unusual design feature was the way in which the fin doubled—or trebled—as an oil tank and cooler. This meant that, while aerodynamically this was a highly effective method of containing and cooling the

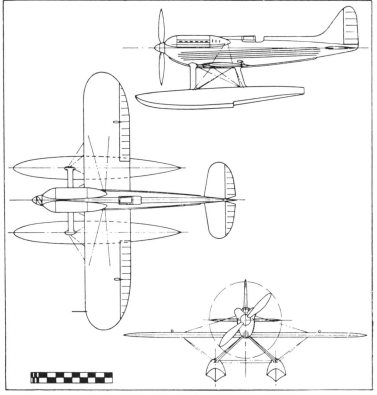

Supermarine S.6

engine oil, it also relied upon the efficacy of many feet of internal 'plumbing'. After the hot oil left the engine it passed rearward along corrugated coolers on each side of the fuselage before entering the top of the fin where it was sprayed out over the tinned-steel inner skin of the fin. From the fin tank it was pumped back to the engine.

The mainplanes were built up around two duralumin spars, with ribs made of flat duralumin sheet, with integral flanged lightening holes, and skin attachment flanges made of extended angle section. One leg of this angle section was drilled and tapped to accept the screws which attached the surface radiators to the mainplane structure. The radiators were built up from two sheets of 24-gauge duralumin which were riveted together with $\frac{1}{16}$-in spacers to provide a very thin cavity for the cooling water flow. The radiators had a completely flat outer surface which conformed to the aerofoil section of the wing, created no drag and were designed to take torsional loads. That part of the mainplane which did not carry a surface radiator had a single duralumin skin. The tailplane was of similar construction to the mainplanes and also was skinned with duralumin sheet.

The floats were carried by four streamlined wire-braced steel tubes which had streamlined duralumin fairings around them. As stated earlier, the forward struts provided support for the two engine bearers, while the rear pair of struts were attached to the fuselage frames through conventional socket attachment points. The floats' centre portions housed the fuel tanks, and engine coolant radiators were carried on their upper surfaces, forward of the front struts, to supplement the radiators carried on the mainplane. The basic float structure was the same as that adopted for the S.5. The two banks of cylinders of the big vee R engine were closely cowled with the upper surface of the top engine cowling panels continuing rearwards to a tunnel-like windscreen and the open cockpit. All the flying control push-rods and cables were carried internally.

The first of two S.6s built (N247) was nearing completion at Supermarine's Woolston factory by the time Rolls-Royce at Derby had finally coaxed the R engine to run for 100 minutes and deliver 1,850 hp. This aeroplane was launched on 5 August, 1929, after some preliminary engine running ashore, and was then taken in tow by a Supermarine launch for the journey down Southampton Water to Calshot where the RAF High Speed Flight was based. As recorded elsewhere, when Sqn Ldr Orlebar attempted to get airborne in N247 he found that the whole of the aircraft was covered in spray to an extent he believed to be three times that created by earlier Supermarine and Gloster floatplanes. The increased propeller torque caused the port float to bury itself in the water, bringing the wing tip down to within inches of the surface as the aircraft swung to the left. However, once the speed had managed to build up a little, this swinging stopped, only to be succeeded by porpoising as the floats lifted out of the water and began running on the surface.

In an effort to mitigate the effects of torque on take-off, the starboard float tank was topped off with more fuel than the port tank and this helped to cure the earlier dipping and yawing. Orlebar also found that, even when hydroplaning in a take-off attitude, his S.5 technique of holding the control column central until flying speed had been reached and allowing the S.6 to fly itself off the water simply would not work. He decided to try instead an older established floatplane take-off in which he applied firm backward pressure on the control column when the S.6 had reached flying speed of around 120 mph (193 km/h) and literally pulling the aeroplane off the water.

N247, the Supermarine S.6, with Flt Lieut H.R.D. Waghorn snugged down in the cockpit, en route to the water at Calshot. (*Flight*)

Close-up of the S.6's nose showing the carefully cowled cylinder banks of the Rolls-Royce R engine, the oil coolers on the fuselage sides and the two-blade metal propeller. (*Flight*)

When Orlebar tried this for the first time, on 10 August, aided by a 'popple' on the water and a stiffish breeze, it was an immediate success. Orlebar subsequently reported that the S.6 handled extremely well in the air and conformed to all predictions. As flying time with N247 was built up in the ensuing days, so a number of minor snags were encountered. These included some tendency to pitch-up, a stiffness in the aileron control circuit, and engine overheating. This last problem was caused by an inability to disperse the great heat generated by running the engine at full power for protracted periods. It was ultimately overcome by adding extra radiator surfaces on the top of the floats, and by fitting small air scoops to help cool the inside surfaces of the wing radiators.

Until these handling and engineering problems had been solved, Orlebar did not allow Flt Lieut H. R. Waghorn and Flg Off R. L. R. Atcherley to make their first flights in N247; thus Waghorn did not get airborne until 19 August, with Atcherley making his first flight on the following day.

Meanwhile the second S.6 (N248) was launched at Woolston on 23 August and was taken to Calshot where Orlebar began some preliminary flight testing two days later.

A feature of the pre-contest practice flying by the High Speed Flight pilots was that the certificates of airworthiness for the practice R engines of their two S.6s had contained a clause limiting them to only five hours running time between overhauls. As this included ground running and taxi-ing time, it left very little flying time. In a typically effective manner Rolls-Royce prepared a special Phantom I motorcar chassis with a cradle to bring replacement engines to Calshot and to return to Derby those needing stripping and overhaul. This high-speed shuttle service between the industrial Midlands and the South Coast became part of the Schneider story, with Rolls-Royce transport department crews vying with each other for the record time between Derby and Calshot. It has been reported that a police speed trap stopped one Phantom after it had roared through some sleepy Hampshire village at around 80 mph. It ensured,

The Supermarine S.6 N247 taxi-ing off Calshot. (*The Aeroplane*)

The S.6 N247 with its 1929 contest number on the rear fuselage.

however, that the S.6s were always available for their pilots to fly them when weather and other considerations permitted.

Waghorn was assigned to fly N247 in the contest and he was keen to push both the airframe and engine to near their limits in practice flights. However, when his S.6 was prepared in contest trim with a full fuel load he found to his alarm that he was unable to make the aircraft unstick. It was only after making five or six attempts, and, no doubt, burning off quite a lot of fuel in the process, that he managed to get airborne. Clearly, in spite of delivering more power than had ever been provided for a British Schneider Trophy entrant, the R engine still lacked enough to lift the S.6's 5,771 lb (2,617 kg) off the water. It was therefore agreed that a small reduction in the pitch of the metal propeller would enable the engine to turn over faster at take-off speed and produce the extra bit of power required. But the price to be paid for this was an increase in engine speed in the air, with its concomitant increase in fuel consumption, and higher running temperature. The answer was for the pilots to use full throttle for take-off but to throttle back slightly, to around 97 per cent, once airborne and settled into the contest circuit.

As practice flying progressed and Waghorn and Atcherley flew their S.6s again and again through high-speed turns, the joints in the wing radiator system began leaking as the wings flexed under the loading. However, it is recorded that a popular brand of radiator sealing compound, used for motor cars, was introduced into the S.6s' cooling system and apparently proved an effective cure for this problem. This and other recurrent snags kept busy the Supermarine, Rolls-Royce and RAF mechanics, plus the technical staffs of some of the equipment manufacturers, during the days before the contest. The most traumatic experience was when a sharp-eyed Rolls-Royce mechanic saw a small piece of white metal on the electrode of a sparking plug which he was changing in N247's engine. Had there not been a party of his colleagues from Derby night-stopping in Southampton before watching the following day's contest, then his discovery could have ended Britain's chances of retaining the trophy. But the right people were in the right place at the right time, and they saved the day by changing one of the R engine's cylinder blocks during the night. The rest is history.

Single-seat twin-float racing monoplane. Pilot in open cockpit.
One 1,900 hp Rolls-Royce R twelve-cylinder water-cooled, geared and supercharged vee engine driving a 9 ft 6 in (2·89 m) diameter Fairey Reed fixed-pitch two-blade metal propeller. Fuel: 58 gal (263 litres) in starboard float and 48 gal (218 litres) in port float; oil: 10 gal (45 litres); water: 20 gal (91 litres).
Span 30 ft (9·14 m); length 26 ft 10 in (8·17 m); height 12 ft 3 in (3·73 m); float length 19 ft 5 in (5·91 m); wing area 145 sq ft (13·47 sq m).
Empty weight 4,471 lb (2,028 kg); loaded weight 5,771 lb (2,617 kg); wing loading 40 lb/sq ft (195·29 kg/sq m).
Maximum speed 357·7 mph (575·65 km/h)—world speed record; stalling speed 90 mph (144·83 km/h).

Production—two S.6s built by Supermarine Aviation Works Ltd, Southampton, in 1928–29. Both airframes modified to S.6B standard with the designation S.6A in 1930–31.

Colour—blue fuselage sides, fin and underside of floats; overall silver wings, tailplane and elevators, fuselage, and float tops and float struts; RAF stripes on rudder; black serials N247 and N248 on rudder with white contest number 2 (N247) and 8 (N248) on fuselage sides.

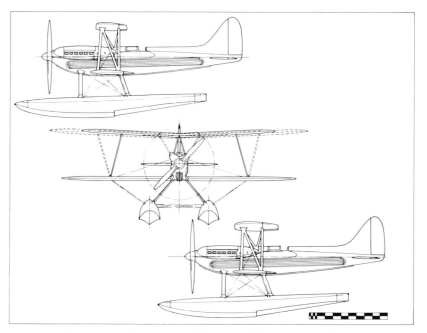

A proposal to convert a Supermarine S.6 into a biplane as part of an experimental programme to reduce the alighting speed was not proceeded with. As can be seen from the drawing, upper mainplanes of different spans and chords were proposed, plus inward and outward canted interplane struts. (*Courtesy C. F. Andrews*)

The prototype Macchi M.67 being manoeuvred by swimmers on Lake Garda during test flying for the 1929 contest. Note the way in which the after ends of the floats sit low in the water. (*Courtesy Richard Ward*)

# Macchi M.67

Mario Castoldi's M.67, built for the 1929 Schneider contest, was the third stage of development of the old well proven and successful M.39 configuration. It differed principally from its predecessors in that Castoldi forsook Fiat as his engine supplier and chose to power the M.67 with an 1,800 hp Isotta-Fraschini Asso eighteen-cylinder broad-arrow engine driving a three-blade metal propeller. In addition he used a straight wing rather than the swept wing of the M.52. The fuselage was of mixed construction, the engine bay and support cradle and the forward section in front of the cockpit, housing the main fuel tank, being all-metal while the rear fuselage and the cruciform integral tail unit was wooden. The three cylinder banks were enclosed in massive cowlings which dominated the entire aircraft. A geared push-rod control was used for the elevators and cable controls for the rudder. The mainplane was built up around a two-spar wooden structure which was almost entirely covered with coolant radiators; only the tip sections and the push-rod-operated metal ailerons were covered with marine plywood. The alighting gear was conventional, consisting of two wooden-clad metal floats, containing duralumin fuel tanks, carried on inverted-V struts, the whole gear being wire-braced to the mainplane and with bracing wires being used in place of float spreader-bars.

A major consideration in the design phase of the three M.67s (MM.103—105) which were built was efficient dissipation of the great heat generated by the eighteen-cylinder engine. Thus, in addition to the great radiating area of the wing surface, coolant radiators and oil coolers were mounted flush in the lower surface of the nose and on each side of the rear fuselage. One of the M.67s had additional radiators on the float struts and between the struts on the top surfaces of the floats.

Engine running with Giovanni Monti's Macchi M.67 at Calshot. Note the very large floats, oil coolers on the fuselage sides, and the coolant and oil tanks behind the engine. (*Flight*)

Construction work began late in 1928 but the Italian high-speed flight pilots at Desenzano had to do much of their practice flying on the M.52s until early August 1929 when the first M.67 was delivered. Then bad weather delayed flying, but Capt Giuseppe Motta made a first flight some six days later and got airborne on several subsequent occasions. However, the weather clamped down again and it was not until 22 August that Motta resumed flying. Then, when he was practicing some high-speed runs and cornering, the M.67 is reported to have stalled and plunged into Lake Garda, Motta being killed. The exact cause of this loss of control is unknown but it may have been caused by exhaust fumes entering the cockpit during the turn; to prevent a recurrence, special ventilators were fitted in the two other M.67s.

These two aircraft and their crews arrived at Calshot, where the contest was to be held, on 29 August, and Lieut Giovanni Monti made the first flight in an M.67 in Britain on 4 September. He made a good take-off, even though he was partially baulked by a meandering motor launch, and went far out over the Solent to keep away from observers on the shore during some practice runs at quite modest speeds. After some ten minutes he alighted when it could be seen that one of the bracing wires had snapped. This was a fairly minor snag compared to that which faced Lieut Remo Cadringher the following day when he attempted to take-off in the other M.67. He found that the port float dug into the water, the aircraft progressed in a series of arcs across the surface and he could not unstick. Some careful addition of fuel in the starboard float and some rigging adjustments helped to cure this problem and, eventually, Cadringher got airborne.

The big engines also gave trouble, refusing to run smoothly at full throttle. For this reason the stops were brought back to reduce the maximum revolutions by some 400 rpm.

Single-seat twin-float racing monoplane. Metal and wood construction. Pilot in open cockpit.

One 1,800 hp Isotta-Fraschini Asso eighteen-cylinder water-cooled direct-drive normally-aspirated broad-arrow engine driving a 2·18 m* (7 ft 2 in) diameter fixed-pitch metal propeller.

Span 8·98 m (29 ft 5½ in); length 7·77 m (25 ft 6 in); height 2·97 m (9 ft 9 in); wing area 13·3 sq m (143·2 sq ft).

Empty weight 1,765 kg (3,891 lb); loaded weight 2,180 kg (4,806 lb); wing loading 163·9 kg/sq m (33·56 lb/sq ft).

Maximum speed 584 km/h (363 mph).

Production—three M.67s (MM.103—105) built by Aeronautica Macchi at Varese, Italy, during 1928–29.

Colour—overall red with white float bottoms; green, white, red national rudder stripes and insignia. White contest numbers 7 and 10 and black M.67 and serial numbers carried on fuselage sides.

*Propeller diameter also reported as 2·52 m (8 ft 2½ in). MM.103 is known to have had a two-blade propeller and MM.105 a three-blade unit.

Calshot scene in 1931 with, left to right, Supermarine S.6B S1596, S.6A N248 and S.6B S1595.

# Supermarine S.6B

While the S.6B was the main instrument which finally won the Schneider Trophy for Great Britain, it could not be said it was the ultimate in high-speed floatplane design technology nor was it revolutionary in concept or construction. It was operating at the frontiers of knowledge and experience and represented the peak of a long programme of airframe, engine and component development by Supermarine, Rolls-Royce and many other companies. The earlier S.6 airframe design had been refined with great skill and its lines were made sleeker than any other previous entrant; the R engine had been developed to deliver nearly 25 per cent more power with reduced fuel and oil consumption; a special fuel was mixed to help provide the increased power; and a great deal of work had been done on the floats to enable them to meet both hydrodynamic and aerodynamic requirements.

The fuselage was of monocoque construction with 46 'top-hat' section frames, spaced at about seven-inch centres, all covered with duralumin skinning. The engine bearers, which were the only longitudinal structural members in the fuselage, were mounted on the front fireproof bulkhead. These were made of heavy 14-gauge duralumin right-angle section shaped to the contours of the fuselage. The front engine mounting feet were bolted directly to the bearers in a metal-to-metal contact but rubber

148

mounting blocks were used under the rear feet. The securing bolts passed through slots in the engine bearers to allow for longitudinal expansion of the engine as it heated up when running. The fin, which was built integral with the rear fuselage, and part of the long fairing running back from the pilot's headrest, formed the oil tank and cooler. For this reason the fin was constructed of tinned-steel as it was more stable. On leaving the engine the hot oil passed back through long corrugated coolers mounted on each side of the fuselage and into the fin. A number of sloping gutters were attached to the inner face of the fin down which the hot oil trickled for cooling after it had been sprayed out of the return oil pipe at the top of the fin. The angled lines of rivets securing these oilways can be seen in photographs of the S.6B's tail unit. From the fin tank the oil passed forward through a further ribbed cooler on the undersurface of the fuselage before being pumped back into the engine.

The tailplane spars were of box-section with conventional duralumin ribs, the structure being covered with duralumin skinning. The cable-operated rudder was of similar construction, as were the elevators.

By mounting the tailplane and elevators below the bottom line of the rudder the need for a cut-out in the elevators, to allow rudder movement, was avoided. Mass balances were carried internally and a small ground-adjustable trim tab was fitted to all flying surfaces. The mainplanes, which were wire-braced to the fuselage and alighting gear, were a two-spar structure with ribs spaced at $9\frac{1}{2}$ in and apart from the extreme tips were clad in surface radiators, screwed directly to the main structure, which formed the main lifting surfaces. The box-section spars were built up from two vertical channel-section webs to which flat strips were riveted top and bottom to form the booms. The duralumin ribs had

S1595, first of the two Supermarine S.6Bs, and winner of the last contest, in 1931.
(*Vickers-Armstrongs*)

149

flanged lightening holes and were stiffened by extruded right-angle section duralumin strip having legs of different thickness. The thicker $\frac{3}{16}$-in leg lay flush with the spar booms and was drilled and tapped to take the long screws securing the surface radiators to the structure. Local stiffening of the rib diaphragms was provided where engine coolant flow and return pipes passed through them. A shaped leading-edge lapping-strip covered the joints between the main structure and the upper and lower radiator surfaces. Two shrouds faired-in the leading edges of the ailerons, which were operated by push-pull rods running from the pilot's control column via bell-cranks to the aileron spars. Streamlined external mass balances were fitted on the ailerons.

The surface radiators were constructed from two sections of 24-gauge duralumin sheet and were arranged in pairs. They were made with a very thin water space between each sheet and with their seams running longitudinally, parallel to the ribs, to act as baffles so that the engine cooling water had to flow across the mainplane rather than pass diagonally from its point of entry at the forward wing root to the collector pipe along the trailing edge. The radiators had completely smooth outer surfaces and created no additional drag in flight.

The floats were carried by four steel tubes, of two-inch outside diameter, with a streamlined duralumin fairing. They were very complex, housing fuel tanks in their mid-section and carrying coolant-radiators over virtually the entire top surface above the chine-line. The forward float struts were attached to and helped support the engine mounting, and the rear struts were attached to the fuselage structure through

The S.6B S1595 taxi-ing off Calshot in 1931. (*The Aeroplane*)

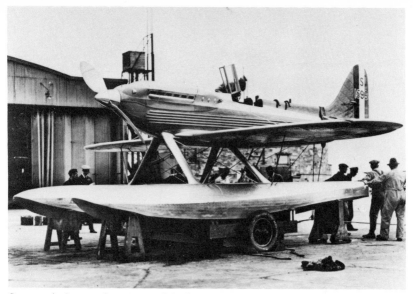

Supermarine's ground crew at work in the cockpit of the S.6B S1596 which has its hinged windscreen swung clear. The diagonal rivetting on the fin indicates the position of the internal oil-cooling baffles. (*Vickers Ltd*)

conventional sockets. The lower ends of the strut tubes were built rigidly into the float structure, passing through duralumin mounting blocks bolted to the double frame main keel member. Heavy steel sleeves stiffened the tubes at the point of maximum bending where they entered the float structure.

The fuel tanks were of the full cross-section of each float which had a duralumin main structure of longitudinal and transverse frames with tinned-steel skinning. Where the internal duralumin float frames came in contact with the skin, tinned-steel angle-pieces were used so that the rivets could be sweated-over to ensure that the float was watertight.

The radiators were built in the same way as those on the mainplane and were assembled in five sections on each float, necessitating a complicated piping system to connect them. For this reason a series of access doors was provided adjacent to each pipe connection. It is a tribute to the skill of Supermarine's sheet-metal workers—the 'tin-bashers'—that although the floats and the radiators were built simultaneously and thus could not be matched one to the other, when the various float components were finally assembled they fitted perfectly. Holes in the radiators for the attachment screws lined up exactly with the tapped bosses in the float structure, and the varying contours of the radiator sections fitting snugly on the tanks and main structures.

The two banks of the R engine's cylinders were carefully cowled and faired into the fuselage nose, and the top line of the nose was continued

Before the 1931 contest. Taken at Calshot this picture shows the Supermarine S.6A N248 flanked by the two S.6Bs, with S1596 nearest the camera. (*The Aeroplane*)

back between these fairings to a long flat-sided windscreen in front of the open cockpit.

The first S.6B, serialled S1595, was delivered to the High Speed Flight at Calshot on 21 July, 1931, and the first flight was made by Sqd Ldr A. H. Orlebar, leader of the British Schneider Trophy team. His early attempts to get airborne were a carbon copy of his experiences with the S.6 as he was repeatedly frustrated by what he described as the aircraft's 'imitation of a kitten chasing its tail'. Each time Orlebar opened the throttle the torque reaction from the powerful engine caused the port float to dig into the water so much that S1595 kept yawing hard to the left. Only once did he manage to achieve sufficient airspeed to hold the swing, and that was by going down wind; but the aircraft yawed again and he abandoned the attempt to fly. Two days later Orlebar collided with a barge in an uncontrollable swing and the mainplanes had to be changed, causing a delay in the working-up programme.

While this work was in hand, some investigative work traced the cause of the problem to the use of an 8 ft 6 in (2·59 m) diameter propeller, which was 1 ft smaller than those used in the 1929 contest. Because the blade pitch of these propellers was fixed to give maximum efficiency in the air, they were in an almost stalled condition at take-off speeds. One of the larger propellers used in the previous contest and which had suffered spray damage at its blade tips, was cropped to 9 ft 1½ in (2·78 m) diameter and fitted to S1595. It enabled enough power to be developed for take-off coupled with a controllable yaw, and made this the first-choice aeroplane for the contest. The volatile fuel mixture, specially compounded by Rod Banks, was found to be attacking the fuel system sealing compound which was clogging the fuel filters and causing engines to cut-out in the air. However, it was found that the joints were still sound and it was only beads of the compound, exuded when the pipes were being connected, which were polluting the system, and the problem passed.

On 11 August the second S.6B, serialled S1596, arrived at Calshot and was test-flown on the following day by Orlebar. Unfortunately, bad weather stopped practice flying for nearly a week; then the loss of Lieut R. L. Brinton, in a take-off accident in the S.6 N247 on 18 August, followed by continuing bad weather until 5 September, did not provide ideal conditions for proving the new Supermarine aircraft. However, modifications and changes in the trim on the two S.6Bs enabled both aircraft to be flown on 6 September. They proved much more controllable on take-off and some longitudinal instability experienced in turns was cured. Orlebar had developed a technique for successful take-off which he instructed his team to adopt. They were to hold the control column hard back when they became airborne until, as the airspeed increased, the nose tried to point even higher. Every instinct was to release backward pressure, but this was to be resisted as, although the aircraft seemed to be on the point of stalling, there was still plenty of lift and the angle of attack was not too great. This was similar to the technique which had been adopted by the pilots of the S.5, and there were no further problems with instability at take-off.

Although both S.6Bs had had only about three hours' flying between them by the day of the contest, they proved themselves equal to the demands made upon them. After S1595 had won the Trophy for Great Britain, a special sprint version of the R engine, which had not been ready for the contest itself, was fitted. Developing some 2,600 hp it enabled Flt Lieut G. H. Stainforth to set a new world speed record in S1596 of 407·5 mph (655·79 km/h) on 29 September, 1931.

Flt Lieut George Stainforth's Supermarine S.6B S1596 in which he established a new world speed record of 407·5 mph. (*Flight*)

Single-seat twin-float racing monoplane. Pilot in open cockpit.
One 2,300 hp Rolls-Royce R twelve-cylinder water-cooled geared and supercharged vee engine driving either a 9 ft 6 in (2·89 m) or 9 ft 1½ in (2·78 m) diameter Fairey Reed fixed-pitch two-blade metal propeller. Fuel: 75 gal (341 litres) in starboard float, and 55 gal (250 litres) in port float with 5 gal (22·7 litres) pressure tank in the fuselage. Oil: 15 gal (68 litres); water: 25 gal (114 litres).
Span 30 ft (9·14 m); length 28 ft 10 in (8·79 m); height 12 ft 3 in (3·73 m); float length 24 ft (7·31 m); wing area 145 sq ft (13·47 sq m).
Empty weight 4,590 lb (2,082 kg); loaded weight 6,086 lb (2,760 kg); wing loading 41 lb/sq ft (200·18 kg/sq m).
Maximum speed 407·5 mph (655·79 km/h)—world speed record; stalling speed 90 mph (144·83 km/h).

Production—two S.6Bs, built by Supermarine Aviation Works Ltd, Southampton, in 1930–31.

Colour—blue fuselage sides, fin and underside of floats; overall silver wings, tailplane and elevators, fuselage and float tops, and struts; RAF stripes on rudder; black serials S1595 and S1596 on rudder with white contest number 1 (S1595) on fuselage sides.

154

# The Non-Starters and Projects

In addition to the forty-seven aircraft which started in the twelve Schneider Trophy contests there were very many more which, for numerous reasons, were withdrawn from the lists. There were, too, a number of projects which never progressed much beyond the Design Office door.

Listed hereafter, in chronological order of the contests, are the names and some details of these aircraft as well as a number of projects.

## 1913

A total of three Nieuports and two Deperdussins, which were among the French entries for the first contest, were withdrawn because of damage or total loss caused mainly by bad weather during the days before the contest took place.

## 1914

Three Deperdussins and one Nieuport were held as reserve aircraft for the French team. Lord Carbery's Morane-Saulnier was replaced by a borrowed Deperdussin, and a Curtiss flying-boat, flown by William Thaw of the United States, was withdrawn.

A German Aviatik Arrow floatplane, flown by Ernst Stoeffler, was damaged during a test flight and, in any event, had proved slower than the Nieuports. The Aviatik was the only aircraft to be entered in a Schneider contest by Germany, and it was a clean-looking biplane having a central main float with balancer floats under the lower mainplane and a small tail float. It was powered by a 150 hp Benz eight-cylinder water-cooled inline engine driving a two-blade wooden propeller. Take-off weight was 900 kg (1,984 lb), wing area was 45 sq m (484 sq ft) and the Arrow was reputed to have a maximum speed of 120 km/h (75 mph).

## 1919

France withdrew one Nieuport 29-C-1 which crashed into the English Channel en route to Bournemouth, plus a second Nieuport and a Spad-Herbemont both of which sustained float damage during pre-contest flying.

This Nieuport 29G, pictured here at Monaco in 1920, was of the same three-float configuration as one of the French entrants for the 1919 Schneider contest which made a forced alighting in the English Channel en route to Bournemouth. (*Musée de l'Air*)

# Nieuport 29

As recorded earlier, when Henri Deutsch de la Meurthe died in 1919 and his son-in-law, M Gradin, was appointed managing director of the Nieuport company, it acquired a new name following a merger in 1921, to be known as Nieuport-Astra. However, the aircraft types emanating from this new company took the name Nieuport-Delage, which title recognized the surname of the organization's chief engineer, Gustave Delage, who had joined it in January 1914 and created a number of renowned military aircraft for the Allied air forces during 1915–18.

Delage's famed Nieuport 29 racer variants, which won many grands prix in the air, established world speed and altitude records and were developed as highly effective fighter type aircraft—some reported to be in service in 1936—were based on his 1918 design for a single-seat scout biplane used by the Aviation Militaire. Powered by the 275 hp Hispano-Suiza 8Fb modèle 42 eight-cylinder water-cooled inline vee engine, this aircraft's very slender fuselage was built up round 16 spruce longerons over four plywood ring formers and covered with tulip wood strips. These strips, tapering in thickness, were applied in a clockwise and anti-clockwise spiral over the basic structure and then fabric covered. Reinforced plywood bulkheads carried the laminated poplar undercarriage struts and attachment points. The wings had spruce box spars with spruce-reinforced plywood ribs, this structure being strengthened by steel compression tubes, braced with wire and fabric covered. With the aircraft rigged, a feature of the two-bay wings was the double pairs of lift wires and the large ailerons, the latter fitted only on the lower wings where their large aerodynamic balance surfaces overlapped the wingtips. The wood and fabric tail unit had a curved wire-braced fin and tailplane with large horn-balanced rudder and elevators. A duralumin fairing over the undercarriage spreader-bar was of aerofoil section. Two Lamblin 'lobster pot' radiators were mounted between the undercarriage struts. Armament was two fixed forward-firing Vickers 11 mm machine-guns.

The Nieuport 29's handling characteristics and top speed of around 200 km/h (125 mph) prompted Gustave Delage and one of the company's test pilots, Jean Casale, to envisage this weapon of aerial combat as a high-speed competition aeroplane. Their first action was to remove the armament from two basic airframes and apply a smooth black finish; their second was to replace the wheeled undercarriages with floats. The first modified airframe had a pair of short, wide, all-wood floats with a two-step keel, a gently rounded top and a deep vertical transom. The floats were carried on ten streamlined struts, arranged in two sets of four, each set in an M configuration, with a pair of fore-and-aft bracing struts and with two slim spreader-bars. Because the float transom was positioned just forward of the wing trailing edge, a large teardrop-shaped float was carried on a broad-chord streamlined strut under the tail unit. This aircraft retained the two-bay wings of the military Nieuport 29.

The second airframe underwent some more fundamental modifications in that the two-bay wings were replaced by single-bay wings, and longer single-step floats were fitted, making unnecessary the tail float. These changes produced a much more modern and business-like seaplane and although it was subsequently destroyed in an accident when being test flown by Casale, and the three-float variant was heavily damaged while alighting after a test flight by Henri Mallard, another Nieuport pilot, two single-bay twin-float seaplanes designated Nieuport 29-C-1, were prepared and entered for the 1919 Schneider Trophy contest at Bournemouth. The structure of these aircraft, with race numbers 2 and 4, followed closely that of the early military variants but there was greater attention paid to weight control and external finish.

Single-seat twin-float racing biplane. Wood and metal construction with wood and fabric covering. Pilot in open cockpit with windscreen and faired headrest.
One 275/300 hp Hispano-Suiza 8Fb modèle 42 eight-cylinder water-cooled inline vee engine driving a two-blade fixed-pitch wooden propeller.
Aircraft No. 2—span 8 m (26 ft 3 in); length 7·29 m (23 ft 10¼ in); float length 4·62 m (15 ft 2 in); maximum wing chord 1·5 m (4 ft 11 in); wing area 22 sq m (236·8 sq ft).
Empty weight 905 kg (1,995 lb); loaded weight 1,220 kg (2,689 lb); wing loading 55·45 kg/sq m (11·35 lb/sq ft).
Aircraft No. 4—span 9·77 m (32 ft 1 in); length 7·29 m (23 ft 11¼ in); float length 3·35 m (11 ft); maximum wing chord 1·5 m (4 ft 11 in).
Empty weight 945 kg (2,083 lb); loaded weight approx 1,236 kg (2,725 lb).
Maximum speed 250 km/h (155·34 mph) estimated.

Production—two Nieuport 29-C-1 seaplane racers were built for the Schneider Trophy contest by Société Anonyme des Établissements Nieuport in 1919.

Colour—the colour scheme of the 1919 Schneider Trophy aircraft is not known with certainty, but it is believed to have been a black overall finish with yellow rudder, interplane and float struts, with a black contest numeral 2 on the rudder.

Sadi Lecointe's Spad-Herbemont S.20bis at Bournemouth, with the starboard float taking water after damage. The locally-applied patching of the starboard upper mainplane tip, after it had been cropped in an effort to improve the Spad's maximum speed, can be seen. (*Musée de l'Air*)

# Spad-Herbemont S.20bis

André Herbemont joined the Spad company soon after it had been reorganized in 1910, and under the tutelage of Louis Béchereau, the company's design genius, he began to blossom as a competent design engineer himself. Before and during the war he was involved with the creation of several Spad aeroplanes including the S.20 of 1918, and when Béchereau left the company early in 1919 young Herbemont succeeded him.

The S.20 was a high-performance two-seat fighter from which stemmed a large number of variants, all inspired by Herbemont, some of which established speed and point-to-point records and won air races piloted by the well-known Sadi Lecointe who had been retained by Spad as the company test pilot. The principal racing variant was the S.20bis, and when the Schneider Trophy contests were re-started in 1919, after their suspension during the war period, it was this aeroplane which was mounted on floats to compete at Bournemouth. While the various sub-types differed in detail design, the basic structure remained almost unaltered. The fuselage, which tapered from the nose-mounted radiator to the rudder, was built up from wooden formers covered with three layers of ply laid in opposing directions. Linen was then glued to the wood surface and the whole fuselage was given a coat of varnish. In the

158

Schneider Trophy S.20bis the rear cockpit was faired over. The fin, tailplane, rudder, elevators, and the ailerons, which were carried only on the lower mainplane, were made of spruce and fabric covered. The mainplane's structure consisted of four spruce spars with plywood ribs, the leading edges were planked with ply while the remainder was covered with fabric. The upper mainplane was built in one piece, was quite sharply staggered forward but swept back, while the lower mainplanes were straight. Single I interplane struts of plywood were used. All of the trailing edges of the mainplanes and of the rudder and elevators were scalloped, a recognizable Spad design feature. The S.20bis was powered by a 260 hp Hispano-Suiza modèle 42 eight-cylinder water-cooled vee engine turning a two-blade fixed-pitch wooden propeller. The ovoid-shaped radiator was mounted in the nose around the propeller shaft and was surrounded by an aluminium cowling ring, while louvred aluminium side panels covered the cylinder block.

The alighting gear consisted of two single-step wooden floats each carried on three streamlined struts, made from several layers of plywood in a complex arrangement, braced by two additional struts each side. The floats were connected by two spreader-bars, and the entire gear, plus the mainplanes and the tail unit were wire braced.

Lecointe first flew this S.20 variant late in August 1919, only two weeks before the Schneider contest in Bournemouth. Lecointe made one or two

The Spad-Herbemont S.20bis, fitted with long-span mainplanes and redesignated S.26bis, taking-off at Monaco in 1920. (*Flight*)

159

flights before the aircraft was shipped to Cowes, accompanied by Herbemont who wanted to see at first-hand how the S.20 floatplane would perform. When the aircraft had been assembled Lecointe got airborne for a practice run over the contest course. Although the S.20bis performed well, Herbemont believed that by reducing the upper mainplane span, and thus the area, he could improve its top speed. He therefore removed the tip bends and the three outer ribs, patched the fabric covering and then varnished over this quite roughly-executed modification. In spite of the sea fog on the following day, Lecointe set out from Cowes for Bournemouth and made a successful alighting—but needed the help of Supermarine's launch which quickly took the S.20bis in tow and prevented its drifting onto an anchored boat. When the S.20bis was secured to a mooring it was discovered that the starboard float was leaking, and the aircraft had to be beached for repairs. Unfortunately, this operation only caused further damage to the floats as well as attracting the unwanted attention of bathers and sightseers on the beach; neither Lecointe nor Herbemont abandoned hope and when the contest's start was delayed by $3\frac{1}{2}$ hr, because of the fog, they redoubled their efforts to effect float repairs. However after only $1\frac{1}{2}$ hr the contest was rescheduled to start in 15 minutes; this caused the French to realize the impossibility of their task and to withdraw from the contest.

During the following year the aircraft was fitted with a larger rudder, the engine installation was altered to improve the exhaust system, and other modifications were embodied. In this form it was redesignated S.26 and, with different sets of mainplanes, set speed and height records at Monaco. With these achievements behind it plans were made to enter the S.26 in the 1920 Schneider contest in Venice but a number of domestic and industrial problems in France caused Spad to withdraw from the lists.

Two-seat twin-float racing biplane. Wood and metal construction. Pilot in open front cockpit, rear cockpit faired over.

One 260 hp Hispano-Suiza modèle 42 eight-cylinder water-cooled direct-drive normally-aspirated vee engine driving a two-blade fixed-pitch wooden propeller of approximately 2·4 m (8 ft) diameter.

Span 7·19 m (23 ft 7 in) (upper wing after modification), 8·9 m (29 ft 2½ in) lower; length 8·07 m (26 ft 5¾ in); height 3·27 m (10 ft 9 in); float length 5·2 m (17 ft 0¾ in); wing area 25·91 sq m (279 sq ft).

Empty weight 850 kg (1,874 lb); loaded weight 1,130 kg (2,491 lb); wing loading 43·45 kg/sq m (8·9 lb/sq ft).

Maximum speed 229 km/h (142 mph) estimated.

Production—one Spad S.20bis landplane was converted to a floatplane for the Schneider contest during 1919.

Colour—it has been impossible to determine the colour scheme used but photographs indicate that the upper half of the fuselage, the fin, and the rudder balance area, could have been dark blue, the lower half of the fuselage silver or grey, the mainplanes, tailplane, elevator and the rest of the rudder white. The alighting gear struts could also have been white with natural varnished wood floats. A black contest number 6 was carried on the rudder. The style of these markings was changed for subsequent competitions.

# Avro 539

With some experience in the design and construction of floatplanes stemming from the manufacture of the Avro 501, 503, 504L and 510, plus an interest in air racing, it was not surprising that A. V. Roe and Co should produce a contender for the 1919 Schneider Trophy contest to be held at Bournemouth.

Construction of the Avro 539, which had been designed by Roy Chadwick, the company's chief designer, was undertaken with great speed at Avro's Hamble factory during the summer of 1919, and it was launched for its first flight on 29 August, only twelve days before the contest.

It was a complete breakaway from previous standard Avro design practices, being a stubby little single-engined single-bay biplane powered by a 240 hp Siddeley Puma six-cylinder water-cooled engine driving a two-blade wooden propeller. It was, however, well finished externally which augured well for its performance in the air.

Constructed of wood and metal, the fuselage was built up around a rectangular wooden wire-braced box girder with wooden formers round it to provide shape. A deep fairing was provided in the top rear fuselage behind the pilot's head. The four longerons were straight and level, providing a good datum for truing up the fuselage during rigging. The engine bay was cowled with aluminium panels, as were the fuselage sides back to the cockpit. These side panels were louvred to assist the passage

The Avro 539 as originally built. (*Courtesy A. J. Jackson*)

161

of engine cooling air through the nose-mounted radiator. The rear fuselage was fabric covered. The complete tail-unit was a wooden structure with fabric covering.

The one-piece upper mainplane and the lower mainplanes were of standard spruce two-spar and rib construction, all fabric covered. Dihedral was included only in the two lower units. Ailerons were carried on upper and lower mainplanes and were interconnected in pairs by an external cable. A single pair of interplane struts was used, inclined outward to the tops for better load distribution. The inner support struts were also splayed outboard to reduce the length of 'free' spar in the upper mainplane. The alighting gear comprised two wooden single-step floats which were carried on four widely-spaced and splayed streamlined steel-tube struts, which, like the wings, were braced with streamlined wires, and two streamlined spreader-bars. The floats were very long, measuring 14 ft (4·26 m) or nearly two-thirds the fuselage length, and their 7 ft (2·13 m) track made tail or wingtip balancing floats unnecessary.

After its first flight, piloted by Capt H. Hamersley, the company test pilot, the Avro 539 was flown a few more times from Hamble before moving to Cowes for the British Schneider team selection trials. Unfortunately, when taking off, Hamersley failed to notice a floating object and damaged a float, so further trials of the Avro 539 were delayed for five days while repairs were made. Clearly Hamersley had not been happy with the directional control or stability for when the aircraft emerged from Hamble the fin had been much increased in size, no doubt to balance the large keel surface forward presented by the flat-sided engine cowling and the floats. In addition, a horn-balanced rudder had been fitted. The civil registration letters G-EALG had been applied to the fuselage sides and the manufacturer's name on the new fin.

The Avro 539 at Bournemouth after undergoing extensive tail modification. (*Flight*)

After the 1919 contest the Avro 539 Falcon floatplane G-EALG was converted to a landplane for the 1920 Aerial Derby and redesignated Avro 539A. (*British Aerospace – Manchester*)

The pre-contest trials showed that the Avro 539's performance was inferior to that of the Supermarine Sea Lion I, the Fairey III and the Sopwith Schneider; it was, therefore, held as the reserve aircraft.

After the debacle of the Bournemouth contest, it was converted into a landplane designated Avro 539A. Subsequently, powered by a 450 hp Napier Lion engine and extensively modified, it was redesignated Avro 539B and re-registered G-EAXM for the 1921 Aerial Derby but was written off in a landing accident on 15 July, 1921, on the eve of the race.

The caption on the reverse of an Avro photograph refers to the Avro 539 as the Falcon.

Single-seat twin-float racing biplane. Wood and metal construction. Pilot in open cockpit.

One 240 hp Siddeley Puma six-cylinder, direct-drive water-cooled normally-aspirated inline engine driving a two-blade fixed-pitch wooden propeller.

Span 25 ft 6 in (7·77 m) (upper), 24 ft 6 in (7·46 m) (lower); length 21 ft 4 in (6·5 m); height 9 ft 9 in (2·97 m); wing area 195 sq ft (18·11 sq m).

Empty weight 1,670 lb (757 kg); loaded weight 2,119 lb (961 kg); wing loading 10·86 lb/sq ft (53 kg/sq m).

No performance figures appear to have survived.

Production—Avro 539 G-EALG (c/n 539/1) built by A. V. Roe and Co Ltd at Hamble Aerodrome, Hants, during 1919. Subsequently redesignated Avro 539A and B.

163

A Macchi M.12 on the still waters of Lake Varese. The wide forward hull and the twin rear booms are just discernible. (*Aeronautica Macchi*)

# 1920

A Spad-Herbemont was withdrawn because of transport difficulties in France, while Italy's industrial unrest, together with repeated aircraft engine failure and poor flying weather, were to blame for the withdrawal of a Macchi M.12 and M.19 and a Savoia S.19.

This view of the Macchi M.12 airborne shows the twin-boom configuration.

The Macchi M.12 was a big 17 m (55 ft 9¼ in) span three-seat reconnaissance-bomber biplane flying-boat powered by a 475 hp Ansaldo-San Giorgio 4E-28 twelve-cylinder water-cooled direct-drive normally-aspirated vee engine which drove a two-blade wooden pusher propeller. The upper mainplane span was considerably greater than the lower and the interplane struts were arranged in a Warren girder configuration. The hull was very wide and almost flat-bottomed, and the twin fins and rudders and tailplane were carried on two booms which were extensions of the hull. The M.12's loaded weight in its military form was 2,560 kg (5,643 lb) and it was credited with a maximum speed of 190 km/h (118 mph). For the contest it was planned to fly with a crew of two, a reduced fuel load, and with much military equipment removed. Little is known of the Savoia S.19 except that it was a biplane powered by an Isotta-Fraschini engine.

One of the classic Savoia flying-boats, the S.19 was withdrawn from the 1920 contest.
(*SIAI Marchetti*)

# 1921

From a long list of sixteen aircraft entered in the eliminating trials, Italy removed three Macchi M.7s and two M.18s, six Savoia S.13s, an S.21, and the S.22, which crashed before the contest. France's Nieuport 29 wrecked its alighting gear during the seaworthiness tests, and an Italian project, the Pegna P.c.1, never came to fruition.

The M.18, like the M.12, was a large military three- or four-seat biplane flying-boat used for reconnaissance, transport and training. With a similar mainplane configuration, but smaller, 15·8 m (51 ft 9 in) span, and a conventional single hull, it was powered by a 250 hp Isotta-Fraschini Asso six-cylinder water-cooled direct-drive normally-aspirated vee engine driving a two-blade pusher propeller. Weighing 1,780 kg

An open-cockpit Macchi M.18. Two similar aircraft were intended to participate in the 1921 contest but were withdrawn following engine trouble. (*Aeronautica Macchi*)

(3,924 lb) it had a top speed in its military rôle of 187 km/h (116 mph). This aircraft would have been flown in the contest with a crew of two, reduced fuel, and with military equipment removed.

The Nieuport 29 was very similar in design and appearance to the aircraft which was withdrawn from the 1919 contest and is believed to have been fitted with short main floats and a small tail float.

## Savoia S.21

From the aesthetic point of view, Alessandro Marchetti's racing biplane flying-boats were, undoubtedly, the most appealing of their type to be produced for the Schneider contest, and of these the little S.21 with its novel inverted sesquiplane layout was perhaps the most memorable. It

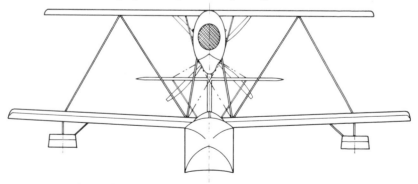

Front elevation of the unusual Savoia S.21. (*Clem Watson*)

166

The 475 hp Ansaldo engine emphasises the small size of the 1921 Savoia S.21. The lower wing had a span of only 7·69 m (25 ft 3 in) and the short upper wing measured 5·1 m (16 ft 9 in). (*SIAI Marchetti*)

was designed and built specially for the 1921 contest. The S.21 was virtually a shoulder-wing monoplane having a small additional mainplane of considerably shorter span carried on long Warren girder style inverted-vee struts high above it.

The slender, beautifully proportioned, single-step hull was 7 m (22 ft 11½ in) long and carried a tall triangular fin built integral with the very shallow-draft rear hull section. The hull was of wooden construction and had a concave undersurface. The pilot's open cockpit was positioned in front of the mainplanes. The tailplane was carried high on the fin and was supported by a Y-strut each side attached to the hull. A large horn-balanced rudder was fitted. The entire tail unit was of wooden construction and fabric covered.

The mainplanes were conventional wooden spar and ribs and were fabric covered. Both upper and lower units had markedly curved aerofoil sections and were of narrow chord. Ailerons were carried only on the lower mainplane, the roots of which were thickened where they joined the hull. Comparatively large symmetrical-section stabilizing floats were carried on struts under the lower surface.

A 475 hp Ansaldo-San Giorgio twelve-cylinder water-cooled engine, driving a four-blade pusher propeller, was mounted on a pair of N-struts and with its radiator was carried in a large flattened-oval nacelle close below the upper mainplane. A pair of light N-struts attached to the engine struts supported the upper mainplane.

Guido Jannello, who had flown the S.13 in the 1919 contest, made the early flight tests of the S.21 and achieved speeds in excess of 240 km/h (149 mph), making it the fastest of the sixteen aircraft which Italy had nominated for the elimination trials to select three for the contest.

Unfortunately, Jannello became ill and could not fly the S.21; his replacement was F. Guarnieri but on the day of the trials engine trouble prevented this potential winner from taking part.

Single-seat racing biplane flying-boat. Wood and metal construction. Pilot in open cockpit.

One 475 hp Ansaldo-San Giorgio 4E-28 twelve-cylinder normally-aspirated direct-drive vee engine driving a four-blade fixed-pitch wooden pusher propeller of about 2·13 m (7 ft) diameter.

Span 7·69 m (25 ft 3 in) (lower), 5·1 m (16 ft 9 in) (upper); length 7 m (22 ft 11½ in); height 2·94 m (9 ft 7½ in).

Empty weight 700 kg (1,543 lb); loaded weight 900 kg (1,984 lb).

Maximum speed 290 km/h (180·19 mph).

Production—one S.21 built by Società Idrovolanti Alta Italia at Milan in 1921.

Colour—believed to have been overall red hull, lower fin and floats with white upper fin and rudder, mainplanes and engine nacelle. Blue and white pennant on side of hull nose, and Savoia below cockpit.

# Savoia S.22

The S.22 was one of the two handsome flying-boats entered by Italy in the 1921 contest. An unlikely contender, as it was a twin-engined two-seat passenger aircraft, the S.22 nevertheless had a maximum speed of some 225 km/h (140 mph). Its design was, perhaps, something of a compromise for it is reported that its concept was conditioned by the terms of contemporary contests.

A slender all-wood hull, with integral fin, supported equal-span two-bay biplane mainplanes of fabric-covered wooden construction. Ailerons

The Savoia S.22 with tandem Isotta-Fraschini engines has been reported as an eight-seater. (*SIAI Marchetti*)

168

appear to have been fitted only on the lower mainplanes. The tailplane was carried high on the fin and was strut-braced to the hull. The outer pair of interplane struts were of substantial broad-chord proportions but the inner pair were much more slender. The entire mainplane structure was braced by diagonal and adjustable streamlined-section tie-rods.

Two 260 hp Isotta-Fraschini V.6 water-cooled engines were mounted under the upper mainplane in tandem configuration and supported on two pairs of V struts. The engines, which from photographs of this installation appear to have been 'handed' so that, viewed from the front, they both rotated in an anti-clockwise direction, drove four-blade propellers. When entered for the Schneider Trophy it was planned to replace the Isotta-Fraschini engines with two 300 hp Fiat A.12 six-cylinder inline engines.

Two-seat biplane flying-boat. Pilot plus one crew in open cockpit.
Two 260 hp Isotta-Fraschini V.6 six-cylinder water-cooled direct-drive normally-aspirated inline engines mounted in tandem driving four-blade propellers.
Span 13·5 m (44 ft 3½ in); length 10·78 m (35 ft 4¼ in); height 3·52 m (11 ft 6½ in).
Empty weight 1,600 kg (3,527 lb); loaded weight 2,500 kg (5,511 lb).
Maximum speed 225 km/h (139·8 mph).

Production—one S.22 built by Società Idrovolanti Alta Italia in 1920.

Colour—unknown, but believed to have been overall red hull and fin; silver mainplanes and rudder; natural metal engine cowlings and spinners; green, white and red national stripes on fin; blue and white pennant with name Savoia on hull nose.

# Pegna P.c.1

While aircraft and engine designers in the United States and Great Britain concerned with creating high-speed seaplanes for the Schneider contests rarely produced unconventional or avant-garde designs, in Italy several projects were at the forefront, or even in advance, of contemporary technology. The most adventurous of these were projected by Giovanni Pegna. Although some Italian designs involved the use of very large engines to achieve high performance, Pegna was aware of the restrictions these imposed when used with large hulls or twin floats; thus he drew on his earlier experience of designing hydrofoils when projecting a series of seaplanes for the contests.

His first proposal for the 1921 contest was the all-wood P.c.1 which was to have a flat-sided slender hull, a shoulder-mounted cantilever wing of medium thickness-chord ratio and with sharply curved back tips, and a fin-mounted tailplane. The pilot would have sat well aft immediately in front of the fin. The engine was to be mounted almost amidships and drive the propeller through a long shaft connected to the engine by a universal joint. The P.c.1 was intended to float in the water with little freeboard, and propeller clearance for take-off and alighting was to have been achieved by tilting up the propeller shaft and the top of the forward hull which carried the radiator, but the aircraft was never built.

# 1922

The Savoia-MVT S.50 selected for the Italian team crashed before the contest, and its pilot was killed; and because of an Italian railway strike neither of France's two CAMS 36s arrived in Naples. Alessandro Marchetti's design for the S.50 biplane was based on a wartime fighter powered by a 250 hp SPA 6-2A six-cylinder water-cooled inline engine, and designated the Marchetti-Vickers-Terni. It is believed that only a handful were built but one was put on floats in 1922, fitted with a 280 hp 6A-S engine. It was an ungainly single-bay biplane, with the fuselage mounted clear of the lower mainplane on the float struts. Single interplane struts were used between the very thick narrow-chord wings which were of complex planform, being swept back and having sharply tapering tips, with the entire trailing edge being scalloped. Lateral control was by wing warping. The tailplane and rudder were overhung from the end of the fuselage. Two large box-section floats had Conflenti-type concave bottoms.

# CAMS 36

The marked similarities between the French CAMS flying-boats, produced for the 1922 and 1923 Schneider contests, and the earlier Italian Savoia flying-boats of the 1919–21 era was no accident. All stemmed from the drawing-board inspiration of designer Raphaël Conflenti who had been the Savoia company's chief of design under its founder and president D. Lorenzo Santoni from about 1917 until 1921. In that year he left the Italian factory on Lake Maggiore and moved to France to join a new company named Chantiers Aéro-Maritimes de la Seine—or CAMS. Here he renewed his association with Santoni, who had made a similar move a little earlier.

Like many other aircraft manufacturers, CAMS believed that a victory in the Schneider contests could enhance its reputation, thus Conflenti was soon at work on a racing flying-boat designated CAMS 36. Its layout drew heavily on its designer's earlier work in Italy and it is recorded that it was little more than a refined and modified version of a basic licence-built Italian aircraft. There were, however, several significant differences which served to stamp some individuality on the graceful French flying-

F-ESFC, the CAMS 36bis with the modified rudder shape and stabilizing floats for the 1923 contest, being taken in tow at Cowes.

boats. Chief among these was the concave shape of the planing bottom, the single I-interplane struts, and the position of the pilot's cockpit.

The CAMS 36's hull was not unique, as Conflenti had used it on some of his Savoia flying-boats, and Alessandro Marchetti, who had joined the Savoia company as its chief engineer after Conflenti had moved, also used concave undersurfaces on the floats of his S.50 floatplane which was a 1922 Schneider aspirant for a few months. In the CAMS 36, however, Conflenti seems to have deepened the concavity and, in so doing, greatly reduced the spray and wash created by the conventional hull shapes. However, this was not achieved until the hull reached planing speed, when the big bow wave which it produced subsided and the aircraft ran cleanly along the surface before lifting off.

The single-step hull was built up from wooden frames and covered with a marine ply skin, with the tall fin and the pilot's head fairing built integral with the basic structure of the hull. The hull frames were doubled and the skin was reinforced at the lower mainplane spar attachment points and at the foot of the engine mounting struts. A large removable hatch was provided in the top surface of the long, beautifully clean, hull just forward of the lower mainplane. The pilot's cockpit was positioned aft of the mainplanes and offset to starboard, presumably to give a better view along the side of, rather than over, the long nose, and more leg room in the deeper side section of the hull. The thin-section wooden tailplane and elevator structure was fabric covered; it was mounted half-way up the fin and was braced to the hull by a single strut and two bracing wires on each side. A quite small square-topped unbalanced rudder of similar construction was used.

171

The mainplanes were built around the conventional two spruce spars and multiple rib structure with fabric covering. Both upper and lower units were rectangular in shape, unswept and of equal span, with the lower mainplane being of narrower chord. Ailerons were carried only on the lower mainplane and were of narrow chord and long span occupying more than two-thirds of the trailing edge. The upper mainplane was carried on a pair of N-struts attached to the engine mounting which were, in turn, cross braced to the centre section. Tall, slender, single I-interplane struts had wide-chord mounting feet at their extremities. Two broad stabilizing floats of deep aerofoil-section were fitted closely under the lower mainplane below the interplane struts.

The 320 hp Hispano-Suiza modèle 42 eight-cylinder vee water-cooled engine was mounted on a pair of massive N-struts and was housed in a remarkably clean nacelle of streamlined shape. It drove a four-blade wooden propeller having a very large spinner. Oil coolers were fitted in the lower curved surface of the nacelle behind the spinner and two Lamblin 'lobster pot' type water radiators were strut-mounted from the main engine supports. The entire wing and engine installation was wire-braced. All the control cable runs from the cockpit to the flying surfaces were within the hull and wings.

Two CAMS 36 flying-boats (F-ESFA and F-ESFB) were built for the 1922 Schneider contest, but their construction took longer than anticipated and their preliminary flying trials had to be curtailed only a few days before the contest, on 12 August, to enable them to be dismantled and prepared for transport by rail to Naples. Unfortunately, neither aircraft arrived in time to compete. For the 1923 Schneider contest Conflenti embodied some small modifications in the previous year's aircraft to create the CAMS 36bis (F-ESFC) by fitting a top rudder with more curve and twin interplane struts, using more streamlined stabilizing floats and slightly changing the rigging wires between the upper and lower mainplanes. An uprated Hispano-Suiza engine producing 360 hp was fitted and two strut-type Lamblin radiators on the engine supports replaced the 'lobster pots'. After some problems associated with the shipping of the CAMS 36bis across the Channel from France to Cowes, the site for the 1923 contest, bad weather interrupted some of the practice flying. However, when Lieut de Vaisseau G. Pelletier d'Oisy was taxi-ing out to the contest starting line his view appeared to be obstructed by the engine-mounting struts and long nose and his aircraft collided with a yacht riding at anchor. The aircraft's hull was only slightly damaged but it was enough to prevent the CAMS 36bis taking part in the contest. This aircraft was flown during 1924 by Lieut de Vaisseau Maurice Hurel to establish a world seaplane altitude record of 6,200 m (20,340 ft).

It should be mentioned that F-ESFA and F-ESFB were the registrations quoted for the 1922 CAMS 36s but they also appeared on the CAMS 33. It would seem that these pre- C of A, or test, registrations were used more than once, as are the present day F-W registrations.

Single-seat racing biplane flying-boat. Wood and fabric construction. Pilot in open cockpit.

One 320 hp Hispano-Suiza modèle 42 eight-cylinder water-cooled direct-drive normally-aspirated vee engine driving a four-blade fixed-pitch wooden propeller of about 2·05 m (6 ft 9 in) diameter. Fuel: 295 litres (65 gal) (estimated).

Span 8·6 m (28 ft 2½ in); length 8·32 m (27 ft 4 in); height 2·76 m (9 ft 0½ in); wing area 20 sq m (215·28 sq ft).

Empty weight 941 kg (2,075 lb); loaded weight 1,260 kg (2,777 lb); wing loading 63 kg/sq m (12·89 lb/sq ft).

Maximum speed 257 km/h (159·69 mph).

Production—two CAMS 36 (F-ESFA and F-ESFB) built by Chantiers Aéro-Maritimes de la Seine at St Denis, France, during 1921–22. One CAMS 36bis (F-ESFC) which could have been one of the earlier aircraft, prepared for the 1923 Schneider contest.

Colour—believed dark blue hull, fin and stabilizing floats; natural linen wing; silver or white interplane, engine and upper mainplane support struts; natural mahogany laminated propeller and spinner. Gold CAMS company wings motif on sides of hull nose. Photographs show registration letters only under lower mainplane (CAMS 36). Overall white; black registration letters on hull sides and under lower mainplanes; believed red contest number 10 on sides of hull nose and rudder (CAMS 36bis).

# 1923

A Sopwith-Hawker, which was the old 1919 contest Sopwith Schneider G-EAKI with a wheeled undercarriage but scheduled to be remounted on floats for this year's Schneider contest, was wrecked when it turned over on landing during trials before its conversion. The Blackburn Pellet crashed on take-off before the seaworthiness trials. France's two Latham L.1 and one CAMS 36bis flying-boats were withdrawn because of damage while afloat or engine failure, and neither of the two Blanchard-Blériot C.1 reserve aircraft were sent to England. Italy's Savoia S.51 and a new Macchi flying-boat failed to materialize as entrants. The United States NW-2 crashed during practice flying over the Solent and the TR-3A wrecked its engine when attempting to start up.

# Blackburn Pellet

Robert Blackburn was quick to appreciate the commercial value of a victory in the Schneider contests. He had formed The Blackburn Aeroplane Co at Leeds in 1911 and only six years later had produced a floatplane version of his Improved Type I monoplane, powered by an uncowled 100 hp air-cooled Anzani radial engine, and known as the Land/Sea monoplane.

In 1916 the company—then known as The Blackburn Aeroplane and Motor Co Ltd—designed a handsome flying-boat to meet the Admiralty

The little Blackburn Pellet being eased down Fairey Aviation's slipway to the water of the Hamble River for initial flight trials. This view shows the outsized stabilizing floats, the well-cowled Lion engine and the small wind-driven generator between the engine support struts. (*Blackburn Aircraft*)

N.1B requirement for a single-seat fleet escort bomber. With the Supermarine Aviation Works at Southampton and the Westland Aircraft Works at Yeovil, who also submitted designs, Blackburn received a contract to build three of the eight prototypes ordered. All were designated N.1B, but while the three Supermarine aeroplanes, serialled N59, N60 and N61, were small pusher-engined flying-boats similar to Blackburn's three prototypes, which were serialled N56, N57 and N58, the two Westland aircraft, serialled N16 and N17, were twin-float seaplanes.

The outstanding feature of the Blackburn N.1B was its two-step hull designed by Lieut Linton Hope RN. It consisted of circular wooden formers and stringers planked diagonally with narrow mahogany strips one-eighth of an inch thick. Two laminations were used, crossing each other at 90 degrees. This method of construction produced a hull of classic hydrodynamic and aerodynamic shape.

Powered by a single 200 hp liquid-cooled Hispano-Suiza engine driving a two-blade fabric-covered mahogany propeller, the top speed of the N.1B was estimated to have been 114 mph (183·46 km/h). Although both Supermarine and Westland completed and flew their five prototype N.1Bs during 1917–18, production of the Blackburn aeroplanes was somewhat slower due largely to the fact that the company could not obtain the engines. However, the contract was cancelled in November 1918 when the Sopwith Pup performed well in flight trials.

By this time Blackburn had built only the hull of N56 and this was wisely put into store. It was to form the basis of the Pellet, a small single-seat flying-boat designed as an entrant for the 1923 contest.

174

There is no doubt that, like a number of manufacturers, Blackburn had not entered the lists earlier because of the comparatively high costs involved in building and flying a one-off design in the contest, particularly when the event was held overseas. It was only when Great Britain became the host country that Blackburn decided to build the Pellet. Even then it is reported that the directors had to make the decision whether to enter the contest or pay a dividend to shareholders. While competitive spirit was strong in the Board members, for they chose the former course, the reaction of the shareholders that year was not recorded. However, this move enabled Blackburn to renew its earlier development of marine aircraft which had ceased when the N.1B programme had been cancelled. As previously mentioned it was that aeroplane's hull, which had been retained and stored at Brough for five years on Robert Blackburn's instructions, which formed the basis of the small single-seat flying-boat announced by the company in March 1923.

This was the second Schneider Trophy contender to have its roots in the N.1B competition; when creating the Supermarine Sea Lion I in 1919, R. J. Mitchell drew heavily on the design of that company's Baby flying-boat. With only six months remaining before the 1923 contest was scheduled to take place, work began on designing the rest of the aeroplane. These were the mainplanes and engine installation and the tail unit. They materialized as single-bay narrow-gap unequal-span wings of

The Blackburn Pellet being fitted with a new metal propeller and with a Lamblin radiator installed during the night before the 1923 contest navigability trials.

175

suitable racing section and wooden construction. There was dihedral on only the upper mainplane which carried the very wide-span ailerons, which occupied more than two-thirds of the trailing edge, and which were operated by internal push-pull rods connected to the cockpit via a cable and chain and sprocket control run. Wooden wingtip floats, believed to have been constructed for the N.1B and put into store with the hull, were attached under the lower mainplane immediately below the reversed N-type interplane struts. Support for the upper centre section, which carried flush-mounted radiators and the engine installation, was provided by canted reversed N-struts. The whole wing cellule was wire-braced. The tail unit consisted of a heavily strut-and-wire-braced tailplane mounted halfway up the fabric-covered fin. The broad-chord unbalanced elevators and rudder were cable operated.

The wooden hull was circular in section with a forward single-step planing-bottom structure built onto it. A second small step with a tiny skeg aft of it was also added at the normal aft waterline. These excrescences on an otherwise almost smooth symmetrical hull provided the essential hydrodynamic qualities. The only other excrescence was the long windscreen which was hinged at its forward edge to provide easier access to the small open cockpit. A small streamlined headrest completed the cockpit fairing, and a wind-driven generator, mounted immediately behind it on the lower wing, provided power for the instrument panel. The power was provided by a 450 hp Napier Lion engine driving a two-blade wooden propeller. This unit was mounted on top of the upper mainplane, was closely cowled and was faired in with a large removable tailcone. It was, in fact, the same engine which had equipped the Gloster Bamel which, earlier in the year, had won the Aerial Derby at 192·4 mph (309·63 km/h). The pilot for the Blackburn flying-boat, now named the Pellet, was the well-known R. W. Kenworthy and, being aware of the fact that he would be flying a one-off prototype built in only a few months, he had asked that it should be completed and ready for flight trials in August 1923, a month before the contest at Cowes. Accordingly, a great effort was made by Blackburn's production personnel, and during July the civil registration G-EBHF was allocated. Later the Pellet also carried the contest number 6 on its rudder and hull. Unfortunately, it was not until the first week in September that, following some initial engine runs, the Pellet was launched from the Brough factory's slipway with Kenworthy aboard. Then the ill-luck which characterized this little aeroplane throughout its brief life immediately struck. The strong Humber tide caught the starboard stabilizing underwing float and slowly the Pellet turned over in the water, fortunately allowing Kenworthy enough time to scramble out of the cockpit. Rapidly the aircraft was salvaged and, with only three weeks remaining before the contest, the long and arduous task of stripping the Lion engine, drying out and repairing the airframe and fitting larger underwing floats began.

Because time was so short there was no opportunity to fly the Pellet at

In this picture of the Blackburn Pellet's fateful take-off the hull can be seen just clear of the water. Quite strong back pressure is obviously being applied to the control column. (*Blackburn Aircraft*)

Porpoising on its take-off run, the Blackburn Pellet is pictured split-seconds before it rolled over and plunged into the water. The hull nose is high, with the aircraft in a semi-stalled attitude.

Brough following this work and the aeroplane was sent to Southampton by rail. From there it was taken by road to the Fairey factory at Hamble for reassembly. This was completed on 25 September, 1923, and early the following morning the Pellet went down the slipway into the chill waters of the Hamble river.

With Kenworthy as pilot, taxi-ing began and it was soon apparent that the Pellet's hull was far from sea-kindly, shipping a lot of water before the aeroplane became airborne for the first time. In the air the Pellet proved very nose heavy and Kenworthy had to haul back on the control column with all his strength to remain in level flight before attempting to alight again in the Solent off Calshot Spit. Back on the water he drifted in the Pellet for nearly an hour before he was taken in tow by a motor-boat to S. E. Saunders' factory at East Cowes. There Kenworthy reported his problems, which included the fact that due to insufficient radiator surface the engine coolant had boiled. Working through the night, Blackburn fitters installed a large Lamblin radiator between the centre-section struts and bypassed the wing radiators: they also replaced the wooden propeller with a two-blade metal propeller without a spinner.

This work enabled the Pellet to be readied for the following morning's navigability and mooring-out tests, and despite Kenworthy's unhappy experiences in this aeroplane he seemed quite confident as he headed out for the starting line. Unfortunately he was baulked by a small rowing boat which looked likely to cross his path and he opened up the Lion engine more rapidly than he had intended. Immediately, the Pellet began to porpoise, leaping into the air and then dropping back into the sea, with a resounding smack each time. Then it became airborne in a nose-up semi-stalled condition, turned slowly right-handed when the underwing float touched the water, the nose dug in, and the Pellet turned over and dived almost vertically below the surface. Although Kenworthy was strapped in the cockpit, some trapped air gave him a tiny breathing space, but it was 61 seconds by the time-keeper's stop watch before Kenworthy's head bobbed to the surface! He climbed onto the inverted Pellet's hull and was picked up by a motor-launch. The wrecked aeroplane was brought ashore and returned to Saunders' factory.

Single-seat racing biplane flying-boat. Wooden construction with wood skinning. Pilot in open cockpit.

One 450 hp Napier Lion twelve-cylinder water-cooled broad-arrow engine driving a 7 ft 8 in (2·33 m) diameter two-blade wooden propeller.

Span 34 ft (10·36 m) (upper), 29 ft 6 in (8·99 m) (lower); length 28 ft 7 in (8·71 m); height 10 ft 8 in (3·25 m).

Empty weight 2,150 lb (975 kg); loaded weight 2,800 lb (1,270 kg).

Maximum speed 161 mph (259·1 km/h).

Production—one Pellet built by Blackburn Aeroplane and Motor Co, Brough, in 1923.

Colour—believed overall pale blue with dark blue engine nacelle and black registration G-EBHF.

# Latham L.1

The rules of the Schneider contests, while they were changed and amended from time to time during the 18 year-long series, were specifically aimed at preventing the construction and participation in the contests of freak or sprint type aeroplanes. The navigability and mooring-out tests and load-carrying requirements were intended to ensure that only sound practical seaplanes would be judged worthy of getting to the starting line. In the event there were many impractical aircraft designed and built which, during elimination trials, failed to reach even the preliminary basic requirements for an airworthy seaplane.

Although the Latham L.1 flying-boats were known as No.1 and No.2, the example seen here bears 01 on its bow. (*Courtesy Jacques Gambu*)

In 1922, after the two CAMS 36 flying-boats had been prevented from reaching Naples for that year's Schneider contest, France determined to mount a thoroughly pragmatic approach to its preparations for the 1923 contest at Cowes. From its careful examination of the CAMS 36bis and the newer CAMS 38 flying-boats it was clear that, while both aircraft were of conventional design and construction, they were not wholly suited to the rigours of the heavy weather which the British Isles can produce at almost any time of the year. For this reason it was decided to adopt a belt-and-braces policy with regard to the French team aircraft and build a more robust design better equipped to face bad weather conditions in the Solent. Accordingly, the Société Industrielle de Caudebec-en-Caux (SICC) was given an order for two flying-boats to meet this requirement.

They materialized as 12·39 m (40 ft 8 in) span 2½ tonne twin-engined aircraft (F-ATAM and F-ESEJ) with their 400 hp Lorraine-Dietrich modèle 13 twelve-cylinder vee engines in a tandem installation. The single-step hull was of conventional construction with its wooden formers overlain by wood strips. The hull had a deep vee bottom with hard chines which swept forward up to the stemhead, while the rear hull curved up to the integral fin. The pilot's cockpit was positioned between the two front engine-mounting struts and behind the front propeller and had an air dam rather than a transparent windscreen. The tailplane was carried on top of the fin and a comma-shaped rudder extended above and below the tailplane which was braced to the hull by a single swept broad-chord strut.

The single-bay rectangular plan mainplanes had the usual two spruce main spars with plywood ribs, all fabric-covered, and single I broad-chord

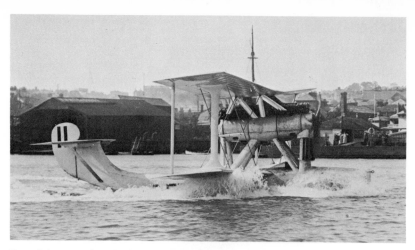

One of the two robust Latham L.1 flying-boats which failed to reach the starting line at Cowes in 1923, creates a great flurry of water while taxi-ing.

interplane struts. Long-span ailerons were carried on the upper and lower mainplanes and were interconnected by a streamlined rod. The arrangement of the engine mounting struts differed on the two aircraft; on No. 1, F-ATAM, the engines were mounted on a pair of single struts at the front—to which two long Lamblin radiators were attached—and by a pair of V-struts at the rear. Two pairs of inverted V-struts on each side supported the upper mainplane centre-section. The front engine was housed completely within the bulky nacelle but the aircraft was some-

The No. 1 Latham L.1, F-ESEJ, showing the massive engine mounting struts and large stabilizing floats.

180

times flown with the top of the rear engine uncowled. On Latham L.1 No. 2, F-ESEJ, two pairs of V-struts supported the engines' nacelle front and rear and it is believed that the tops of both engines were permanently uncowled as indicated in contemporary drawings. On both aircraft a fin-type oil cooler was fitted in the bottom of the nacelle between the two engines. The whole of the wing cellule was braced by streamlined wires. Two 'trousered' stabilizing float structures were attached directly under the lower mainplanes.

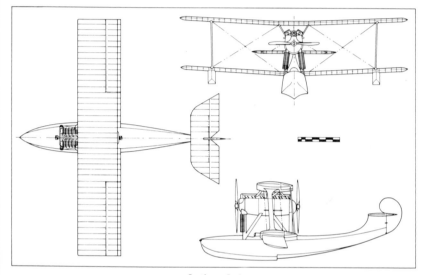

Latham L.1

The two engines were not 'handed' and thus both rotated in the same direction; as they were mounted back-to-back they turned their respective two-blade wooden propellers, which had curved scimitar-like blades, in opposite directions and cancelled out the torque reaction.

As the date of the contest drew near it began to be apparent that there could be a repetition of the previous year's non-appearance of the French entries; however, both L.1s were readied for their journey to Cowes aboard ship only two days before the all-important navigability trials were scheduled to begin. When the ship which was to have taken the two CAMS flying-boats went unserviceable, it was decided to switch the shipping arrangements and fly the Latham L.1s across the Channel, leaving the one available ship to bring the more frail CAMS aircraft.

As recorded on page 16 the enthusiastic but misguided assistance of eager Britons rendered F-ATAM unserviceable almost at the moment it reached English shores and a magneto failure on one of F-ESEJ's engines prevented its participation in the contest.

181

Single-seat racing biplane flying-boat. Pilot in open cockpit.

Two 400 hp Lorraine-Dietrich modèle 13 twelve-cylinder water-cooled direct-drive normally-aspirated vee engines mounted in tandem and driving two-blade fixed-pitch wooden propellers.

Span 12·39 m (40 ft 8 in); length 10·92 m (35 ft 9¾ in); height 4·26 m (14 ft); wing area 50 sq m (538·2 sq ft).

Empty weight 1,533 kg (3,380 lb); loaded weight 2,700 kg (5,952 lb); wing loading 54 kg/sq m (11·05 lb/sq ft).

Maximum speed 257·49 km/h (160 mph).

Production—two Latham L.1s (F-ATAM and F-ESEJ) built by Société Industrielle de Caudebec-en-Caux during 1922–23.

Colour—not definitely established but believed to have been pale blue overall with dark blue registration letters on sides of hull and under lower mainplanes; contest number 11 (F-ESEJ) on each side of nose and on upper part of rudder.

# Blanchard-Blériot C.1

The design of the Blanchard-Blériot C.1 flying-boats intended for the 1923 contest was based on that of a French military fighter type. Of pleasing, if slightly unusual appearance, the C.1 was a parasol monoplane powered by a 380 hp Gnome-Rhône built Jupiter nine-cylinder air-cooled direct-drive unsupercharged radial engine. The slender all-wood hull had an almost flat top-decking, a broad-vee undersurface with the chine line curving up at the front to meet the deck line in a scow bow shape. The fin was built integral with the hull and carried the tailplane,

The Blanchard-Blériot C.1. Note the aft cockpit, interesting stabilizing-float mounting, and the comparatively bulky engine installation compared to the generally slender lines of the hull. (*Musée de l'Air*)

182

which was wire braced to the top of the fin and supported by a pair of struts attached to the hull on each side. The rudder and elevators were of wooden construction and fabric covered.

The mainplane was a conventional two-spar structure in wood and was fabric covered, and it is believed that the leading edge was of formed plywood. It was carried above the hull on a pair of wooden wire-braced N-struts which also supported the engine. The outer panels of the mainplane were braced on each side by a pair of parallel struts attached at their lower ends to the hull sides. Square-section stabilizing floats were attached to the undersides of these struts, quite close to the hull, and each float had a pair of smaller wire-braced struts attached to the hull.

The Jupiter engine was mounted in the front of an all-metal cowled nacelle, with its thrust-line above the mainplane, and drove a two-blade wooden propeller. The cylinders protruded through the cowling, and there was an oil-cooler below the nacelle between the N-struts.

The pilot's cockpit was positioned well aft of these N-struts and was provided with a small windscreen and a head fairing. Two C.1s were built, one of which, F-ESEH, proved disappointingly slow, with a maximum speed of only 219 km/h (136 mph). A more powerful Jupiter engine of 540 hp was fitted in the second C.1 but, unfortunately, before it was registered, it was involved in a collision and written off.

Single-seat racing parasol-monoplane flying-boat. Predominantly wood and fabric construction with some metal components. Pilot in open cockpit situated aft of the wing.

One 380 hp Gnome-Rhône STAe 9Aa bis Jupiter nine-cylinder air-cooled direct-drive normally-aspirated radial engine driving a two-blade fixed-pitch wooden propeller.

Span 12·25 m (40 ft 2¼ in); length 9·71 m (31 ft 10 in); height 3·3 m (10 ft 9¾ in); wing area 21 sq m (226 sq ft).

Empty weight 950 kg (2,094 lb); loaded weight 1,280 kg (2,822 lb); wing loading 60·95 kg/sq m (12·48 lb/sq ft).

Maximum speed 219 km/h (136 mph).

Production—two Blanchard-Blériot C.1s (F-ESEH, plus one unregistered) built by Société Aéronautique Blanchard at Les Coteaux de St-Cloud during 1923.

Colour—cannot be established but might have been blue hull, tail unit, floats and struts with silver or white mainplane and engine nacelle.

# Wright NW-2

As recorded elsewhere, the construction of racing aircraft in the United States was often wrapped around with mystery, the work involved and often the designations of the aeroplanes themselves were deliberately misleading; moreover, the production of a racing design sometimes was the means of providing a flying testbed for powerful new engines. A batch of four aircraft built during 1922–24 by the Wright Aeronautical Corporation owed their creation to all of these.

The pugnacious-looking Navy-Wright NW-2 ashore, showing the mainplane surface radiators, the complex strut arrangements, and the two-blade wooden propeller.

Basically and ostensibly their raison d'être was to be testbeds for the new T-series of Wright Tornado engines, the first of which, the T-2, began ground test-running during May 1922. The success of these preliminary trials was such that the US Navy decided to fund the building of not one but two aircraft with the T-2 to carry Navy colours in that year's Pulitzer Trophy race.

Drawing heavily on the layout and design detail of the French Nieuport-Delage sesquiplane racer of 1921, Commander J. Hunsaker, of the Navy's Bureau of Aeronautics, produced drawings for the first Wright 'testbed'. It was, almost unashamedly, a racing aeroplane which bore the designation NW, for Navy-Wright. The fuselage was built up from steel tube, welded and diagonally wire-braced, with metal formers which were fabric-covered aft from the front edge of the sharply sloping windscreen. Metal cowling panels enclosed the big 600 hp twelve-cylinder vee engine and main fuel tank. The two-blade wooden propeller was dwarfed by the engine installation. The upper mainplane, mounted on the fuselage in the mid-position as on a mid-wing monoplane, was spruce-ply covered from the leading edge back to the rear spar. The trailing-edge section and the metal ailerons were fabric-covered. The wire-braced broad-chord tail unit also was a steel frame structure with fabric covering. The short-span narrow-chord lower wing, without ailerons, was positioned far below the fuselage, carried on N-struts attached to the fuselage and braced to the upper wing by a single diagonal strut on each side. This very unusual lower wing was ply-covered and carried the main undercarriage units which were encased in large aluminium spats. Two large Lamblin 'lobster pot' radiators were carried by the N-struts which braced the lower wing. The small cockpit opening had a tiny windscreen and faired headrest.

184

Because of the speed with which the first aeroplane was built and the manner in which both the Navy and the Wright company kept secret details of its design and subsequent performance, the NW earned itself the soubriquet 'mystery racer'. The first aircraft, serialled A6543 and with the official designation NW-1, made its first flight on 11 October, 1922, only three days before the Pulitzer race, piloted by Marine Corps 2nd Lieut Lawson H. Sanderson. Such was the urgency to fly the NW-1 that it completed this initial test without the upper engine cowling panel. Even so it is recorded that it achieved a speed of 209 mph (336·34 km/h). In the race the T-2 engine overheated, because the oil cooler was too small, and seized. Sanderson crash-landed in shallow water on the edge of Lake St Clair in Michigan, but he surfaced with only a few cuts and bruises as a result.

The second aircraft, serialled A6544, was completed in December and differed mainly in a re-styled engine cowling, aimed at improving the cooling, and the removal of the wheel spats. This aircraft was flown on a series of engine tests from Mitchel Field, Long Island, after which it was returned to the factory for conversion to a floatplane and participation as a US Navy entrant in the 1923 Schneider Trophy as the NW-2.

Its conversion resulted in an almost complete rebuild of A6544 for not only were floats fitted but the sesquiplane configuration was changed to a more conventional equal-span biplane layout. The multi-spar-and-rib structure had plywood skinning with surface radiators on the inboard

As prepared for the 1923 contest, the NW-2, afloat at Cowes, carries its contest number 5 and has a three-blade metal propeller.

185

sections of the upper mainplanes and at mid-span on the lower ones. Fabric-covered ailerons were fitted on upper and lower mainplanes and were interconnected by tie-rods. Large single inward-canted I-shaped interplane struts with very broad chord sections top and bottom were used. The tailplane was increased in size and a ventral fin was added to balance the large keel surface presented by the 11 ft (3·35 m) long floats which had shallow-vee planing-bottoms with four longitudinal strakes. The floats were each carried on four struts, and the alighting gear was heavily braced through the lower wing to the fuselage by N-struts. The fuselage was raised clear of the lower wing on a long-chord pylon. Power was provided by a new higher-powered T-2 engine driving a two-blade wooden propeller for the early test flights of the NW-2 as a floatplane. This propeller later was changed for a three-blade adjustable-pitch metal propeller, and yet another new T-2 was selected for installation before the Schneider contest at Cowes.

The pilot chosen for the NW-2 was Navy Lieut Adolphus W. Gorton who quickly proved the capabilities of the aircraft by achieving speeds of more than 180 mph (290 km/h), some 5 mph faster than the new world's speed record established a few days earlier with a Curtiss CR-3. However, the Curtiss aircraft destined for the contest were flying even faster than that and, in an effort to coax more power and speed out of the NW-2, it was decided to adjust the propeller blades to a finer pitch and so increase the engine rpm. Ground tests of the T-2 in the United States showed that it could be expected to run for five hours—and then probably disintegrate, as did the test engine.

In order to preserve engine running life for the contest itself Gorton did all his practice flying in a reserve aircraft. However, it was agreed that he should make one practice run over the course in the NW-2. Unfortunately the T-2 blew up some 20 minutes after take-off and A6544 crashed into the water and was a complete write-off. Gorton was rescued by a small fishing boat.

Single-seat twin-float racing biplane. Wood and metal construction with wood and fabric covering. Pilot in open cockpit.

One 600 hp Wright T-2 twelve-cylinder liquid-cooled direct-drive normally-aspirated vee engine driving a 7 ft 6 in (2·28 m) diameter three-blade adjustable-pitch metal propeller. Fuel: 106 US gal (401 litres). Oil: 8 US gal (30 litres).

Span 27 ft 11 in (8·5 m); length 28 ft 4 in (8·63 m); height 11 ft 7 in (3·53 m); wing area 266 sq ft (24·71 sq m).

Empty weight 3,565 lb (1,617 kg); loaded weight 4,444 lb (2,015 kg); wing loading 16·7 lb/sq ft (81·54 kg/sq m).

Maximum speed 204 mph (328·3 km/h); stalling speed 74 mph (119·08 km/h).

Production—one NW-2 converted by Wright Aeronautical Corp from second NW-1, A6544, in 1923.

Colour—fuselage, floats and struts medium grey; wings and tail unit silver with white rudder. Black serial, USN and contest number 5 on fuselage sides and rudder. Regulation US Navy markings on upper wing surface.

The Naval Aircraft Factory TR-3 after being extensively modified for the 1923 contest as the TR-3A. (*Smithsonian Institution*)

# Naval Aircraft Factory TR-3A

The TR-3A was the last and most specialized variant of the series of five US Navy TS and TR fighter-scout and racing floatplanes built during 1921–23 by the Curtiss Aeroplane Company to a basic design concept by Cdr J. Hunsaker of the Naval Aircraft Factory. The TS-1, the US Navy's first postwar fighter-scout and the progenitor of the TR-3A, was powered by a Lawrence J-1 nine-cylinder air-cooled direct-drive unsupercharged radial engine driving a two-blade fixed-pitch propeller. Struts abounded in the general construction of this aeroplane and gave the impression of keeping apart, rather than joining, the main constituent sections of the airframe. The fuselage and tail unit were all fabric covered apart from the forward top decking, and the front bay immediately aft of the uncowled radial engine, which had louvered metal panels. The pilot's cockpit had a small windscreen but a very large head fairing and was positioned under the trailing edge of the upper mainplane.

The prototype TS-1 (A6248) was designed to be fitted with either a wheeled undercarriage or floats, and it retained its tailskid when equipped as a floatplane.

For the 1922 Curtiss Marine Trophy race, four TS-1 airframes were taken from the Curtiss production line for modification by the Naval Aircraft Factory. One TS-1 (A6248) with a J-1 radial engine remained almost in its standard Service form; a second aircraft (A6303) redesignated TR-1, also had a J-1 engine but was fitted with thinner 'racing wings'. The third aircraft (A6446), redesignated TS-2, retained the standard high-lift mainplanes but was powered by a 200 hp Aeromarine

187

eight-cylinder water-cooled direct-drive unsupercharged vee engine, while the fourth aircraft (A6447), redesignated TR-3, was fitted with the special thinner mainplanes and a 225 hp Wright E-3 eight-cylinder water-cooled direct-drive unsupercharged vee engine. All the TS and TR variants were equipped with two-blade fixed-pitch propellers and, apart from their mainplanes and engines, were almost identical. A major visual feature of the TS-2 and TR-3 was the large rectangular box-shaped coolant radiator carried under the fuselage immediately forward of the lower mainplane. Although the TR-3 retired during the Curtiss race, when its propeller securing bolts slackened, this aeroplane was selected as the reserve aircraft for the US 1923 Schneider Trophy team. Accordingly, towards the end of 1922 work began at the Naval Aircraft Factory on an extensive modification programme to clean up the TR-3 design. The major changes were in the choice of engine and in the upper mainplane. While the cylinder heads of the TR-3's Wright E-3 engine had protruded through the cowling, the new E-4 engine chosen was completely enclosed, with large close-fitting streamlined fairings covering the cylinder heads. The upper mainplane was of a new design, its inboard sections being covered with surface radiators, and a small 'blister' header-tank was mounted on the upper surface on the centre line. The mainplane was lowered, so that it was attached directly to the top of the fuselage, and the earlier heavy strutting was replaced by a pair of interplane struts each side, which were wire-braced to the fuselage. The fuselage support struts and those in the alighting gear remained unaltered. The pilot's head fairing was removed.

Redesignated TR-3A, this aeroplane emerged a business-like racer, and not belied when it achieved a maximum speed of 160 mph (257·49 km/h) during initial flight trials. However, having been shipped to Cowes in readiness for the Schneider Trophy contest, a backfire wrecked its engine inertial starting system. As it was found impossible to hand swing the engine, the TR-3A was unable to fly in the contest as the replacement for the US Navy's NW-2 which crashed during pre-contest practice flying.

Single-seat twin-float racing biplane. Wood and metal construction with fabric, wood and metal covering. Pilot in open cockpit.

One 210 hp Wright E-4 eight-cylinder water-cooled direct-drive normally-aspirated vee engine driving a two-blade fixed-pitch wooden propeller.

Span 23 ft (7·01 m); length 26 ft (7·92 m); height 9 ft 3 in (2·81 m).

Empty weight 1,700 lb (771 kg)—estimated; loaded weight 2,129 lb (965·7 kg).

Maximum speed 160 mph (257·49 km/h).

Production—one TR-3A (A6447) converted from a TR-3 by the US Naval Aircraft Factory, Philadelphia, during 1922–23.

Colour—believed to be overall silver, with red, white and blue national rudder stripe markings, black serial A6447 and contest number 5 on fuselage sides.

# 1924

The Supermarine Sea Urchin flying-boat project was not completed although manufacture was planned, and the Gloster II crashed at Felix-stowe during early flight trials. A number of Italian projects, including the Pegna P.c.2/Piaggio P.4 and P.c.3/P.4 floatplanes, the S.4 from Dornier-Italy, remained as such. The French CAMS 45 did not progress beyond the drawing board stage and the Wright F2W-2 crashed during test flying in the United States.

## Supermarine Sea Urchin

Although the Supermarine company had achieved mixed results in the 1919, 1922 and 1923 contests, with the venerable Sea Lion, the runaway victory of the United States CR-3 floatplanes in this last encounter indicated that the days of the racing flying-boat were numbered. Never-

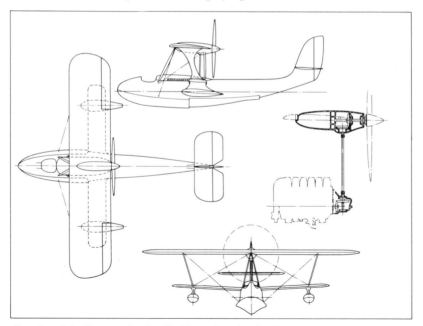

Drawing of the Supermarine Sea Urchin project showing the proposed shaft-drive to the propeller and the internal mounting of the engine in the hull. (*Courtesy C. F. Andrews*)

theless R. J. Mitchell proceeded with the work of scheming another potential Schneider contest entrant as a 'Sea Lion replacement', and in December 1923, less than three months after that year's contest at Cowes, the layout of the Sea Urchin was finalized.

Mitchell, learning a lesson from the Curtiss designs, had paid great attention to reducing frontal area and had taken this almost to its ultimate for a biplane by burying the engine in the hull. It was this feature which finally killed this project for it was found impossible to design and manufacture the power transmission system, embodying two sets of right-angled bevel gears and shafts, which linked the big 600 hp Rolls-Royce Condor engine and the pusher propeller carried on the upper mainplane. Nevertheless, as can be seen in the drawing, the streamlining of the Sea Urchin was of a high order, particularly of the interplane struts, underwing stabilizing floats and the propeller installation. The use of a comparatively high thickness/chord ratio upper mainplane coupled with a very small thinner lower wing in a sesquiplane configuration, and the design of the two-step hull, are noteworthy design features.

# Gloster II

When the Aerial Derbies were discontinued after the 1923 race, which was won by the Gloster I—piloted by Larry Carter—at a speed of 192·4 mph (309·63 km/h), the Gloucestershire Aircraft Company decided to follow its earlier policy of building high-speed aircraft in an effort to focus public attention and that of the Air Ministry on the company's products. The first result of this important decision came in 1924 when the company was invited to design and build two floatplanes to meet specification 37/23, calling for high-speed entrants for the Schneider Trophy contest.

The first of the two examples of the Gloster II, each costing about £3,000, was completed by the end of August 1924. Of very similar

J7504, the Gloster II, taking-off for the flight after which it sank at Felixstowe.

The Gloster II, bearing its contest number 1, at Felixstowe. Note the protective covers over the strut-mounted radiators and the polished wooden floats.

appearance and construction to the earlier Gloster I, it embodied many design features aimed at improving its aerodynamic efficiency, its speed and general handling characteristics. The 585 hp Napier Lion VA twelve-cylinder water-cooled broad-arrow engine, the most powerful of its type, drove a Fairey Reed two-blade fixed-pitch metal propeller. The Lion's three cylinder blocks were carefully faired in, all external pipework was re-routed internally, and the short centre-section struts of the earlier Gloster I were enclosed by a fairing which unfortunately effectively obscured the pilot's view directly forward. Two Lamblin strut radiators were mounted on the forward faces of the front float struts, and long graceful floats, with small frontal area, were fitted.

The prototype, J7504, went to Felixstowe on 12 September and was prepared for test flying by Capt Hubert Broad. Unfortunately, a week later on 19 September, before the pre-contest trials could be completed, this Gloster II sank and was a complete loss after one of the float struts had collapsed after porpoising while alighting on rough water in Harwich Harbour.

In the air, the Gloster II had performed well. Even though it had proved rather tail-heavy, making it impossible for Broad to fully open the throttle, the little floatplane had achieved a speed near to 200 mph (320 km/h). Its loss could have had a major effect on the entire Schneider Trophy series because the Italian entries had been withdrawn due to recurring engine problems, leaving the United States alone in the contest

191

needing only a fly-over to win the Trophy. However, in a most sporting gesture, the National Aeronautic Association wrote to the Royal Aero Club waiving the United States' right to a fly-over and postponing the Baltimore-based contest until the following year.

The second Gloster II, G-EBJZ, was converted to a landplane and was prepared for testing metal propellers and radiators and for an attempt to establish a new world speed record. Unfortunately, it was wrecked when, on 11 June, 1925, it crashed at Cranwell after elevator flutter developed at about 240 mph (386 km/h). Larry Carter, the pilot, sustained a fractured skull, spent a year in hospital but never flew again. He died from meningitis in a Cheltenham nursing home on 27 September, 1926.

Single-seat twin-float racing biplane. Wooden construction with fabric covering. Pilot in open cockpit.

One 585 hp Napier Lion VA twelve-cylinder water-cooled broad-arrow engine driving a Fairey Reed two-blade fixed-pitch metal propeller.

Span 20 ft (6·09 m); length 26 ft 10 in (8·17 m); height 11 ft (3·35 m); wing area 165 sq ft (15·32 sq m).

Empty weight 2,500 lb (1,134 kg); loaded weight 3,100 lb (1,406 kg); wing loading 18·79 lb/sq ft (91·74 kg/sq m).

Maximum speed about 225 mph (362 km/h) at sea level.

Production—two Gloster IIs built by Gloucestershire Aircraft Co Ltd at Cheltenham during 1924.

Colour—Cambridge blue fuselage, remainder ivory except floats believed to have been brown. Black contest number 1 on undersurface of lower wing.

# Piaggio-Pegna P.4/P.c.2 and P.4/P.c.3

Although Giovanni Pegna's designs for racing seaplanes were generally imaginative and adventurous in the extreme, his first projected design for a 1922 Schneider Trophy entrant appeared quite conventional by comparison. When it failed to materialize from the Pegna-Bonmartini-Cerroni factory in time for the contest, the pace and interest in the aeroplane slackened. Then, in August 1923, its manufacture was taken over by Società Anonima Piaggio following Pegna's appointment as technical manager of that company. Two prototypes, designated P.2, appeared later that year as low-wing cantilever monoplanes with wheeled undercarriages and bearing military serial numbers MM.26 and 27.

Pegna's new employers were keen to capitalize on his design skills and urged him to use them in creating another design for a Schneider Trophy entrant. Pegna quickly adapted the P.2 layout and incorporated a twin-float undercarriage. This project, which bore the twin designation P.4 and P.c.2, featured a deep, rather bulbous ovoid-section front fuselage which tapered sharply to a quite small rounded fin and rudder. The pilot's open cockpit was set well aft of the mainplane trailing edge and had a long vee-windscreen and a long head fairing. Like the one-piece ply-covered mainplane, the tailplane was a cantilevered surface. It is believed that the P.4/P.c.2 was intended to have a ply-covered movable tailplane without elevators. The two single-step floats, which had broad-vee bottoms, were each carried by a pair of struts and were wire-braced to the fuselage and mainplane. The P.2s had been powered by 200 hp Hispano-Suiza modèle 42 eight-cylinder water-cooled vee engines licence-built in Italy; however, it is believed that Pegna had in mind the acquisition of a Curtiss D-12 engine driving a four-blade propeller for his Schneider Trophy project which had a calculated high loaded weight of 2,910 kg (6,415 lb).

The adaptation of the P.2 was not Pegna's last word in the matter of a 1924 contest entrant. While retaining the basic cantilever mainplane and tailplane configuration, he reshaped the fuselage, reducing its frontal area to produce a much more refined profile. The mainplane was reduced in span, the planform was slightly modified, and it is believed that Pegna may have intended to use surface radiators. The restyled tailplane was fitted with conventional elevators. The floats were reshaped and increased in length and were almost as long as the fuselage. Power was to have been provided by a 470 hp Curtiss D-12 engine driving a two-blade propeller.

The result of these design refinements produced a very handsome project; unfortunately, neither the P.4/P.c.2 nor the P.c.3—the designation by which this latter project was known—came to fruition.

Single-seat twin-float monoplane. All-wood construction with wood and fabric covering. Pilot in open cockpit.

The type of engine is not known, but it is believed that a Curtiss D-12 may have been specified for the P.4/P.c.2. One 470 hp Curtiss D-12 twelve-cylinder water-cooled direct-drive normally-aspirated vee engine driving a two-blade fixed-pitch propeller was chosen for the P.4/P.c.3.

Span 10·107 m (33 ft 1¾ in); length 7·8 m (25 ft 7 in); height 2·99 m (9 ft 9½ in); wing area 19·5 sq m (209·89 sq ft)—P.4/P.c.2.

Span 9·35 m (30 ft 8 in); length 7·75 m (25 ft 5 in); height 2·96 m (9 ft 8½ in); wing area not known—P.4/P.c.3.

Estimated loaded weight 2,910 kg (6,415 lb)—P.4/P.c.2.

Performance estimates are not known and the aircraft were not built.


# Dornier S.4 Greif (Griffon)

In 1924 the Dornier company at Pisa Marina in Italy revealed some brief details and illustrations of the wind-tunnel model of a twin-float project for that year's contest. Designated S.4 and powered by an undisclosed water-cooled vee engine of about 500 hp, it was a mid-wing cantilever monoplane with a cantilever tailplane. The fuselage had a deep oval section forward, tapering aft to a substantial fin and rudder, and with the pilot's cockpit positioned above the mainplane trailing edge. Each of the

This head-on view of the Dornier S.4 wind-tunnel model shows the proposed cantilever mainplane. (*Dornier GmbH*)

single-step floats was carried on a pair of slim struts with a pair of spreader-bars between them. Presumably the alighting gear was wire braced and some illustrations appear to indicate that Forlanini-type floats were to be used. However, although aesthetically pleasing, the S.4 did not advance beyond the design and wind-tunnel model stage.

Single-seat twin-float cantilever monoplane. Pilot in open cockpit.
An unknown engine of about 500 hp was specified.
Span 8·8 m (28 ft 10½ in); length 7·7 m (25 ft 3 in).
No other information has survived.

A wind-tunnel model of the Dornier S.4 project which is believed to have been allotted the name Greif (Griffon). (*Dornier GmbH*)

# Wright F2W-1 and F2W-2

If the Navy-Wright NW-1 and NW-2 had made few pretensions to being anything but high-speed racing aircraft, their successors at least received pseudo-military designations; moreover, the Wright corporation publicly proclaimed its interest in winning production contracts from the US Army and Navy for fighter-type aircraft. Indeed the F2W-1, as the first of the new aircraft was designated, looked much more like practical fighting machines than did either the NW-1 or NW-2. But Wright was, first and foremost, an engine manufacturer and when its new engine, the T-3, delivered more than 760 hp during bench tests, the urge to prove it under racing conditions was too strong. Accordingly, plans were made to use the 1923 Pulitzer Trophy race.

The designers of the F2W-1, or the TX (Tornado Experimental), were A. L. Thurston and H. T. Booth, two engineers with experience of designing successful racing aircraft. The fuselage of their new creation was an all-wood monocoque structure built up from four spruce longerons with plywood bulkheads closely positioned, all covered with spruce two-ply skinning. The single-bay biplane mainplanes had spruce spars and ribs with spruce skinning and carried surface radiators inboard of the single I-shaped interplane struts. Short-span broad-chord ailerons were fitted on upper and lower mainplanes and were interconnected by heavy tie-rods. A small streamlined coolant header tank was carried on the centre-line of the upper mainplane. The tailplane had spruce spars and ribs with mahogany skinning and was adjustable on the ground for trimming. The fin was of similar construction and both fixed surfaces carried fabric-covered metal-framed control surfaces. Two V-struts carried the main-wheels whose axle was covered by a streamlined spreader-bar. The only metal used was in the cabane structure which was welded steel-tube with wood skinning, and a steel strut bracing each side of the wood engine bearers.

The first TX, serialled A6743, flew for the first time on 27 August, 1923, piloted by Sanderson who repeated the pattern of his early flights in the NW-1 by carrying on a running speed battle with the contemporary Curtiss racers. Navy Lieut S. Calloway flew the second aircraft, A6744, on 18 September and achieved more than 230 mph (370 km/h) on this first flight.

In the Pulitzer Trophy, Sanderson flew A6743, now redesignated F2W-1, to continue the myth that this aircraft, with fuel for only a little over half-an-hour's flying, was a fighter prototype! After finishing in third position he promptly ran out of fuel and force-landed, wrecking the aeroplane. A6744 finished in fourth place and subsequently, during 1924, was converted for that year's Schneider Trophy contest. While in the

The Wright F2W-2 intended for the 1924 contest, but crashed during pre-contest trials. (*US Navy, courtesy Smithsonian Institution*)

factory a new set of mainplanes, with thinner aerofoil section and reduced gap, was fitted; in addition the surface radiators were redesigned, float strut radiators were added, a large header tank was mounted on top of the fuselage in front of the windscreen, and metal interplane struts replaced the earlier wooden units. With these modifications A6744 became known as the F2W-2.

This work was completed during early October and the aircraft was moved to the Naval Aircraft Factory for preliminary flight trials by Lieut Gorton. Immediately, Gorton found the F2W-2 showed a marked reluctance to unstick from the water; when he applied full throttle the only result was that the port float dug into the water, in response to engine torque, and the aeroplane merely travelled in semi-circles because the rudder was ineffective at the low airspeeds. When a larger rudder of about 10 per cent increased area was fitted after the design figures had been checked, Gorton finally got the F2W-2 on the step, going straight and became airborne. As the aircraft accelerated he found himself in a steep and rapid climb, but managed to level out and began a steady descent for landing. He discovered that the trim was wrong, that A6744 was very tail-heavy and it did not handle well. As Gorton touched down, a wrongly installed vent pipe in the header tank blasted scalding steam in his face. He accidentally pulled back on the control column, A6744 bounced off the water at around 140 mph (225 km/h) and, as Gorton applied full power to go around again, the aircraft torque-rolled onto its back and plunged into the water. Gorton survived the crash with a minor bruise.

So ended the Wright company's efforts to produce high-speed racing aircraft and its engineering skills were then directed toward the development of a highly successful series of air-cooled radial engines.

Single-seat twin-float racing biplane. Wood and metal construction with wood and fabric covering. Pilot in open cockpit.

One 680 hp Wright T-3 Tornado twelve-cylinder water-cooled direct-drive normally-aspirated vee engine driving a 7 ft 8 in (2·33 m) diameter Standard three-blade adjustable-pitch metal propeller. Fuel: 95 US gal (360 litres). Oil: 9 US gal (34 litres).

Span 23 ft (7·01 m); length 26 ft 1 in (7·95 m); height 10 ft 10 in (3·3 m); wing area 170 sq ft (15·79 sq m).

Empty weight 3,296 lb (1,495 kg); loaded weight 4,160 lb (1,887 kg); wing loading 24·47 lb/sq ft (119·5 kg/sq m).

Estimated maximum speed 320 mph (514·98 km/h); stalling speed 90 mph (144·83 km/h).

Production—one F2W-2 converted by Wright Aeronautical Corp from second F2W-1, A6744, in 1924.

Colour—details not available.

# 1925

The Supermarine S.4 crashed during pre-contest practice flying, and a Gloster IIIA was damaged when alighting during seaworthiness trials and was withdrawn. A Macchi M.33 developed trouble with its tired Curtiss D-12A engine; the P.c.3/P.4 was still not built; neither were the Macchi M.27 and a second Dornier project.

# Supermarine S.4

Although the 1926 Schneider contest had been won by a Macchi M.39 monoplane, the first monoplane winner since the original contest in 1913, Great Britain was the first country to revive interest in and use of this configuration for racing seaplanes.

The aircraft which wrought this change was the Supermarine S.4, serialled N197/G-EBLP, designed by R. J. Mitchell, who, realizing that his plans and designs for a flying-boat racer, with the engine in the hull driving a remotely positioned propeller, would never come to fruition, had made a great leap forward and produced not only a monoplane but one embodying cantilever flying surfaces and alighting gear. In fact, Mitchell, in his design of the S.4 went beyond the state of the art in structures and in aerodynamics; nevertheless, this aeroplane established a world speed record, although it did not survive to compete in the Schneider contest at Baltimore later that year.

For the first time, too, the British Government had decided to support the construction of racing floatplanes for the contest, and agreed to buy the S.4 if the Supermarine and Napier companies would initially finance the manufacturing cost of the airframe and its Lion engine. After some discussions between them and the Air Ministry, on 18 March, 1925, the companies decided to press ahead with the construction of one aircraft to meet specification 2/25, and work began on 25 March.

The S.4 fuselage was built in three sections; the engine bay and mounting, the centre, and the rear monocoque. Wood was used throughout for construction, with the exception of two massive A-frames of tubular steel, which formed the main load-carrying structure for the aircraft, and some steel fittings. The rear monocoque shell was made of spruce skin laid diagonally and attached to light ply formers and was secured at its forward end to the rear A-frame. The small circular cockpit opening was well aft of the wing trailing edge and had a small semi-circular windscreen. The wooden centre fuselage with duralumin skinning was mounted between the two A-frames and the engine mountings were hung onto the front frame. The all-wood tail unit was built as one piece with wood-covered flying surfaces. The monoplane wing was constructed as a single unit. It embodied two spars having spruce booms and plywood webs, and similarly constructed ribs. A number of spanwise stringers were let into the ribs so that they lay flush with the spar boom flanges and those on the ribs. This structure was skinned with plywood sheeting which tapered in thickness from the aircraft centreline, where the skin was thickest, out to the wingtips. Two spanwise troughs were provided in the lower surface of the wing to house the two Lamblin-type radiators, which were the only excrescences to mar the otherwise clean lines of the

The Supermarine S.4 on the Woolston factory slipway with engine cowling panels removed. Note the web of panel mounting rails around the Lion engine, and the underwing radiators. (*Courtesy Eric Morgan*)

The Supermarine S.4 N197 on its launching trolley, being prepared for engine running. Note the fairings at the top of the float struts and the radiators partly recessed into the mainplanes' undersurfaces. (*Vickers Ltd*)

S.4. The RAF 30 wing section had been developed by Supermarine in collaboration with the Royal Aircraft Establishment at Farnborough, where a full-scale example of this monoplane wing had been tested to destruction in the 'Temple' structural test-rig. The single-piece wing was mounted in the mid-position between the two A-frames to which it was attached. The central bay above and below the spars housed fuel tanks which were shaped to conform to the fuselage contours. A finned oil-cooler was positioned under the centre-fuselage between the float struts.

A unique feature of the S.4's flight controls was the provision of flaps interconnected with the ailerons, which could be operated independently or together. Because of the higher wing loading of a monoplane, about 23 lb/sq ft (112·29 kg/sq m) and the higher take-off and alighting speeds which resulted, Mitchell had embodied this feature to overcome this disadvantage. It is not clear whether this system was effective, as no record has been traced of a report upon it by Henri Biard, Supermarine's pilot; it is interesting and perhaps significant, however, that Mitchell did not incorporate flaps in any of his subsequent Schneider floatplanes in spite of their even higher wing loadings of as much as 41 lb/sq ft (200·18 kg/sq m).

The S.4 was powered by a 680 hp Napier Lion VII direct-drive engine, driving a Fairey Reed two-blade metal propeller having a small pointed spinner. The three banks of the Lion's cylinders were closely cowled with duralumin cowling panels carried on rectangular section cowling rails, and with the cowling of the two outer banks being carefully blended into the leading edge of the wing. Duralumin skinning also was used on the centre fuselage section.

Already bearing its contest number the Supermarine S.4, in this view, shows the thin spreader-bar mounted high between the rear float struts and the broad-chord fairings at their tops. (*Courtesy Eric Morgan*)

The tubular-steel A-frame legs which formed the alighting gear struts had duralumin fairings of a streamlined section around them, and their junctions with the fuselage also were faired in with broad-chord duralumin 'gloves'. The single-step floats, which were of all-metal construction, were built up from a central fore-and-aft keel member with two chine members to form the deep concave vee bottom. Double watertight bulkheads were used throughout the float structure which was, nevertheless, sufficiently flexible to absorb the take-off and alighting loads. The

Launching the Supermarine S.4 at Baltimore. It carries its contest number 4, and a small Union flag on the rudder.

200

four legs of the A-frame were built into the structure, with small fairings at the point where they passed through the duralumin upper skin of the floats.

Yet another surprising feature of the S.4 was the speed with which this aeroplane of such revolutionary design was built in Supermarine's factory at Woolston. On 25 August, 1925, only five months from the official go-ahead, the S.4 made its first flight from Calshot, the Royal Air Force flying-boat base. The pilot was Biard who, with Mitchell, had lived closely with the day-to-day design and construction of the aeroplane. Although Biard was impressed with the advanced design of the S.4 and the apparent potentialities, he was concerned about the cantilever wing and the position of the cockpit from which the view forward was completely blocked by the mid-mounted wing and the long cowling over the Lion's central cylinder block. Although the S.4 handled well in the air he sensed that at times he was flying on a knife-edge, particularly in turns where he believed that he experienced wing flutter. Ever a pragmatist, he dismissed this as stemming from an overworked imagination.

Whatever the handling characteristics, there was no doubt that the S.4 was fast. On 13 September Biard established a new world floatplane speed record and a British air speed record of 226·75 mph (364·91 km/h), making one run over the three-kilometre course above Southampton Water at 231·4 mph (372·39 km/h).

When the S.4 arrived at Chesapeake Bay, Baltimore, for the Schneider contest, bad weather and unsatisfactory aircraft servicing facilities merely

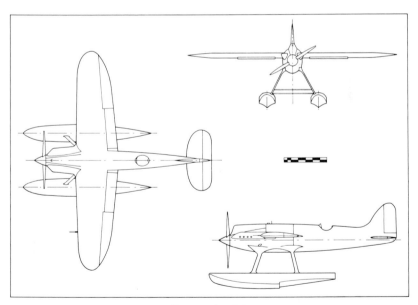

Supermarine S.4

201

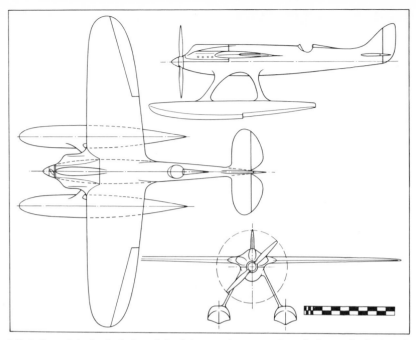

Mitchell used the basic design of the S.4 to produce a number of schemes for improved developments of it, one of which is illustrated here. In spite of the flutter problems which almost certainly led to the destruction of the S.4 at Baltimore, this preliminary scheme for a high-speed development not only retained a cantilever mainplane but also a cantilever alighting gear. A major change was to the shape of the tail unit, with the rudder extending below the tailplane, with a resulting change in the elevator shape to provide for rudder movement. A faired headrest was added behind the cockpit. The absence of radiators may infer the use of mainplane surface units. (*Courtesy C. F. Andrews*)

added to Biard's problems of a wrist broken on the voyage to the United States. These were compounded when he contracted influenza and, on 18 October, was confined to bed. Fortunately he had made two check flights in the S.4 before this calamity, but he was still not fully recovered when he took off for the navigability trials on 23 October. There is much doubt about what occurred during the ensuing few minutes of the flight. To the onlookers the S.4 was seen to go into a series of vertical banks, appearing to stall, and then sideslip in an apparently uncontrolled descent, before falling into the water, from about 100 ft, in a flat 'super-stalled' attitude. Fortunately Biard was rescued, badly shaken but unharmed apart from bruising and a re-fractured wrist. Biard was convinced that wing or aileron flutter had caused him initially to lose control but he believed he regained control and got the S.4 into straight and level flight—at which point the aircraft stalled, crashed into the water and was completely wrecked. If the wing structure had not been sufficiently stiff, large aileron movements could have twisted the wing causing aileron reversal, a condition which Biard may have failed to recognize or had not experienced before. The failure of the flap and aileron interconnection system is another possible cause which seems not to have been investigated or reported on.

Suffice it to say that, thereafter, Mitchell never used cantilever wing structures for his Schneider Trophy aircraft, preferring to employ braced wings of thinner and lighter construction which, he claimed, added some 5 mph to their maximum speeds.

Single-seat twin-float racing monoplane. Pilot in open cockpit.

One 680 hp Napier Lion VII twelve-cylinder water-cooled direct-drive normally-aspirated broad-arrow engine driving a 7 ft 10 in (2·38 m) diameter Fairey Reed two-blade fixed-pitch metal propeller. Fuel: 45 gal (205 litres); oil: 5 gal (23 litres); water: 10 gal (45 litres).

Span 30 ft 7½ in (9·33 m); length 26 ft 7¾ in (8·12 m); height 11 ft 8½ in (3·56 m); float length 18 ft (5·48 m); wing area 139 sq ft (12·91 sq m).

Empty weight 2,600 lb (1,179 kg); loaded weight 3,191 lb (1,447 kg); wing loading 23 lb/sq ft (112·29 kg/sq m).

Maximum speed 231·4 mph (372·39 km/h)—during world speed record flight; stalling speed 80 mph (128·74 km/h).

Production—one S.4 (c/n 1215) built by Supermarine Aviation Works at Southampton in 1925.

Colour—overall white with natural metal engine cowling, centre fuselage panels and alighting-gear struts. Blue contest number 4 on fuselage sides below cockpit and undersurface of wingtips. Union flag on rudder.

*        *        *

Few details of the M.27 and Dornier projects are known but it is most likely that the Macchi design was based on the M.26, a very clean single-bay biplane fighter flying-boat powered by a 300 hp Hispano-Suiza eight-cylinder water-cooled vee engine; it is believed that the Dornier project was a developed version of its S.4 project of 1924.

# 1926

The Supermarine S.5 and Gloster IV floatplanes which were being built were entered but withdrawn from that year's contest when their Lion VII engines were not delivered in time for them to compete.

Two other British private-venture projects were abandoned during their early planning stages. A Curtiss R3C-3 was severely damaged when alighting and an R2C-2 crashed during test flying.

# 1927

The Short-Bristow Crusader crashed on take-off during pre-contest flying. The Kirkham-Williams aircraft was withdrawn.

## Short-Bristow Crusader

Drag was the all-time enemy of the designers of Schneider Trophy high-speed floatplanes and flying-boats, particularly in the later years of the contest series when speeds were mounting. An important factor in the battle against drag was the maintenance of a low frontal area, typified in the biplanes by the Curtiss designs of 1924—25 which showed the advantage of using an inline water-cooled engine.

In Britain, from 1920, another running battle was being fought between Armstrong Siddeley Motors and Bristol Aeroplane's aero-engine division with their Jaguar and Jupiter radial air-cooled engines. However, it was a foregone conclusion in 1926 that the highest performance could be attained with an inline engine, but neither company wanted the entire initiative in the creation of engines for fighter aircraft, and other high-speed designs, to pass either to Napier or Rolls-Royce.

At Bristol Roy Fedden, then the company's chief engineer, was work-

A dominant feature of the Short-Bristow Crusader was the individual helmeted cylinder heads of the Mercury radial engine. (*Short Bros*)

ing on the design of a new nine-cylinder air-cooled radial engine based on the earlier Jupiter. Named Mercury, it had the same bore as the Jupiter but a reduced stroke and with a higher rotational speed. By the spring of 1925 the first engine was running in the Filton testbed. Now Fedden was looking for a suitable vehicle in which he could show off his new power unit which promised to provide around 950 hp. Frank Barnwell, Bristol Aeroplane's chief engineer, had produced some preliminary sketches of a Jupiter-powered racing floatplane in 1924 but this project was not pursued. Armed with a preliminary brochure on the Mercury, Fedden went to the Air Ministry and suggested that it was a suitable engine for use in an entrant in the 1927 Schneider contest. To his surprise he was awarded a £13,000 contract to build three short-life uprated Mercuries for this purpose.

The design of a Mercury-engined project for the contest was begun under the general supervision of Col W. A. Bristow, a well-known and respected consultant aircraft engineer, who obtained, rather reluctantly, the services of W. G. Carter who had recently parted company with Hawker Aircraft's design office. George Carter had been hoping to have a holiday from design work before joining the de Havilland team at Stag Lane. However, he became intrigued with the plan to put a radial engine in a racing floatplane and he soon got down to work. By the spring of 1926 the design was sufficiently far advanced for Bristow and Carter to submit to the Air Ministry their twin-float strut-braced monoplane which they believed could compete on equal terms with the inline-engined Supermarine and Gloster entrants for the following year's Schneider contest. Specification 7/26 was drafted around the Mercury-powered design and the aircraft was allocated the serial number N226.

A quarter-scale model was tested in the National Physical Laboratory's Duplex wind-tunnel at Teddington but, unfortunately, the aeroplane which 'flew' so well on paper was a failure when the wind-tunnel performance was calculated. Clearly the drag was too high, as much as 50 per cent stemming from the radial engine but some produced by the wing and its strut bracing. The very existence of a suitable radial engine had created a fundamental problem for Carter, but he at once made a major structural change by reducing the wing span by 18 in (45 cm) and by replacing the bracing struts with streamlined wires. Another important refinement was the addition of long helmet fairings around each of the Mercury's cylinders. It was the shape of these fairings which gave the name Crusader to the aeroplane, known variously as the Short-Bristow, the Bristow/Carter or the Short-Bristol Crusader, only the first combination of names being the correct one. The revised scale-model was approved during November 1926 and the final layout drawings completed. It was immediately apparent that only a well-equipped manufacturer with experience of marine aircraft construction could undertake the complex task of producing all the detail design drawings and building the airframe in the time available. Short Brothers at Rochester, with a wealth

Maximum mainplane thickness occurred at about mid-span on the Crusader. (*Short Bros*)

of experience of hull and float design and of construction, was to build the Crusader's floats, as they had those for the Supermarine and Gloster aeroplanes. It was logical, therefore, that this company should do all of the remaining work on the Crusader's airframe. Fortunately, two young engineers had recently joined the Short design team; they were C. T. P. Lipscomb and Arthur Gouge. Lipscomb became responsible for all the detail design work while Gouge supervised the work of the draughtsmen.

While the airframe manufacture was in progress the Mercury engine was being built and by the autumn of 1926 was achieving some satisfactory results on the test bench. However the crankshaft was found to be too light in construction and so the Jupiter III's crankshaft was substituted. There were, too, some ignition problems which, with carburetion difficulties, were to plague the Crusader throughout its short life.

By the middle of February 1927 the airframe was very near to completion at Rochester; meanwhile the Mercury had been transferred to the RAE at Farnborough for some final running checks on the carburetion system. Early in March it went to Rochester to be installed in the airframe.

The Crusader's fuselage was of composite construction, mainly of wood. The rear fuselage aft of the pilot's seat bulkhead was a monocoque-type structure built up from spruce ring frames and stringers which were skinned with two layers of mahogany veneers laid diagonally with the grain opposed. This skin was covered with silk, doped on, and then given a fine enamelled finish. The fin and tailplane were of similar construction. The rudder and elevators also were of wood with fabric covering and the whole shape of the cantilever tail unit stamped it as emanating from George Carter's drawing board. Forward of the seat

206

bulkhead the fuselage structure consisted of a strut-braced frame of high-tensile steel-tube which carried the engine-mounting plate at its front end. Detachable duralumin panels were carried on this frame which housed the main fuel and oil tanks.

The pilot's cockpit had a totally suppressed windscreen at the rear of a long fairing running back from the engine's top cylinder helmet, and the headrest was at the front of a fairing which continued down the top of the fuselage to the base of the fin.

The mainplanes, which originally were 28 ft (8·53 m) span but which were reduced to 26 ft 6 in (8·07 m) following the wind-tunnel tests of the model, had two spruce box spars with multiple spruce ribs all skinned with 1 mm three-ply mahogany sheets. These were covered with doped-on silk, like the rear fuselage, and given a high-gloss enamelled finish. The wooden ailerons were fabric covered and had a swept forward hinge-line. The elliptical planform of the mainplanes, their bi-convex RAF 27 aerofoil section with a sharp leading edge, and the location of their maximum thickness and chord at mid-span, again reflected Carter's design thinking. This wing shape was to appear again on another Schneider Trophy floatplane designed by Carter, the Gloster VI produced for the 1929 contest. It provided good turning capability at speed, which was a prime requirement for an aeroplane of this type.

The alighting gear consisted of twin duralumin floats, similar in design and construction to those produced for the Gloster IV by Shorts, each mounted on a pair of sharply forward-raked tubular steel struts with streamlined fairings to produce a low-drag section. An auxiliary fuel tank was carried in the starboard float. The wing and alighting gear were

The bullet-shaped fuselage and the unusual elliptical wing are apparent in this top view of the Short-Bristow Crusader as it rests on the waters of the River Medway at Rochester.
(*Short Bros*)

braced by streamlined-section wires, and similar wires were used between the floats in place of spreader-bars. All the flying control cables from the cockpit to the control surfaces were carried inside the fuselage and mainplanes. Each of the nine cylinders of the 860 hp Bristol Mercury I air-cooled supercharged radial engine had slender individual helmets sharply swept back. Their design was derived from the cowls on the 1923 French Jupiter-engined Gourdou-Leseurre monoplane racer. They admitted only sufficient air flow to cool the cylinders. The Mercury initially drove a 7 ft 4 in (2·23 m) diameter two-blade fixed-pitch wooden propeller fitted with a very pointed spinner, but this was replaced by a two-blade metal unit.

With construction completed at Short's Rochester factory, the Crusader N226 was launched on the Medway during the afternoon of 18 April, 1927. The Air Ministry would not allow any flight trials with the Crusader to take place from Rochester so only preliminary taxi-ing and water handling trials were scheduled to be completed on the river—but the Mercury, which fired on the first swing of the propeller, could not be persuaded to run smoothly before it became too dark for them to begin. The following morning John Lankester Parker, Shorts' test pilot, again climbed aboard and almost immediately the engine started and ran with little trouble. He taxied away and soon had the Crusader running nicely on the step at around 65 mph (105 km/h) for about half a mile, after which he executed a few turns.

A few days later the Crusader was dismantled and crated for the road journey to Felixstowe where it was immediately dubbed 'Curious Ada' by the RAF High Speed Flight pilots, and where Bert Hinkler, rather than an RAF pilot, was detailed to undertake the preliminary flight trials. After a careful examination of the aeroplane, now powered by a derated 650 hp Mercury, and some discussions with Lankester Parker about the longitudinal control, Hinkler asked, arbitrarily, for a 70 per cent increase in the rudder area before he flew it. In the event, the size of the rudder was increased but not by the amount which Hinkler demanded. On 4 May he got airborne in the Crusader and later was timed at an average of 232 mph (373·36 km/h) over the measured mile. However, on alighting, the Crusader dropped a wing and touched down on one float which caused it to swing wildly to port, narrowly missing an attendant launch before coming to rest. Back on the slipway it was found that the alighting gear struts were buckled and all their bracing wires loose, making the Crusader 'wobble like a jelly' according to a contemporary report. Hinkler later admitted that the larger rudder was 'hunting' in flight and that the original smaller area rudder was correct.

When the Crusader had been repaired and returned to the flight line, the float struts had been repainted white instead of their original royal blue. There then began a long series of snags with the Mercury which included carburettor air-intake surging and overheated plugs which caused intermittent cutting out.

When Flt Lieut S. N. Webster of the High Speed Flight flew the Crusader, he liked the general handling characteristics but not the repeated power loss from the spluttering Mercury. Later, with Flg Off Schofield at the controls, he reported that the supercharger stopped and then cut in again immediately after take-off. Schofield was also very critical of the visibility and gave the aeroplane his own descriptive title 'The Blind Wonder.' Following the installation of a new engine, and modifications to the Mercury's air intake and the fitting of special high-temperature plugs,

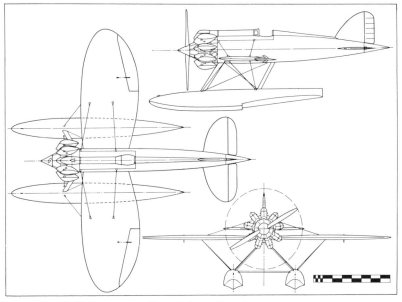

Short-Bristow Crusader

Schofield again flew N226, which performed well until at nearly 240 mph (about 385 km/h) the engine began cutting out again. In mid-July, when the six Supermarine and Gloster floatplanes were moved with their pilots to Calshot for final working-up trials before being shipped to Venice, the Crusader remained at Felixstowe where great efforts were made to cure the engine problems. Eventually it, too, moved to Calshot but without a complete solution to the Mercury's malfunctioning.

On 17 August N226 was loaded aboard the ss *Eworth,* with the S.5 N219 and the Gloster IVA N222, and left Southampton for Venice, arriving at San Andrea on 31 August. When flying was resumed at Venice the Crusader, even powered with an uprated Mercury of some 960 hp, proved to be slower than any of the Supermarine or Gloster aeroplanes and so was used as a practice machine to save flying hours on the contest aircraft. On 11 September, as Schofield took off in N226, the starboard wing dropped in a gust but when he applied corrective aileron the rate of

209

roll increased until the wingtip, going over the vertical, hit the water, the fuselage broke in two, and the Crusader disappeared below the surface. Schofield was found, clinging to the floating tail section, very badly bruised and with an injured face, but happily was soon able to walk again with the aid of sticks. This loss of an aircraft, even one relegated to practice flying as the Crusader had been, had a temporarily demoralizing effect on the British team but did not affect the final result of the contest in Venice. The loss of the Crusader was caused by the crossing of the aileron cables during assembly.

Perhaps the most important contribution made by the Crusader was not to be fully realized until some years later. Then the work which had been put into developing the Mercury by Roy Fedden and his design team at Filton began to pay off as design, development and production of the Pegasus, Perseus, and Hercules single- and twin-row air-cooled radial engines became vital to Britain's continuing prosecution of the war.

Single-seat twin-float racing monoplane. Wood and metal construction with wood and fabric covering. Pilot in open cockpit.

One 860 hp Bristol Mercury I nine-cylinder air-cooled geared and supercharged radial engine driving a 7 ft 4 in (2·23 m) diameter two-blade fixed-pitch metal propeller. Fuel: 80 gal (363 litres).

Span 26 ft 6 in (8·07 m); length 24 ft 11½ in (7·6 m); height 8 ft 3 in (2·51 m); wing area 120 sq ft (11·14 sq m).

Empty weight 1,935 lb (878 kg); loaded weight 2,706 lb (1,227 kg); wing loading 22·55 lb/sq ft (110·14 kg/sq m).

Estimated maximum speed 270 mph (434·51 km/h); achieved maximum speed 232 mph (373·36 km/h); alighting speed 85 mph (136·79 km/h).

Production—one Crusader (N266 c/n S.736) built to specification 7/26 by Short Bros. at Rochester in 1926–27.

Colour—overall gloss white; dorsal 'spine' fairing, fin and rudder and float struts, royal blue. No record of serial or contest number having been carried.

# Kirkham-Williams floatplane

When official United States Government support for a 1927 contest entrant was not forthcoming, a group of businessmen revealed that it was providing $100,000 to build an aircraft capable of winning the Schneider contest and taking the world's speed record from France.

The aircraft was designed mainly by Charles Kirkham, the creator of the designs for the Curtiss K-12 engine, who had established his equipment company, Kirkham Products, on Long Island, New York. The pilot was to be Navy Lieut Alford J. Williams, a renowned air-racing pilot, who also contributed money towards the construction of the new biplane racer. But these funds were insufficient, and the Packard company agreed to loan an engine to keep the project alive; in addition, many components

The powerful-looking Kirkham-Williams floatplane racer which failed through shortage of financial backing. (*Smithsonian Institution*)

and man-hours of work were given free of charge in an attempt to ready a US representative for the contest.

An all-wood structure with ply covering, the Kirkham-Williams looked like an enlarged Curtiss racer. The oval-section fuselage was very deep at the front, to accommodate the big Packard X-2775 engine, but tapered gently to the tail cone and the broad-chord dorsal fin and large rudder. A small ventral fin also was used. The tailplane and elevator were of broad-chord, with the tailplane being wire-braced to the fin. The pilot's cockpit, which was immediately aft of the mainplanes, had a windscreen and a headrest which faired into the leading edge of the fin.

The upper mainplane overhung the lower unit by some 3 ft (91 cm) each side and was mounted directly to the top of the fuselage. A single massive broad-chord interplane strut, which was widened top and bottom where it joined the wire-braced mainplanes and splayed outward at its top, was used on each side. Surface radiators covered almost all of the mainplanes, oil coolers being built into the outboard sections. The very long floats were carried on a pair of N-struts and were wire-braced to the mainplanes.

The engine consisted of two 650 hp Packard V-1500 twelve-cylinder vee units—one upright and the other inverted—mounted on a common crankcase to form a four-bank X power unit delivering 1,250 hp. But time was short, there were difficulties with the floats and the engine, and the sponsoring consortium, being businessmen above all else, decided that as the aircraft's performance was not good enough to beat the anticipated Italian and British contenders, it would not go to the added expense of sending the aeroplane to Venice. Accordingly, this US private venture entry was withdrawn, but the aircraft was later converted into a landplane

211

and is reputed to have achieved a speed of 322·6 mph (519·166 km/h), an unofficial world record.

Single-seat twin-float racing biplane. Wooden construction with some metal components. Pilot in open cockpit.

One 1,250 hp Packard X-2775 twenty-four-cylinder water-cooled direct-drive normally-aspirated X-engine driving an 8 ft 6 in (2·59 m) diameter two-blade metal propeller. Fuel: 60 US gal (227 litres). Oil: 15 US gal (57 litres).

Span 29 ft 10 in (9·09 m); length 26 ft 9 in (8·15 m); height 10 ft 6 in (3·2 m); wing area 217 sq ft (20·15 sq m).

Weights and performance unknown.

Production—Kirkham-Williams racer built by Kirkham Products, Long Island, New York, in 1927.

Colour—fuselage, floats. struts, fin and tailplane were blue; mainplanes, rudder and elevators were gold. Wing radiators were natural brass.

# 1929

The Gloster VI was withdrawn when its engine would not run satisfactorily during turns. Italy's highly unconventional Pegna P.c.5 tandem-engined and P.c.6 retractable planing bottom projects were not built; the P.c.7 was built but would not fly; the Savoia S.65 suffered engine overheating problems; one Fiat C.29 crashed on test and the second was not readied for the contest in time to participate. A Dornier project did not advance beyond the wind-tunnel model stage.

None of France's Bernard or Nieuport-Delage floatplanes arrived at Cowes for the contest. Time and money ran out for the Williams-Mercury floatplane which could not be coaxed off the water for more than a hundred yards.

# Gloster VI

In November 1927 design work began on the Gloster V, a development of the earlier Gloster IV biplane. It was intended for use by the RAF High Speed Flight pilots in the 1929 Schneider contest, and in the preliminary wind-tunnel tests the models proved very satisfactory. However, some problems were encountered at a later stage when it was discovered that the supercharger on the 1,320 hp Lion VIID largely contributed to the weight increase of nearly 300 lb (136 kg) over earlier Lions. When the airframe design was modified to move the mainplane forward to compensate for the shift in the centre of gravity, it was found that the front spar boom of the upper mainplane would foul the Lion's centre cylinder block. Thus it was impossible, without a radical re-think on the basic design, to re-position it in this manner and provide an adequate view forward for the pilot. For this reason Folland reluctantly abandoned the biplane layout, and the Gloster VI, the last of his high-speed racing floatplanes was a monoplane.

Design and construction began in May 1928, and when a £25,000 Air Ministry order for a new racer was received in November the work was well advanced.

The Gloster VI's structure was wood and metal. The fuselage was of all-metal semi-monocoque construction having oval formers and flush-riveted duralumin skinning. The mainplane, with six spars, was of the multi-spar and multi-rib type of construction, all built in spruce, with two-and three-layer spruce laminations laid over the basic framework as skinning. All-duralumin flush-riveted floats, produced by Gloster, con-tained the main fuel tanks and were carried on steel-tube struts with duralumin fairings. Two engine-driven pumps raised the fuel in equal proportions from each float tank and fed it into a 2 gal (9 litre) collector tank in the fuselage. Surface radiators, of thinner section than earlier types, were carried on the mainplane, and oil cooling was achieved by a cooler and tank encircling the fuselage aft of the cockpit and laying flush with the skin. Additional flat-tube oil coolers in the upper surfaces of the floats could be brought into use if necessary, the oil passing via oilways in the leading edges of the struts.

Mainplane thickness was increased on the outer portions to improve the lateral control at lower speeds because the thinner inboard portion began to lose lift before the outer part. The trailing edge was curved and maximum chord occurred at the point of maximum thickness which was

Certainly among the more beautiful of the Schneider Trophy floatplanes, the Gloster VI, pictured being taken to the water at Calshot.

213

well outboard, and the design aimed at combining the advantages of a low-drag thin wing with the greater lift of a thick one.

The 1,320 hp Napier Lion's new supercharger was rear-mounted on the engine to keep the frontal area to a minimum. The cylinder banks were carefully cowled to blend into the fuselage shape, and although the cockpit, initially, was open, with a small suppressed windscreen continuing the line of the centre cylinder block fairing, it was later enclosed under a metal cover with a large oval cut-out on each side of the pilot's head position.

Construction of two Gloster VIs, N249 and N250, was completed by July 1929 and their appearance raised paeans of praise from the daily and technical press in which they were described as 'the most beautiful aeroplanes ever built'.

The Gloster VI N249 on its launching trolley at Calshot. This view shows its very beautiful lines. (*Flight*)

Sadly, the hitherto highly reliable Lion engine plagued Gloster and the High Speed Flight engineers with a succession of failures. In an effort to provide great power, coupled with a small frontal area, to offset the 300 lb increase in weight, the Lion had been over-boosted, being rated at 1,320 hp for limited periods when standard Lions of identical capacity were delivering only 500 hp.

N249 was delivered to Calshot on 12 August, 1929, and N250 five days later, when they were assembled and successfully completed flotation tests. Bad weather delayed flight trials but on 25 August Sqn Ldr A. H. Orlebar got airborne in N249, only to have engine failure immediately after take-off. After further ground running of both engines, Orlebar got

214

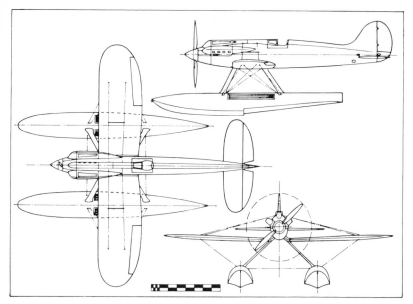

Gloster VI

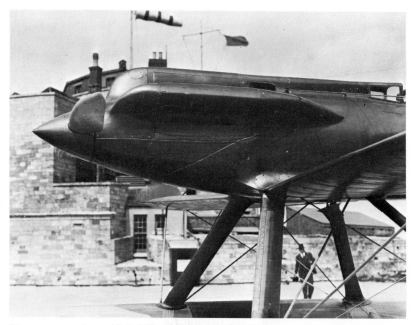

The great attention paid to achieving minimum-drag skinning and structure can be seen in this close-up view of the Gloster VI nose. Note the loose cuff at the top of the starboard rear float strut where a connection occurred in the fuel line from the float. (*Flight*)

This view shows to full advantage the superb lines and minimal frontal area of the Gloster VI. The very thin wing roots and deeper outer sections appear to be an early example of area-rule. (*The Aeroplane*)

in one flight in N250 just before dark on 31 August; but although the aircraft handling was satisfactory, the Lion cut out on turns and occasionally in level flight. During the next five days both aircraft were flown by High Speed Flight pilots but they were unable to trace the cause of the problem. Teams of Napier and Gloster engineers worked round the clock for three days and nights but were equally unsuccessful, and neither of the two Lions could be kept running at full throttle. For this reason the Gloster VIs were withdrawn from the contest.

The Gloster VI N250 built for the 1929 contest. (*The Aeroplane*)

On 10 September, the day after the Supermarine S.6 had won the contest, Flt Lieut G. H. Stainforth made five runs in N249 over a three-kilometre course from Calshot Spit to Agwi Pier. Although he still experienced some engine problems in the turns, the Lion performed well, straight and level with a first run at 351·3 mph (565·35 km/h) and an average speed on the five runs of 336·3 mph (541·21 km/h). This was ratified as an Absolute Speed Record. Just a month afterwards, on 9 November, a Gloster VI took part in the traditional Lord Mayor's Show in London. In 1930, N250 was exhibited in the New and Experimental Types Park at the RAF Display at Hendon and afterwards went to Felixstowe where, with a new engine and further modifications to improve the airflow through the carburettor intake, it was used for limited flying, but full power still could not be sustained. N249 was similarly

217

Gloster, Napier and RAF ground crews, hard at work trying to cure the Gloster VI's fuel system problems. This view shows N250. (*Flight*)

modified with the same results; thus, when the High Speed Flight returned to Calshot in May 1931, although this Gloster VI was still on charge and listed as a training aircraft, it was rarely flown.

So ended the Gloster line of pure racing floatplanes. Was their design and production worth the expenditure of much time, effort and money, for such a limited return in terms of contest results? With the benefit of hindsight, there is no doubt that, apart from the prestige attached to such esoteric aeroplanes, their creation helped to keep a design team together, provided much needed work in the factory, and built a storehouse of knowledge on which the company drew in later years.

Single-seat twin-float racing monoplane. Metal and wood construction with metal and wood covering. Pilot in open faired cockpit.

One 1,320 hp Napier Lion VIID twelve-cylinder supercharged liquid-cooled broad-arrow engine driving a 7 ft 8 in (2·33 m) diameter Gloster two-blade fixed-pitch metal propeller.

Span 26 ft (7·92 m); length 27 ft (8·22 m); height 10 ft 9½ in (3·28 m); float length 22 ft 2 in (6·75 m); wing area 106 sq ft (9·84 sq m); maximum chord 4 ft 8 in (1·42 m).

Empty weight 2,284 lb (1,036 kg); loaded weight 3,680 lb (1,669 kg); wing loading 34·7 lb/sq ft (169·61 kg/sq m).

Maximum recorded speed 351·3 mph (565·35 km/h) at 100 ft (30 m); alighting speed 110 mph (177 km/h); stalling speed 92 mph (148·05 km/h).

Production—two aircraft, N249 and N250, built by Gloster Aircraft Co Ltd at Hucclecote during 1928–29.

Colour—Cambridge blue floats, remainder old-gold, with regulation RAF rudder stripes and black serial number N249. This aircraft was named *Golden Arrow*. Old-gold wings and tailplane, Cambridge blue fuselage, fin and struts, white floats, regulation RAF rudder stripes and black serial number N250.

# Fiat C.29

For Italy, 1928 was a watershed year. The Schneider Trophy, which was in Italian hands, had been lost to Great Britain in Venice the previous year and this had been a shock, not just to Italy's team but to the nation as a whole. In particular, it showed that Benito Mussolini's Fascist state could not sweep all before it in international competitions. Thus Italy's Air Minister, General Balbo, decided to change the entire course of his country's Schneider Trophy planning and preparations. He had an historic meeting in London in December 1927 with British Government officials, and thereafter, in January 1928, the FAI announced that the Schneider contest would be staged every two years, with three victories in five successive contests to be regarded as an outright victory.

Another change was Balbo's decision to harness the design skills of several manufacturers rather than rely on Macchi to produce high-speed floatplanes. As a result, Fiat, Savoia Marchetti, and Piaggio, produced designs for and built three aeroplanes to compete with the latest Macchi development as contenders for places in the Italian team. The most orthodox of these was Fiat's diminutive C.29 which was cast very much in the same mould as the Macchi aeroplanes but of very much more modest proportions.

Of mixed wood and metal construction the C.29 fuselage had four steel-tube longerons connected and stiffened by steel-tube frames and wire-braced internally. Duralumin formers provided shape, and the dorsal and ventral fins were built integrally with the fuselage, the whole being

The Fiat C.29 with its original small fin and rudder and open cockpit. The radiator can be seen standing proud of the inboard mainplane surface. (*Centro Storico Fiat*)

219

covered with duralumin sheet. The tailplane, elevators and rudder were of wood, probably spruce, with duralumin covering. The engine was carried on two duralumin fabricated girder beams, braced and supported by diagonal steel-tubes attached to the bulkhead in front of the cockpit. Detachable duralumin cowling panels enclosed the engine.

Originally the C.29 was designed to have a small fin and rudder, similar to that of the earlier Supermarine S.4, and an open cockpit. One aircraft was built to this design, but later photographs show a cruciform tail unit and enclosed cockpit on two aircraft. On these two (129 and 130bis)* a feature unique among Schneider Trophy aircraft was the sliding windscreen which could be moved aft to enclose the cockpit.

The prototype Fiat C.29 with its sliding cockpit windscreen/canopy in the open position. (*Centro Storico Fiat*)

The narrow-chord mainplanes were of medium thickness with a biconvex aerofoil section with very sharp leading and trailing edges. They were built up around two light-alloy spars machined to shape, connected by steel compression tubes and diagonally wire braced. The ribs were of spruce with poplar leading- and trailing-edge strips, and carried small fittings for aileron attachment. The mainplanes and the wooden structure of the ailerons were duralumin covered. The wings were attached to the fuselage by socket joints and were wire-braced to the main engine bulkhead. Quite small surface radiators, occupying less than half the mainplane chord and about one quarter of the span, were carried on the upper and lower surfaces.

The alighting gear was orthodox, consisting of two single-step duralumin-clad wooden floats of deep vee-section, carried on four streamlined steel-tube struts which were wire-braced throughout. Fuel was carried in tanks in the floats.

*These numbers appeared on the rear fuselage. It is not known whether these were constructor's numbers or MM serials.

Engine-running tests on one of the two Fiat C.29s at Calshot. The pipes leading up over the starboard mainplane trailing edge are from external fuel and oil drums. (*Flight*)

Close-up view of the Fiat C.29 engine bay showing the fabricated bearers and some internal plumbing. (*Flight*)

Power was provided by a 1,000 hp Fiat AS.5 twelve-cylinder water-cooled vee engine which drove a two-blade metal propeller. The AS.5 was claimed to have the best power/weight ratio of any engine in the world at that time and was regarded as a most reliable unit with a good record of test running. The C.29 was the third of four new types to arrive at Desenzano, the Italians' high-speed training base on Lake Garda, and made its first flight on, or about, 10 August, 1929. Because of the very small cockpit, Warrant Officer Francesco Agello, the smallest of the team's pilots, was entrusted with the task of test flying the C.29 and he successfully completed its maiden flight. However, he asked for a minor change in the rigging of the floats and then got airborne again. The C.29 appeared to handle well but, as Agello throttled back and prepared to alight, the engine caught fire. Fortunately the fire was soon extinguished and Agello was unharmed but repair work was necessary both to the engine and the airframe. This was soon completed and a few days later Agello was again on the water in the C.29 preparing for a further flight. He found, however, that the aeroplane would not unstick, and although the airframe and floats were checked it refused to get airborne at the second attempt. On the third run the C.29 leapt into the air, following a surprisingly short run, and began to climb away, but suddenly it dropped back heavily onto the water, smashing off the alighting gear and sinking. Rescue boats, which were quickly on the scene, recovered Agello who was unconscious but floating on the surface and only badly bruised and shaken.

With insufficient time to prepare another C.29 for the contest, this ended Fiat's sole attempt to win the Schneider Trophy for Italy.

Single-seat twin-float racing monoplane. Metal and wood construction. Pilot in open/enclosed cockpit.

One 1,000 hp Fiat AS.5 twelve-cylinder water-cooled direct-drive normally-aspirated vee engine driving a 1·98 m (6 ft 6 in) diameter two-blade adjustable-pitch metal propeller.

Span 6·62 m (21 ft 8½ in); length 5·42 m (17 ft 9¾ in); height 2·75 m (9 ft); wing area 8 sq m (86·1 sq ft).

Empty weight 900 kg (1,984 lb); loaded weight 1,160 kg (2,557 lb); wing loading 145 kg/sq m (29·69 lb/sq ft).

Maximum speed 558·43 km/h (347 mph).

Production—Fiat's records show that four C.29s were built during 1928–30. One aircraft had a conventional tail unit and open cockpit but carried no markings. Two aircraft (129 and 130bis) had a sliding windscreen to enclose the cockpit and a cruciform tail unit. The first aircraft listed above could have been modified to become either 129 or 130bis. It has not been possible to establish serial numbers or markings of any other C.29s.

Colour—overall red with white panel around cockpit and down fuselage sides; white float undersurfaces; engine cowlings either white or natural metal. Italian national rudder markings; C.29 and serial number in white on fuselage side below tailplane; fasces symbol, probably in red, gold, blue and white, on fuselage sides below cockpit.

Model of the Piaggio P.c.7, showing the main and tail hydrofoils, the elliptical main-plane, the water propeller, and the water rudder below the main aerodynamic rudder. (*Rinaldo Piaggio SpA*)

## Piaggio-Pegna P.c.7

Giovanni Pegna's last Schneider Trophy design, the P.c.7 was way beyond even his hitherto advanced projects, so much so that it bordered on the fantastic. While most of his designs had been advanced but practical, the P.c.7 had too many untried and revolutionary design features. A high-wing cantilever monoplane in which the conventional floats were replaced by hydrofoils, it was designed—rather like the P.c.1—to float deep in the water with the wing resting on the surface. The engine was mounted well back in the long slim hull/fuselage and drove a two-blade metal propeller, the air screw, through a long shaft and clutch mechanism. If this were not sufficiently unusual, then the rest of the propulsion system took the P.c.7 into the realms of the impossible. In place of his earlier scheme to pivot the propeller upwards to clear the surface of the water until the aircraft had lifted into the air, Pegna decided that while the P.c.7 was waterborne it would be driven by a water propeller connected through another shaft and clutch to the rear of the engine. When sufficient speed had been reached to cause the hull to lift on its hydrofoils and provide clearance for the airscrew, it would be engaged by its clutch and the water propeller would be declutched.

As far as can be established, the long slender fuselage was built of wood and metal. The central section was built up from a metal frame structure supporting the engine, a one-piece mainplane, the cockpit, and the long shaft to the marine propeller. The nose was a wooden semi-monocoque structure containing the shaft and clutch mechanism for the airscrew, and

A heavily retouched photograph of the Piaggio P.c.7. Minor differences between the aircraft and the model were a narrower-chord water-rudder and tail hydrofoil support, a revised windscreen shape, and a modified elevator. (*Rinaldo Piaggio SpA*)

housing the oil cooler. The central portion of the fuselage, which contained a horse-shoe shaped fuel tank, had wooden formers and longerons and was covered with marine ply. The fin was built separately from the remainder of the fuselage and carried a conventional rudder with a deep narrow-chord water-rudder attached to its lower edge. A small skeg was built onto the bottom of the fuselage in front of the marine propeller.

The hydrofoils, which could be either flat or of V-form, were carried on two broad-chord cantilever struts, which in some drawings were cranked and gave the appearance of an inverted gull wing, and on a small strut under the skeg. The open cockpit was placed well aft behind the wing,

The unique Piaggio P.c.7 afloat. The exhaust ports can be seen along the upper surface of the engine bay, the two-blade air screw is just awash and the aircraft bears the number P7-126 on the rear fuselage beneath the tailplane. (*Industrie Aeronautiche e Meccaniche Rinaldo Piaggio*)

which was of similar planform to that on the P.c.1 having an almost elliptical shape and conventional ailerons. The top of the fuselage above the engine was flattened and the exhaust ports vented upward through it. Surface radiators were carried on the wing. In theory, this mixed propulsion proposal may have appeared feasible but in fact would have been impossible if only for the reason that the pilot required three hands to operate the propellers' controls and to fly the aircraft.

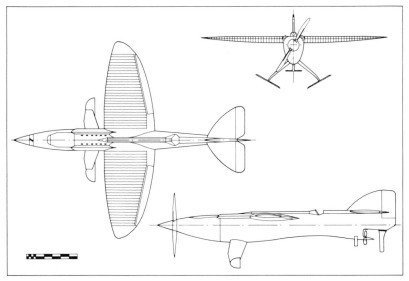

Piaggio P.c.7

A large vertical lever on the port side of the cockpit operated a system of push-rods, rocking levers, and bell-cranks, connected to the clutch at the rear of the engine. A similar system ran aft to the pitch-change mechanism of the water propeller. A horizontal handle, moving in a slide on the cockpit port wall, operated a cable and push-rod system linked to the clutch at the front of the engine and a shaft brake just aft of the propeller. With the throttle open to provide power to the water propeller for take-off, the pilot was required to concentrate on steering the P.c.7 like a boat. When his speed through the water was sufficient to generate enough lift from the hydrofoils to raise the nose clear of the water, he would have had to pull back on the horizontal handle to engage the forward clutch and drive to the air propeller and disengage the shaft brake. Ideally, at the same time he would have needed to push forward the vertical lever to disengage the rear clutch and drive to the water propeller, so that all the engine power was available for the air propeller, and to move the blades of the water propeller to the feathered position where they would produce least drag. If these two actions were not synchronized the engine revolutions would have fluctuated wildly.

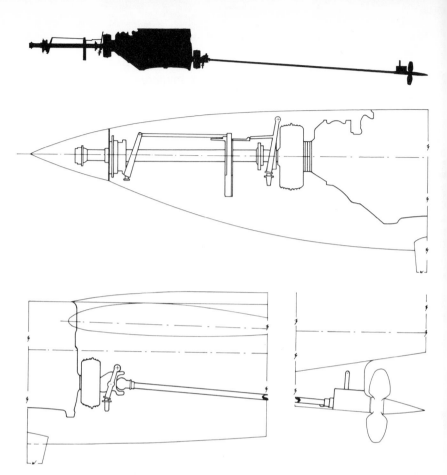

The Piaggio P.c.7's Isotta-Fraschini engine with transmission to air and water screws (*top*), drive to the air screw (*centre*), and drive to the water screw (*base*). (*Clem Watson*)

Alighting would have been equally hazardous as, presumably, it would have been a 'dead stick' operation, with the propeller stopped and the blades horizontal to clear the water.

Pegna carried out a good deal of testing with a P.c.7 model, both in a wind-tunnel and in water-tanks, and on full-size clutch installations. However, although one P.c.7 was built during 1928–29, and underwent trials on Lake Garda with Warrant Officer T. Dal Molin as pilot, it never flew because 'the clutch mechanisms would not work'. It is doubtful, therefore, whether this unique aeroplane was ever driven through the water fast enough to allow the hydrofoils to lift it sufficiently high to enable the airscrew to be engaged. Photographs show the model moving nose-high through the water but with the airscrew stationary and the blades horizontal.

226

Single-seat racing monoplane with hydrofoils. Wood and metal construction. Pilot in open cockpit.

One 970 hp Isotta-Fraschini twelve-cylinder water-cooled vee engine driving a two-blade metal propeller of 2·38 m (7 ft 10 in) diameter. Fuel: 260 litres (57 gal).

Span 6·76 m (22 ft 2 in); length 8·86 m (29 ft 0¾ in); height 2·45 m (8 ft 0½ in); wing area 9·82 sq m (105·8 sq ft).

Empty weight 1,406 kg (3,100 lb); loaded weight 1,738 kg (3,832 lb); wing loading 176·98 kg/sq m (36·22 lb/sq ft).

Estimated maximum speed 580 km/h (360·39 mph).

Production—two P.c.7s built by Società Anonima Piaggio in 1928–29.

Colour—unknown. Probably overall red with stripes in red, white and green on rudder. Italian national insignia and white serials P7–126/127 well aft on fuselage sides.

# Savoia Marchetti S.65

One of a clutch of four new Italian aircraft types intended for the 1929 contest, of which three reached Calshot, the S.65 floatplane was one of the more unusual designs—and certainly the most distinctive—to be built and flown. Designed by Alessandro Marchetti, the S.65 was a low-wing twin-float monoplane with a short nacelle housing two 1,050 hp Isotta-Fraschini Asso twelve-cylinder liquid-cooled engines. Their crankcases and sumps were of a streamlined shape, were externally ribbed and stiffened and were bolted directly to the bulkheads as integral engine mountings. This feature is believed to have been unique among Schneider contest aircraft. The forward engine drove a two-blade fixed-pitch metal airscrew and the rear engine a similar propeller. There were large pointed spinners, and both engines were very cleanly cowled. The cockpit was sandwiched between the two engines and protected by fireproof bulkheads. Oil coolers were flush-mounted in the fuselage sides and above them were long clear-view panels to improve the pilot's view. The whole nacelle was of small cross-section, of metal and metal skinned.

The Savoia S.65 afloat on Lake Maggiore. (*SIAI Marchetti*)

227

The central nacelle with an engine fore and aft, the slender tail booms, and the single central fin and rudder, were features unique to the Savoia S.65. (*SIAI Marchetti*)

The thick rectangular planform mainplane was a wooden structure with two main spars and fabricated ribs and was almost completely covered with surface radiators. The ailerons were fabric-covered. The two slim floats were of all-metal construction, contained the fuel, and were nearly as long as the aircraft itself, being about 6·55 m (21 ft 6 in) in length. They were carried on four slender metal struts and, like the mainplane, were wire braced. The tail unit was mounted on two slender all-metal booms, protruding aft from the trailing edge of the mainplane,

The Savoia S.65's rear engine being test run at Calshot. (*Flight*)

228

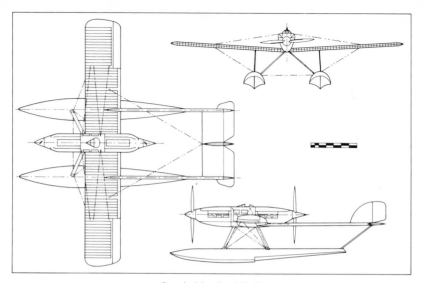

Savoia Marchetti S.65

which were supported on two V-struts fixed to the rear of the floats. The tailplane, horn-balanced elevators, and the unbalanced broad-chord rudder, were of fabric-covered metal construction.

The aircraft was completed during mid-summer 1929 but its early trials were plagued with engine running problems. The major difficulty was heat dissipation, and despite the large radiator surface it was insufficient to keep both engines cool during ground testing. This and fuel system problems prevented the S.65 from coming to the starting line for the 1929 contest but once back in Italy work continued on it throughout the year and into 1930. When flight trials were resumed after the engine problems were partially overcome, there were others with longitudinal control; the aircraft crashed, killing Warrant Officer Dal Molin, its diminutive pilot, believed to be the only available one small enough to fit into the S.65's cramped cockpit.

Single-seat twin-engined twin-float racing monoplane. Pilot in open cockpit.

Two 1,050 hp Isotta-Fraschini Asso twelve-cylinder water-cooled direct-drive normally-aspirated engines driving two-blade fixed-pitch metal propellers of approximately 2·28 m (7 ft 6 in) diameter.

Span 10·05 m (33 ft); length 8·83 m (29 ft); height 2·74 m (9 ft); wing area 12·4 sq m (133·47 sq ft).

Weights and performance unknown.

Production—one S.65 built by Società Idrovolanti Alta Italia, at Sesto Calende in 1929.

Colour—natural metal central nacelle; overall red mainplanes, boom, tail unit and floats; red, white and green national rudder stripes; white S.65, stylized pennant and Savoia Marchetti in capital letters on outer sides of floats.

The Dornier project for the 1929 contest featured a central nacelle with twin engines, and two long floats which extended aft to carry the twin fins and rudders and the tailplane.

# 1929 Dornier

For the 1929 contest Dornier again produced designs and models of an unconventional project. Similar to the Italian S.65, it featured two 500 hp engines arranged in a nacelle in a tandem installation, with a single open cockpit sandwiched between them.

The mainplane was set at the bottom of this nacelle and was heavily wire-braced to it and the floats. The very large single-step floats, which were carried on a pair of V-struts at the front and a single-strut at the rear of the nacelle, extended a long way aft of the rear pusher propeller and terminated in two integral fins and rudders. The tailplane was mounted between the fins. No dimensions, weights or performance details are available for this design which did not advance beyond the project stage.

# Williams-Mercury

The passage of two years failed to soften the United States Government's view of further participation in the Schneider contests and in 1929 it was again left to Alford Williams to carry the nation's hopes. His aircraft, styled the Mercury, a handsome mid-wing monoplane developed from the 1927 biplane, was designed by the Bureau of Aeronautics, Navy Department, and built in extreme secrecy in the Naval Aircraft Factory at Philadelphia. Again, it was a non-profit making organization, the Mercury Flying Corporation, which financed this programme. Wind-tunnel models were tested at the Washington Navy Yard, and construction of the Mercury was supervised by John Keen, a Yard aeronautical engineer.

Of all-wood construction, the fuselage was a semi-monocoque structure with plywood covering. It had a very deep oval-section forward to accommodate the big Packard X-2775 engine but tapered sharply aft of the cockpit. The pilot's headrest was faired into the large oval fin and aluminium rudder unit which had a small ventral portion. The oval tailplane and elevator assembly was a cantilever unit.

The mid-mounted mainplane was a two-spar and multi-rib structure, plywood covered, with aluminium ailerons and carrying surface radiators. It was wire-braced to the fuselage and alighting gear. The aluminium floats were carried on two pairs of forward-raked struts.

The four cylinder banks were housed under aluminium cowlings, the lower ones running aft into a fairing between the pairs of float struts. The Mercury was powered by the same Packard engine used in the 1927 biplane.

Flight trials were scheduled to take place at Santee Wharf, Annapolis Military Academy, and the Mercury was moved there early in August 1929. The Navy Department agreed to transport the aircraft and support crew to Calshot if it could exceed the world's speed record of 318 mph (511 km/h). But far from reaching this speed, Williams found that he was unable even to take-off. Torque reaction was causing the port float to dig in so much that the use of ailerons or rudder to correct the swing created sufficient drag to prevent the floats getting up to a planing position. By chance, Williams found that with the controls in neutral, this situation

The bulky Williams-Mercury, showing the mid-mounted mainplane, the large vertical surfaces of the tail unit, and the massive proportions of the alighting gear. (*Courtesy RAF Museum*)

was overcome, but he was still unable to get airborne. However, it is reported that on 18 August the Mercury lifted off for a few hundred yards on its only flight, keeping only four feet off the water in ground effect. When the design data were checked, they showed that the Mercury was 400 lb (181 kg) overweight and so a new, more powerful, Packard engine was prepared. It was planned to install it on the journey to England, but when the Navy Department suffered a change of heart and withdrew its offer of free transport the whole programme was cancelled.

Single-seat twin-float racing monoplane. All-wood construction with metal components. Pilot in open cockpit.

One 1,250 hp Packard X-2775 twenty-four-cylinder water-cooled normally-aspirated X-engine driving an 8 ft 6 in (2·59 m) diameter two-blade fixed-pitch metal propeller.

Span 28 ft (8·53 m); length 29 ft 6 in (8·99 m); height 12 ft 6 in (3·81 m); wing area 141 sq ft (13·09 sq m).

Dimensions are estimates and no figures are available for weights and performance.

Production—one Williams-Mercury built by the Naval Aircraft Factory, Philadelphia, in 1929.

Colour—believed to have been dark blue overall.


# Bernard H.V.40, 41, 42, 120 and 220

For a company which was conceived in 1916 with such renowned associates as Blériot, Birkigt and Béchereau, plus its founder Adolphe Bernard, it was small wonder that the aircraft it produced were advanced, practical and effective. The pace of its development may be judged from the fact that by 1922 it had had three titles—the last being Société Industrielle des Métaux et du Bois (SIMB)–and been reorganized at least twice. Its first aircraft, the C.1, was a masterly creation in duralumin which took aircraft design and engineering to the frontiers of the then known technology. As an exotic racing aircraft it is possible that the C.1 would have been a success, but attempts to militarize it failed and development was abandoned.

With high speed as its guiding principle, SIMB, generally known simply as Bernard, produced a number of imaginative designs and aircraft before the spring of 1928 when, in parallel with the Nieuport-Delage company, it received an order from the French Ministry of Marine for two high-speed seaplanes. The Gnome-Rhône, Hispano-Suiza and Lorraine engine companies also received orders to produce new racing engines for these aircraft. The intention was to attack the world speed record and to compete in the 1929 Schneider contest.

The Bernard company's designers, Roger Robert and a young Pole named S. G. Bruner, produced designs for two twin-float mid-wing

The first of the Bernard Schneider seaplanes—the Gnome-Rhône Mistral-powered H.V.40. (*Musée de l'Air*)

monoplanes. The first of these was the H.V.40, powered with a new Gnome-Rhône Mistral nine-cylinder air-cooled radial engine developed from the Bristol Jupiter and producing some 600 hp. The second design, the H.V.42, was fitted with an Hispano-Suiza twelve-cylinder water-cooled vee engine of 900/1,000 hp. The H.V. in the designations meant Haute Vitesse (high speed).

The H.V.42 was, therefore, the more realistic contender with its high power/weight engine. Unlike contemporary monoplane racing floatplane designs which featured, almost without exception, a low-wing configuration, both the H.V.40 and H.V.42 had a wire-braced mid-mounted mainplane in which the very deep root section blended smoothly into the slender fuselage. The all-wood fuselage was built up around four spruce and ply longerons, and formers. The fin was built as an integral part of the fuselage and the tailplane was a cantilever unit. The entire fuselage, fin and tailplane were wood covered.

The mainplane centre-section was of multi-spar and rib construction, but the outer panels had the conventional two-spar and rib structure, all of which was wood covered. Fabric-covered metal ailerons were carried on a small false spar. The engine bearers were attached to the front of the centre-section/fuselage structure.

The alighting gear consisted of two single-step duralumin floats which contained tinned-steel integral fuel tanks. They were carried on steel-tube N-struts, with wooden fairings to produce a streamlined profile, which were attached to a rectangular duralumin mounting frame which formed part of the base of the centre-section. Lamblin radiators were carried on the forward float struts. A contemporary report described these aircraft as 'of not very clean design'.

Production began late in 1928 but a number of airframe snags slowed

233

the building programme, although by the spring of the following year these seemed to have been cleared and both types are reported to have flown for the first time during June. However, it was soon apparent that the engines provided were not ready for practice contest flying, they gave trouble and clearly had not had sufficient development running time. At the Gnome-Rhône factory the Mistral was still being ground tested, with much work still to be done to fit it for the rigours of the contest, while development of both the Hispano-Suiza and Lorraine engines was a long way behind schedule.

Like the Italians, the French made thorough preparations for the training of their pilots and set up a lakeside training base at Hourtin on the Gironde where the Armée de l'Air pilots of the Schneider team did their practice flying. Moreover, Adjutant Florentin Bonnet and the renowned Sadi Lecointe had been retained by the French Ministry to undertake the acceptance trials of the Bernard and Nieuport-Delage aircraft. Sadly, the loss of Bonnet in the crash of his Nieuport 62, allied to the mechanical problems being experienced with the aircraft and the engines, led to the withdrawal of France from the list of entrants for the 1929 contest.

This setback did not deter the French from continuing the training programme and making preparations to compete in the 1931 contest. Three companies—Bernard, Nieuport-Delage and Dewoitine—were given preliminary orders for new aircraft, and the Lorraine, Renault, Farman and Hispano-Suiza companies were to produce the engines. In the spring of 1930, Lorraine devoted a special factory to the production of the Radium, an alleged 2,000/2,200 hp twelve-cylinder water-cooled geared and supercharged engine. As far as can be established, not a single

The aerodynamically-clean Dewoitine H.D.412 with Lorraine Radium engine. (*Courtesy Jacques Gambu*)

234

The Bernard H.V.41 with Hispano-Suiza Spécial liquid-cooled engine. (*Courtesy Jacques Gambu*)

Radium was delivered to the Bernard company in time to equip a contest aircraft, only a space model to enable associated systems, such as the coolant system, to be installed.

While confirmation of the order for new aircraft was awaited, some development of the H.V.40 and H.V.42 went ahead; in addition, the H.V.41 variant with the Hispano-Suiza Spécial engine was flown in November 1929 by Antoine Paillard, chief pilot of the Bernard company. A good deal of development effort also went into an interim variant powered by the long-awaited 1,500/1,680 hp Hispano-Suiza 18R geared engine intended for use in the 1929 contest. This variant, which had wing-surface radiators and was designated H.V.120, (F-AKAK c/n 01) made its first flight at Hourtin during March 1930 with Paillard at the controls.

Development of this aeroplane, and the H.V.41, progressed steadily, if slowly, during the subsequent summer months and it was not until November that it arrived at Berre near Marseilles, a new training base for the French Schneider team. Here, it was believed, the weather of the Midi would be better suited to high-speed practice flying than that of the Gironde.

With France confirming its participation in the 1931 contest on the last day of 1930, the French pilots began assembling at Berre early in the new year expecting that the promised delivery of three H.V.42s would have been made. It was not until March 1931 that the first aircraft arrived, with the others being delivered the following month. Then, with the first H.V.120 at Berre and trials of the second (F-AKAL c/n 02) underway, Paillard died on 15 June, thus seriously affecting the flight development programme of the Bernard aircraft, and it was soon apparent that plans to have the new low-wing H.V.220 racing seaplane ready for the contest were hopeless. Thus all efforts were turned to embodying modifications

235

A Bernard H.V.120 which it was hoped would compete in the 1931 contest. (*Courtesy Jacques Gambu*)

in the existing aircraft, which had been intended for the 1929 contest, to ready them for the 1931 event. It was decided to reduce the wing span of the H.V.120 by 1·2 m (3 ft 11¼ in) in order to improve the top speed and, while F-AKAK remained at Berre for further flying, F-AKAL was returned to Bernard's La Corneuve factory for this work to be done.

Meanwhile, a number of different propellers were flown on the H.V.42 and H.V.120, including Levasseur, Chauvière and Ratier types of three- and four-blade configuration, and the H.V.40 joined the Berre establish-

The Bernard H.V.220 awaiting delivery of its 2,000/2,200 hp Lorraine Radium engine, at the factory at Le Corneuve. (*Musée de l'Air*)

236

ment. It was during a test flight of a four-blade Chauvière propeller, that Georges Bougault, one of the French team pilots, was killed when F-AKAL crashed into the Étang de Berre. When the wreckage was salvaged it was found that the air-speed indicator was jammed at 585 km/h (363 mph).

Once again, the Bernard programme had to be changed and the first H.V.120, with the direct-drive Hispano-Suiza 18R engine, which had completed 25 flights was returned to La Corneuve to be prepared to fly in the contest as the first-string aircraft. In six days the wing span was reduced by 1·2 m (3 ft 11¼ in), which cut the wing area by 2·48 sq m (26·7 sq ft), and the surface radiators were modified to suit. With these changes, it was hoped to achieve at least 580 km/h (360 mph), but because of them, new acceptance trials had to be completed before F-AKAK could be handed back to the team pilots. There were some doubts expressed about the effect on the lateral control and whether, in fact, the reduced wing area would make the take-off more difficult for Jean Assolant, who was nominated to do the acceptance tests.

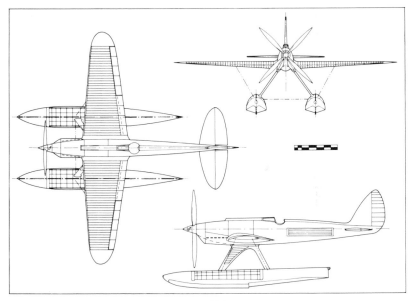

Bernard H.V.220

On 25 August he made four flights in an H.V.42 but a mistral, that notorious French wind, delayed the first flight of the modified H.V.120 for three days. When Assolant got airborne in F-AKAK he flew it fairly gingerly at first but found that it handled quite well; in any event, he is reported as having partially blacked-out in one tight turn. Engine over-heating with the small radiators was a problem which was only partially solved by further modification to the system.

## Bernard Schneider Seaplanes

| | H.V.40 | H.V.41 | H.V.42 | H.V.120 | H.V.220 |
|---|---|---|---|---|---|
| Engine | 600/800 hp Gnome-Rhône 9 Kfr Mistral | 900/1,000 hp Hispano-Suiza Spécial | 900/1,000 hp Hispano-Suiza Spécial | 1,500/1,680 hp Hispano-Suiza 18R | 2,000/2,200 hp Lorraine 12 RCR Radium |
| Span | 8·7 m (28 ft 6¼ in) | 9·2 m (30 ft 2 in) | 9·2 m (30 ft 2 in) | 9·85 m (32 ft 3¾ in) | 9·4 m (30 ft 10 in) |
| Length | 7·4 m (24 ft 3¼ in) | 7·99 m (26 ft 2½ in) | 7·99 m (26 ft 2½ in) | 8·24 m (27 ft 0⅓ in) | 9·455 m (31 ft 0 in) |
| Height | 3·6 m (11 ft 9½ in) | — | 3·6 m (11 ft 9½ in) | 3·6 m (11 ft 9½ in) | 3·955 m (12 ft 11½ in) |
| Wing area | 10 sq m (107·64 sq ft) | 12 sq m (129·16 sq ft) | 12 sq m (129·16 sq ft) | 13·68 sq m (147·25 sq ft) | 13·86 sq m (149·18 sq ft) |
| Loaded weight | — | — | 1,650 kg (3,638 lb) | 2,100 kg (4,630 lb) | 2,370 kg (5,225 lb) |
| Wing loading | — | — | 137·5 kg/sq m (28·16 lb/sq ft) | 153·5 kg/sq m (31·44 lb/sq ft) | 170·99 kg/sq m (35·02 lb/sq ft) |
| Maximum speed | 400 km/h+ (248·5 mph) | 450 km/h (279·6 mph) | 450 km/h (279·6 mph) | 530 km/h* (329·3 mph) | 640 km/h† (397·6 mph) |

* Speed applies to H.V.120-01 after span reduced to 8·65 m (28 ft 4½ in) and area to 11·2 sq m (120·55 sq ft).
† Estimated speed.

But time was running out for the Bernard and on 1 September, when the aircraft should have been ready for dismantling and packing for the journey to Calshot, it was still not contest ready. This was a major factor in France's decision to withdraw from the contest, which was received by the British Air Ministry on 5 September.

An interesting project also planned for the 1931 contest was a racing flying-boat of unusual configuration in which the mainplane was carried high above the hull on a pylon which incorporated surface radiators. The two engines were mounted in tandem in the centre-section. Stability afloat was provided by two large sponsons which gave a sesquiplane appearance to the aircraft. A braced tailplane was carried high on a very tall fin, and the pilot was housed in an enclosed cabin at the base of the pylon.

The H.V.220 was eventually completed and a cleaner version, the H.V.320, was projected.

## Nieuport-Delage ND.450/650

Nieuport-Delage, one of the two companies ordered to produce designs for the 1929 contest, stuck to the conventional low-wing monoplane configuration in its proposal for that year. Like the Bernard company, Nieuport's attempts to complete its aircraft for the contest were foiled largely through the failure of the engine manufacturers to deliver power units in time.

The all-wood aircraft, designated ND.450, appeared as a very handsome, clean design with a slim deep-section fuselage, having a large

The Nieuport-Delage ND.450, showing the three-blade propeller, very long-chord cylinder-bank fairing running aft to the cockpit, heavy-framed and supported windscreen, and the multiplicity of bracing wires on the float struts. (*Musée de l'Air*)

239

The Nieuport-Delage ND.650 (nearest) and two Bernard H.V.120s in the hangar at Hourtin. (*Musée de l'Air*)

dorsal fairing running from behind the pilot's head to the curved fin and the broad-chord rudder. A large cantilever tailplane carried narrow-chord elevators. The very thin section mainplane was wire-braced to the fuselage and alighting gear. Two very long floats, longer than the fuselage, were carried on four heavily wire-braced broad-chord struts. The big 1,680 hp eighteen-cylinder Hispano-Suiza 18R geared broad-arrow engine was neatly cowled and drove a three-blade Ratier propeller. The fairings over the two outboard banks of cylinders were continued aft along the fuselage to a point below the cockpit.

By the summer of 1929 the airframe was ready and waiting for its engine which was a long way behind schedule, but France's withdrawal from the contest at the beginning of August put an end to Nieuport's immediate preparations.

Work was continued on the ND.450 and with the arrival of the engine in the early autumn the programme received a great impetus, and the aircraft went to Hourtin for its first flight, made by Sadi Lecointe. In January 1930, after some modifications required following the initial flight tests, the designation of the aircraft was changed to ND.650. Flying continued through the year at Hourtin and from Étang de Berre, with some further modifications being made and the installation of a direct-drive Hispano-Suiza 18R engine. Early in February 1931 Sadi Lecointe made the first flight of the prototype ND.650 with this engine at Berre. On 12 March he attained a speed of 390 km/h (242 mph) in spite of faulty carburetion.

Meanwhile, a second ND.650 had joined the team at Berre to await flight trials by Lecointe. At the end of June the first aircraft moved from Berre to Caudebec-en-Caux where Fernard Lasne was to continue the flying programme. Unfortunately, on 22 July this ND.650 crashed into the Seine, and although, happily, Lasne was not seriously injured, the aircraft needed almost complete rebuilding.

240

As with the Bernard H.V.120 it was decided to crop the span of the second ND.650 by some 98 cm (3 ft 2 in) in spite of the fact that this would inevitably increase the wing loading and make the take-off and general handling more difficult. It was returned from the Nieuport-Delage factory to Hourtin for flight testing by Lecointe, but the geared 18R engine was not delivering its expected power and even by the last week of August Lecointe had not been able to get the ND.650 off the water. To overcome this fundamental problem the floats were rapidly changed, but these neither enabled the aircraft to get airborne nor even taxi any better.

According to a Reuter report, Lecointe managed a test flight on 1 September, but French Government sources later gave the date as 3 September, crediting the aircraft with a maximum speed of 530 km/h (329·3 mph).

With this first flight completed, the plan was to dismantle the ND.650, crate it and transport it to Cherbourg where it was to be re-erected and taken to Calshot aboard a French naval vessel. Hopes of achieving this were shattered on 3 or 4 September when it was realized that the performance of the ND.650 was insufficient to make it a credible contender in the Schneider contest; in addition it was directionally unstable. On 5 September France confirmed it would not compete, and all of Nieuport's great efforts had been in vain.

# 1931

When the Bernard H.V.120–02 and a Nieuport-Delage ND.450/650 crashed within days of each other, France withdrew from the contest because the H.V.220 was not ready. Italy followed suit through the failure of the Macchi-Castoldi MC.72 to be fully airworthy for the contest. A Dornier flying-boat project did not come to fruition. Because of the continuous development programme, the Bernard and Nieuport-Delage seaplanes are described together on pages 232–241 covering the 1929 contest.

## Macchi-Castoldi MC.72

If there was one lesson which the Italians learned from their Schneider contest efforts in 1929 it was that they had been spread too thinly over too many types; in addition, Fiat, Macchi and Savoia had all worked in almost total isolation on their respective designs and the wide experience of Macchi had not been made available generally. When the time came to plan and create new aircraft and engines for the 1931 contest the Italian Government pinned its faith on the proven team of Macchi and Fiat.

The ultimate in racing floatplanes, the Macchi-Castoldi MC.72, serialled 181, nevertheless failed to come to the starting line for the final Schneider Trophy contest in 1931. The great amount of radiator surface on the floats and the long fuselage-mounted oil-cooler can be seen in this view. (*Courtesy John Stroud*)

The result of their combined experience, skills and facilities was the MC.72. This last of Italy's Schneider contest aspirants, and the ultimate in racing floatplane design, scaled peaks of engineering and performance which no subsequent aircraft of its class has since attempted to climb.

Always seeking to develop and improve upon an existing successful design, Mario Castoldi went further than ever when he schemed a new aircraft aimed at giving Italy the victory essential to keep the contest alive. He was supported in this aim by Tranquillo Zerbi who had created a unique new powerplant, the Fiat AS.6, basically two lightweight 1,500 hp twelve-cylinder AS.5 engines coupled in tandem on a common crankcase. The two engines—or two groups of twelve-cylinders—were not coupled; each drove one half of a counter-rotating propeller through coaxial shafts, the rear engine also powering a centrifugal compressor to supercharge both units. This monster power unit, which had a capacity of 50,000 cc, was designed as a complete entity with a single induction and ignition system, and the only mechanical link between them was the throttle linkage.

Apart from its novelty, the AS.6 produced more power for its frontal area than any engine in a Schneider contest aircraft. Its frontal area was only 0·583 sq m (6·275 sq ft). The AS.6 drove two 2·59 m (8 ft 6 in) diameter counter-rotating two-blade metal propellers at a maximum rotational speed of 2,000 rpm. This propeller installation enabled the diameter to be reduced and the counter-rotating feature eliminated the torque reaction, which was always a problem during the take-off phase. While there was a similarity between the mainplane and tailplane of the MC.72 and M.67, the MC.72's fuselage shape was completely different, being of a much higher fineness ratio and appearing as a long streamlined shape to accommodate the 3·365 m (11 ft) length of the AS.6.

242

The fuselage was of mixed construction, the forward fuselage and the engine bay were all metal, with the engine being supported in a long fabricated aluminium cradle. These two sections were wholly cowled, being covered in aluminium panels. The rear portion of the fuselage, aft of the cockpit, was built entirely of wood, consisting of wooden frames and bulkheads all connected by wooden stringers and longerons. This structure was covered in wood skinning. The tail unit and control surfaces were of similar construction. The wire-braced mainplane was a conventional Castoldi all-duralumin two-spar design which was almost entirely covered with flat-tube surface radiators. The alighting gear consisted of all-metal floats carried on four broad-chord struts covered in coolant radiators. Additional radiators were mounted on the top surface of the floats, and an oil cooler was fitted around the undersurface and sides of the rear fuselage aft of the open cockpit.

Most of the practice flying by the ten new pilots who joined the high speed training school, at Desenzano, was done on the old M.52s during 1930 and the early months of 1931, until the arrival of the MC.72 in June. The first flight was entrusted to Capt Giovanni Monti and he made a perfect take-off, not having to worry about or make allowances for torque-reaction from the propellers. On the test-bench the AS.6 had run very satisfactorily but in the air there were carburetion problems. Thus, on this initial flight, these problems limited it to only two minutes before Monti had to put down on the water. After adjustments, further flights proved that the carburettor functioned quite well at the lower end of the

The Macchi-Castoldi MC.72 displays its fine lines and abundance of cooling surfaces on the floats and struts. (*Courtesy The Royal Aeronautical Society*)

243

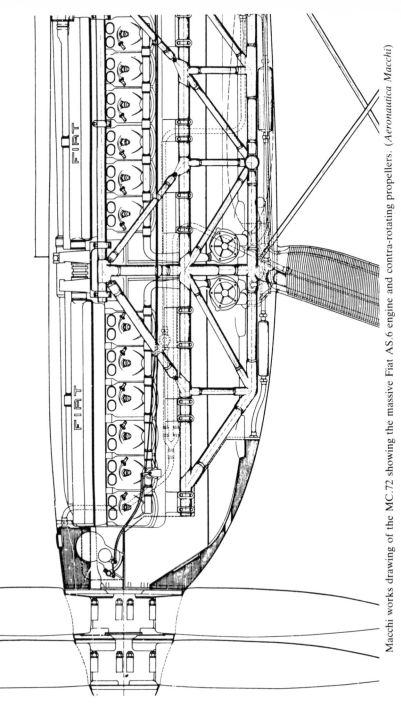

Macchi works drawing of the MC.72 showing the massive Fiat AS.6 engine and contra-rotating propellers. (*Aeronautica Macchi*)

244

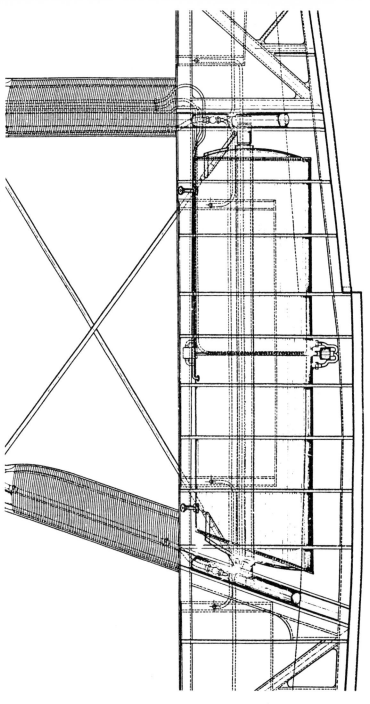

Part of the works drawing opposite, showing the centre portion of the float with fuel tank, and the float attachment struts with their cooling surfaces.
(*Aeronautica Macchi*)

throttle range but toward the top end, at full throttle, there was the ever-present danger of backfiring. In addition, the propellers seemed to be rotating at different speeds and, therefore, not synchronized, and there were engine overheating problems.

On 2 August, Monti was killed when his MC.72 crashed into Lake Garda. This was a sad and severe upset to Italy's pre-contest plans, and as similar carburetion problems were experienced with the second aeroplane there were doubts that Italy would participate in the contest. These doubts became fact on 5 September when both Italy and France confirmed that neither would compete.

But this failure to produce an Italian team in the contest did nothing to lessen the belief of Macchi and Fiat in the MC.72, and two days before the Calshot fly-over by the S.6B, Lieut Stanislao Bellini attacked the world speed record in the MC.72 by endeavouring to exceed the 634 km/h (394 mph) achieved earlier by Lieut Ariosto Neri. Sadly, after one very fast run he flew across the Desenzano air base and into rising ground on the far side of the lake. Subsequent investigations revealed that the engine had backfired into the carburettor air intake and set fire to the gravity fuel tank just behind it. As a result, the aircraft exploded and was entirely destroyed. Further test flying ceased, and hope of establishing a new speed record was deferred.

After Great Britain had taken permanent possession of the Schneider Trophy on 13 September, Italy decided to make a further attempt on the absolute air speed record but, mindful of the continuing problems with the AS.6 carburetion, invited Rod Banks, the British fuel expert, to help solve these difficulties. In Italy he discovered that the engine had not been tested on the ground in conditions which were fully representative

The surviving Macchi-Castoldi MC.72 at the 1934 Salon de l'Aviation in the Grand Palais.

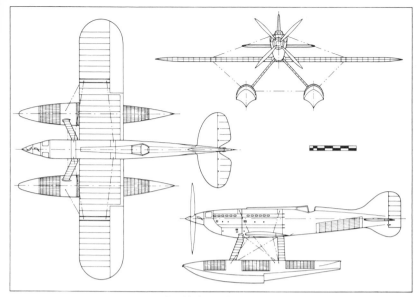

Macchi-Castoldi MC.72

of those to be experienced in the air. Banks persuaded Fiat to install a big blower in the test house to simulate flight conditions and provide the engine with ram air equivalent to the forward speed of the aircraft. He also blended a special fuel, combining benzole, leaded gasoline and ethyl alcohol and, after cyclic testing representing six runs over the 3 kilometre course, the flight engines were checked and sent to Desenzano for installation in the MC.72. In April 1933, with Warrant Officer Agello at the controls, a record speed of 682·078 km/h (423·822 mph) was established. Agello raised this to 709·209 km/h (440·681 mph) on 23 October, 1934, a record which still stands in his name and that of Italy.

Single-seat twin-float racing monoplane. Mixed metal and wood construction. Pilot in open cockpit.

One 2,850 hp Fiat AS.6 twenty-four-cylinder water-cooled geared supercharged vee engine driving two 2·59 m (8 ft 6 in) diameter two-blade fixed-pitch metal counter-rotating propellers. The power was increased to 3,000 hp during 1934.

Span 9·48 m (31 ft 1½ in); length 8·32 m (27 ft 3½ in); height 3·3 m (10 ft 10 in); wing area 15 sq m (161·46 sq ft).

Empty weight 2,500 kg (5,511 lb); loaded weight 3,025 kg (6,669 lb)—1933, 2,907 kg (6,409 lb)—1934; wing loading 201·66 kg/sq m (41·3 lb/sq ft)—1933, 193·8 kg/sq m (39·69 lb/sq ft)—1934.

Maximum speed more than 682·078 km/h (423·822 mph)—1933, 709·209 km/h (440·681 mph)—1934.

Production—five MC.72s (MM.177–181) built by Aeronautica Macchi during 1930–31.

Colour—overall red, aluminium propellers and spinner, natural copper radiators and oil coolers, red, white and green national stripes on rudder; white MC.72 on rear fuselage aft of oil cooler.

# 1931 Dornier

The third and last Dornier racing seaplane project was prepared for the 1931 contest. Unlike all the other participating countries which had long abandoned the flying-boat configuration for Schneider Trophy entrants, Dornier in Germany produced a sleek flying-boat powered by two engines of about 2,000 hp each. Full of unusual features, which so often in the contests had proved to be no substitute for the conventional, the Dornier boat's engines were mounted in the forward part of the circular-section hull, the rear engine facing forward and the front facing aft. Their drive-shafts were connected to a gearbox which drove a vertical shaft running up inside a broad-chord pylon; on the top was mounted the pusher propeller. Radiators were carried on the sides of the forward and rear hull, on the pylon and fin, and almost completely covered the mainplane which was mounted above the hull on the pylon. Two small teardrop-shaped retractable stabilizer floats were fitted on the hull sides, sliding in and out on mounting arms. The tailplane was carried high on the fin and was strut-braced.

Span 11·98 m (39 ft 4 in); length 10·97 m (36 ft); height 4·08 m (13 ft 5 in); wing area 23·96 sq m (258 sq ft); empty weight 3,250 kg (7,165 lb); loaded weight 4,000 kg (8,818 lb); wing loading 166·94 kg/sq m (34·19 lb/sq ft); and estimated maximum speed 650 km/h (403·89 mph).

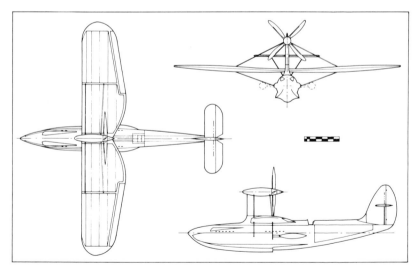

Dornier reverted to the flying-boat configuration for this twin-engined project for the 1931 contest.

# The Engines

If there was one factor of paramount importance to success in the Schneider Trophy contests it was engine reliability. During the early years, when airspeeds were comparatively modest, aerodynamic refinement was hardly considered, and this is apparent from the multiplicity of struts and bracing wires in the winning Deperdussin floatplane and the Nieuports at the first and second contests at Monaco in 1913 and 1914.

It was not until 1919 that streamlined structures began to be in evidence, and the universal adoption of the monoplane configuration for all the aircraft in the contest did not take place until 1929, although the Macchi M.33 monoplane had been placed third in the 1925 contest. Throughout the contest series, while it is true that there were airframe design defects and failures during trials, with resulting withdrawals and some fatalities, it was the high rate of engine and associated systems failure or unserviceability which contributed most to the air and ground crews' problems. Of the 47 floatplanes and flying-boats which came to the starting line of the twelve contests, no less than 18, or 40 per cent, retired with engine or associated system failures. It is difficult to assess accurately the number which were built, with the intention of being flown in the contest, but which failed in selection trials or during flight testing through engine problems. Power output, while of importance, is only one of the requirements of a successful aero-engine, specific weight and power and specific fuel and oil consumption are among others. The first internal combustion engine to fly, a Lenoir-type gas engine fuelled with coal gas to power an 1872 airship, weighed 205 lb (93 kg) for each one horse power it developed. Yet, by the turn of the century this had been reduced to 3·6 lb (1·63 kg) per hp in a remarkable five-cylinder water-cooled radial engine designed and built by Charles M. Manley in the United States, and which developed about 50 hp. The four-cylinder water-cooled horizontal engine designed by Wilbur and Orville Wright and built largely by Charles Taylor, their mechanic, weighed 180 lb (81·64 kg) and was reputed to have produced about 12 hp. It was used to make the world's first successful controlled powered flight by a heavier-than-air craft on 17 December, 1903.

In France Léon Levavasseur's 1905 Antoinette eight-cylinder water-cooled vee engine had fuel injection and evaporative cooling, which were well ahead of their time. This 110 lb (50 kg) engine produced 50 hp and was put into production.

The rate of progress may be judged from the fact that the Rolls-Royce R engine of 1931 weighed a little over 8 ounces (226 grammes) for each one horse power it developed. As engine power outputs slowly increased, a major problem which arose was dissipation of the heat generated by combustion of the fuel/air mixture. Most early aero-engines were water-cooled, requiring watertight jackets around the cylinder or combustion chamber, and a system of pipes to connect these jackets to a radiator in the airflow where the water could be cooled by the transfer of heat to the surrounding air. These, plus the cooling water itself, were heavy and bulky, and the radiator created drag.

The creation of the internal combustion rotary engine by the Frenchman Laurent Seguin and his brother during 1907—8, stemmed from the fundamental problem of overheating and often the subsequent failure of the inline water-cooled and radial engines of the period. Clearly, increased power output was being demanded by all airframe manufacturers and, with the low quality of the fuel then available, this meant increasing the number or size of the cylinders which added to the weight and aggravated the problem of cooling. The Seguins' solution was to reverse the basic design concept of the traditional internal combustion engine with its stationary cylinders and crankcase and rotating crankshaft. Their Gnome rotary engine, as its classification implies, featured a stationary crankshaft, with the cylinders, valve gear and crankcase with the propeller bolted directly to it rotating around it. In this way the cooling of the engine was much improved, particularly when ground running where there was no forward motion to provide an airflow. The first Gnome engines had five cylinders and were rated at 50 hp with a specific weight of 1·2 kg/hp (2·7 lb/hp). It was an expensive engine as each cylinder was a solid steel forging which had to be machined to produce a thin-walled cylinder with integral radial cooling fins. A carburettor fed a fuel/air

100 hp Gnome Monosoupape air-cooled rotary, showing the cam-operated valve gear. (*RAF Museum*)

mixture, to which lubricating oil was added, through the hollow crank-shaft to the crankcase. The oil chosen was castor oil as it did not mix with, and therefore dilute, the fuel. Centrifugal action threw a substantial amount of the lubricating oil into the cylinders, where it was either combusted with the fuel/air mixture or was ejected as a fine spray from the exhaust, blowing back in the slipstream and consequently coating the aircraft and the pilot.

The fuel/air mixture passed into the cylinder through a counterweight-operated valve in the head of each piston. After ignition the burnt gas escaped through a valve in the cylinder head which was opened at the correct moment by push-rods operated by a fixed cam ring inside the crankcase. Oil consumption could be high, varying from two pints up to four pints for every gallon of fuel consumed, which posed a storage problem in the aircraft.

Nevertheless, the Gnome rotary produced high power and, because of the flywheel effect of the rotating engine, high torque; it also overcame the problem of overheating. The Gnome rotary engine was widely used to power Schneider contest entrants and aspirants during 1913—14.

Within three years there were nearly 80 manufacturers of aero-engines, with only a small minority outside of Western Europe, but the market was dominated by the Gnome rotary which was, without doubt, the most efficient and effective type of power unit available for use by aircraft designers and builders of the prewar era. This was underlined by the fact that it was not only produced in France but under licence in Germany as the Oberursel UR.1, in Britain as the Bentley BR.1 and in Sweden as the Thulin. Moreover, it was developed into a nine-cylinder unit and later was built as a fourteen-cylinder twin-row engine.

The main disadvantage with the rotary design was that in turning the propeller the mass of the engine had to be turned for effective cooling and this absorbed almost one-third of its power. That the rotary engine concept was the best of its era, however, was evidenced by the fact that some of the other manufacturers tried—and succeeded—in getting around the Seguins' patented design features, often by embodying im-provements of their own. The Clerget and Le Rhône companies' rotary engines were examples of this, the Clerget engine being built in very large numbers throughout the war years by some 18 manufacturers in France, Germany, Britain and the United States. But the Seguins made a number of design changes to their engine, improving the reliability and power output. Modifications included the replacement of the counterweighted valve in the piston head by inlet ports in the cylinder, uncovered by the piston at the bottom of its stroke, through which the fuel/air mixture entered the cylinder from the crankcase. The single exhaust valve gave the engine its name, the Gnome Monosoupape (single-valve). This en-gine, too, was manufactured in many thousands during the First World War.

In France the Renault company produced an 80 hp, eight-cylinder inline air-cooled vee engine with a reduction gear and from it were developed eight- and twelve-cylinder vee engines, air- and water-cooled, with power outputs of up to 260 hp. An unusual design was the Salmson (Canton-Unné) nine- and fourteen-cylinder water-cooled radial engine producing up to 240 hp; so, too, was an engine in which the cylinders were arranged in a spiral.

Germany, meanwhile, was producing water-cooled inline engines, with four or six cylinders, of which the larger units developed some 300 hp. The main manufacturing companies were Austro-Daimler, Benz, BMW, Maybach and Mercedes. A disadvantage of the upright inline engine was the length of the crankshaft, which tended to bend. Other European engine manufacturers used these basic design configurations for their products; they included Clément-Bayard, Hispano-Suiza, Fiat and Isotta-Fraschini, Wolseley, Green, Sunbeam, and Isaacson. These, then, were the major power producers, the designers and builders of the engines to whom the aircraft manufacturers turned for the means to get their designs into the air; and it was to their products that the designers and pilots of the early Schneider Trophy contenders looked for victory.

At the first contest in 1913 at Monaco, all six aircraft which took part in the trials to select a French team had either Gnome rotary or Salmson/ Canton-Unné radial engines, and the lone entry representing the United States also had a Gnome rotary engine. The following year at Monaco the German entry, the Aviatik Arrow, had a Benz inline engine; all the remaining eleven British, French, Swiss and US aspirants for a place in the contest had rotaries—Gnomes, Gnome Monosoupapes or Le Rhônes. Great Britain's ultimate winner, the Sopwith Tabloid, was powered by a Gnome Monosoupape rotary which, though functioning on only eight of its nine cylinders for more than 12 of the 28 laps, continued to run steadily and produce sufficient power to enable the little Tabloid to finish the course without stopping, something which none of the other competing aircraft could accomplish.

That the British contestant had to rely upon a French engine was readily acknowledged by Tom Sopwith, and it was a quite accurate indicator not only of the lead which France had taken in aviation but of the lack of reliable and effective aero-engines of British manufacture. Only a month before the 1914 contest the fifth Aero Show was held at Olympia in London. Only two of the sixteen British aircraft exhibited were equipped with British engines; one, a Green, was too heavy for its 100 hp output, and the other, an ENV engine, was of inadequate power for the aircraft in which it was fitted. Without exception all the engines exhibited by French and German manufacturers had better power/weight ratios than the British designs.

At the outbreak of the First World War the Royal Flying Corps and the Royal Naval Air Service did not have a single aircraft powered by a British engine; those being used were of French design or manufacture. Moreover, only one type of aero-engine was being produced in any quantity in Great Britain at that time; it was a 100 hp Sunbeam and even then the designer was a Frenchman, Louis Coatalen, who had joined the Sunbeam company in 1910 to design a 200 hp engine based on a Hispano-Suiza unit.

During the four war years, when the Schneider Trophy contests were suspended, there was a dramatic change in the aero-engine industries of the combatant nations. In Great Britain, for example, companies such as Siddeley Deasey (later Armstrong Siddeley), Napier, Cosmos and Rolls-Royce, plus the Royal Aircraft Factory (RAF) at Farnborough (which changed its name to Royal Aircraft Establishment on 1 April, 1918, to avoid confusion with the newly formed Royal Air Force), had built up a great deal of experience and knowledge of aero-engine design and development. In 1914, there was little conscious thought being given to such things as the effects of stress concentrations in components, of detonation, of the importance of adequate cooling, carburetion and lubrication or of synchronous vibration; four years later they were everyday features of an engine designer's work. The development of improved materials was another facet of work at the RAE; better steels for crankshafts and connecting rods, and better light alloys for castings and forgings, stemmed from that source; as did work on supercharging and liquid coolants. There had been failures, like the ABC Dragonfly and the Sunbeam Arab, but there were many successes too. The 450 hp Napier Lion twelve-cylinder water-cooled broad-arrow engine, for example, which, conceived in 1916, remained in production until 1932, powering ten of the thirteen British aircraft which came to the starting lines in postwar Schneider contests. Its record was two first places (1922 and 1927), two seconds (1925 and 1927), and two thirds (1923 and 1929), which was unequalled by any other engine in the contest series.

The manufacturer of this remarkably successful engine was D. Napier and Son Ltd, which was formed in 1808, the year David Napier went to London from his native Scotland. The company soon became highly regarded for precision engineering, first with the design and manufacture of printing machinery, then bullet-making machinery and coin-sorting machines. Two generations later the company turned its interests toward motor-cars. But first, in 1899, came the progenitor of the long line of Napier engines for cars, boats and aircraft. It was a two-cylinder vertical engine of about 8 hp, with the two cylinders firing one after the other. The cranks went round together so that there were two firing strokes followed by two idling strokes. Total engine weight including all the accessories was about 320 lb (145 kg). The first Napier car took part in the Automobile Club's Thousand Miles Trial, which began on 23 April, 1900, and after some vicissitudes was placed first in its class and second overall in the Trial.

The First World War swept Napier cars off the road and the market and ultimately sounded the death knell of the company's car interests. However, military vehicles were produced in large numbers. Then in

August 1915 Napier's Acton factory became a 'controlled' establishment. All automobile work stopped and the company's entire efforts were directed to the production of aero-engines and airframes—but neither to Napier designs. The engines originally were the RAF 3a twelve-cylinder water-cooled engines, designed by the Royal Aircraft Factory at Farnborough, and then the eight-cylinder Sunbeam Arab.

Napier believed that it could produce better engines, and in July 1916 A. J. Rowledge, the company's chief designer, began designs of a twelve-cylinder water-cooled geared broad-arrow aero-engine. Rowledge aimed to produce a compact engine, and the broad-arrow configuration, in which the cylinders were disposed in three inline banks of four cylinders each, enabled a short, stiff crankshaft and crankcase to be used. It required a fairly complex master connecting rod but this was outweighed by the other mechanical advantages of this configuration.

Although the broad-arrow provided these benefits, aerodynamically it was far from ideal as it presented a much larger frontal area than did the more conventional vee engine layout. This problem was compounded by the amount of external 'plumbing', such as the air-intake pipes of the carburetion system, which had at least been designed to fit in the vees between the three cylinder blocks rather than on the outer flanks of the engine. In the early marks of Lion the frontal area amounted to almost 50 per cent more than the classically slender Curtiss D-12. The Lion used aluminium monobloc castings for the cylinder heads, steel cylinder barrels with individual steel water jackets, and a cast aluminium crankcase. The design of the complex master connecting rod in the vertical cylinder bank and the tubular rods in the two other banks

A 585 hp Napier Lion VIIA broad-arrow engine. Note the twin-choke carburettor and the induction manifolds on the near side of the engine. (*RAF Museum*)

254

produced different strokes. The Lion was a particularly smooth-running engine, attributable in part to the roller and ball bearings used in its construction.

During the fourteen years of its production life the power of the Lion was increased from its original 450 hp to more than 1,300 hp in the supercharged VIID variant which was achieved in 1929 when fitted in the Gloster VI. This increase was accomplished by supercharging and regular increases in compression ratio from around 4:1 for the 'cooking' Lions, intended for the steady grind of day-to-day military and civil flying, to more than 8:1 of the Series VII Lions with short lives and intended solely for Schneider Trophy racing.

In addition to the supercharging and other purely mechanical modifications made to the old Lion design to boost its power output, there was the inevitable 'secret ingredient' supplied by Napier engineers which came from the company's long history of producing reliable and finely engineered machinery.

The Lion was chosen by both Folland and Mitchell for all their Schneider contest aircraft between 1919 and 1929, two of which—the Supermarine S.4 of 1925 and the Gloster VI of 1929—set world absolute speed records. There were many other achievements by Lion-powered aircraft, the last, in 1935, being an 11,000 mile (17,700 km) flight from Aden to West Africa and return by four Fairey IIIFs of No. 8 Squadron, RAF.

In 1914, when war began Rolls-Royce had been urged by the Admiralty to produce the Royal Aircraft Factory's version of the highly regarded 80 hp Renault eight-cylinder air-cooled inline vee engine and

A cutaway example of a Napier Lion engine, showing the valve-gear. (*Courtesy Charles Cain*)

other derivatives, but Rolls-Royce resisted, being critical of the basic design concept. However, the water-cooled Mercedes engine removed from a successful Mercedes racing car, brought to London for a show-room display, was sent to Rolls-Royce's Derby factory where it was test run, stripped and every part subjected to careful examination and evaluation. From this study of the German engine came the design for Rolls-Royce's first aero-engine, the Hawk, from which was developed the Falcon, which powered many Bristol Fighters, and the Eagle, a twelve-cylinder water-cooled inline vee engine which was developed to produce 375 hp, and which equipped many RAF aircraft including the Vickers Vimy which made the first direct aerial crossing of the Atlantic in 1919.

The 295 hp Siddeley Deasey Jaguar fourteen-cylinder twin-row air-cooled radial, which was the world's first supercharged engine to enter production, typified the advances made in Great Britain under the stimulus of war.

In the United States the 285 hp Liberty eight-cylinder inline vee engine was another power unit which drew heavily on Mercedes design principles. Schemed and drawn during the early months of the war, it was intended to be a simple, easily produced, engine but, because of the speed with which it was conceived, it was a collection of design features from earlier power units. Nevertheless, it was redesigned and developed into a 400 hp twelve-cylinder engine of which some 18,000 were built during the last year of the war to power a number of renowned aircraft.

Possibly the most important United States engine was designed by Charles Kirkham in 1916–17; this was the 400 hp Curtiss K-12 twelve-cylinder water-cooled inline vee engine. It featured a very small frontal area; monobloc and wetsleeve construction, which allowed maximum surface contact between the sleeve, or cylinder barrel, and the cooling water to provide highly efficient engine cooling, and double overhead camshafts operating the exhaust and inlet valves. Indirectly, this engine, which had been influenced by the Hispano-Suiza design, plus the earlier Mercedes engines, was to colour the concept of inline engines for nearly 40 years.

Mercedes, BMW (Bayerische Motoren Werke) and Junkers in Germany; Fiat and Isotta-Fraschini in Italy; and Renault, Peugeot and Hispano-Suiza in France; all produced aero-engines of advanced design for their military needs and came out of the war with some highly effective and reliable power units. In 1915 Hispano-Suiza, whose name reflects the Spanish site and the Swiss engineer, Marc Birkigt, who established his first factory there, produced an exquisitely engineered yet practical 150 hp eight-cylinder water-cooled inline vee engine, the first to employ his monobloc construction, which was later developed as a geared engine to produce 220 hp. This engine was also built under licence in the United States, in Italy, and by Wolseley in England where it was known as the Viper. Hispano-Suiza also produced the 300 hp modèle 42 eight-cylinder water-cooled inline direct-drive vee engine which was, in 1917, another excellent power unit, used in some British and French aircraft for a number of years after the war.

The advances made were apparent from the power and the configuration of the engines which were installed in the British, French and Italian aircraft entered for the first postwar Schneider Trophy contest at Bournemouth in 1919. The 450 hp Napier Lion and Cosmos Jupiter were nearly three times as powerful as the Gnome and Le Rhône rotary engines of the 1914 entrants, and inline water-cooled engines predominated, the sole radial engine being the Jupiter in the Sopwith Schneider. Sadly this 'fiasco in the fog', as the 1919 contest at Bournemouth has been described, caused so many entrants to retire through poor visibility that no worthwhile comparison of engine performance or reliability could be made.

With these very substantial increases in power, however, came the problem of heat dissipation which was to bedevil the designers of Schneider contest aircraft for the ensuing twelve years. As will have been seen, the different engine configurations—rotary, radial, inline—were the result of different methods of cooling the cylinders. The Seguins' rotary design helped to overcome the problem of insufficient airflow around the cylinders of the stationary engine in slow-moving aircraft; the radial engine configuration put the heavily finned cylinders directly in the airflow behind the propeller. Other designers believed that, because of the low quality of the available fuel and the low rpm achieved by the engines, the best way to develop adequate power was to have cylinders with a large swept volume. The air-cooled radial engine, in spite of its large frontal area, had certain advantages for military aircraft in that it was more easily maintained, it had no lengthy and heavy water-cooling system which was vulnerable in combat, and the short single-crankpin crankshaft was more reliable than the long crankshafts of the early multi-cylinder inline engines, which tended to bow and whip.

It followed, therefore, that the only way to obtain streamlining and a small frontal area in an engine having large cylinders and a crankcase housing a large throw crankshaft was to place the cylinders, one behind the other, in a row. This virtually ruled out air-cooling as only the first cylinder, and possibly the second, would be cooled adequately, the airflow around the remainder being already hot as it dissipated the heat from the cylinders in front. But water-cooling meant using large radiators to dissipate heat from the cooling water, which needed to be maintained at a temperature less than 212 deg Fahrenheit (100 deg Centigrade) to prevent it boiling. The parasitic drag of the radiators was high. The large, bulky honeycomb structures generally were mounted in the nose of the aircraft, where they could face into the airflow, but on some aircraft they were moved beneath it—in the 'chin' position—or were side mounted. The drag of the radiators, their weight and that of the piping and the coolant, plus their vulnerability to damage, were the penalties of this type of engine cooling. And as engines became more powerful and generated more heat, so radiators became larger. Nevertheless, inline engines and water-cooling benefited from the experience which had been gained by the development of motor vehicle engines, and designers of high-speed aircraft were of the opinion that the advantages of a comparatively streamlined installation outweighed the penalties.

With the return to peace and something approaching normality in sport, air racing began again, replacing in some measure the immediate needs of war as a spur to aviation development and progress. As in so many other fields of aeronautical pioneering and endeavour it was a Frenchman who was first to tackle the problem of radiator drag, and to produce a practical solution. He was A. Lamblin who, in 1918, had designed a radiator of completely new configuration. Because of its external appearance it quickly earned itself the soubriquet 'lobster pot', being generally cylindrical in shape and composed of a large number of radially-mounted hollow copper fins around which the air could flow freely to cool the water circulating inside them. Lamblin's claim that his 'lobster pot' was as effective as other radiators of at least double the size was proved in laboratory tests; this stemmed from the fact that the radiating surface was around 100 times that of the projected frontal area of the radiator.

The first Schneider contest entrant to be so equipped was the French Nieuport 29-C-1 of 1919, a floatplane variant of the standard Nieuport 29 landplane racer which had been developed from a single-seat scout or fighter aeroplane. All used the Lamblin 'lobster pots'.

The remaining Trophy aspirants that year almost ran the gamut of engine-cooling methods, with radiators side-mounted, nose-mounted, nacelle-mounted with pusher propellers, and with one surviving rotary engine. While the Nieuport 29-C-1 was undoubtedly fast, even on the modest power of its 300 hp Hispano-Suiza modèle 42 engine, it was not, in the event, put to the test at Bournemouth. The 1920 Nieuport-Delage 29, which failed the contest's navigability trials, had the same Lamblin radiators.

In the United States, where there were a number of rich sponsors of air races—even if some of the contests they funded were flown over courses in Europe—the design and development of a number of racing land-planes and seaplanes was pressed ahead with much vigour and some competence. In the matter of cooling, the year 1922 was a watershed for it was then that the Lamblin radiator began to be replaced almost entirely by wing-surface radiators. Initially, the Curtiss company had in mind a method of using the wing skinning as a means of dissipating heat from the engine cooling water, and had first flown this concept on an Oriole two-seat biplane in 1921. In October 1922 the Curtiss R-6s (AS68563 and 68564) and CR-2s (A6080 and 6081) which took the first four places in the Pulitzer race were all equipped with a developed form of this skin radiator which, it was claimed at the time, permitted a 20 mph (32 km/h) increase in maximum speed.

Attempts to produce a low-drag radiator did not come to fruition in Great Britain until 1925 when a Gloster III floatplane (N195) was retrofitted with wing-surface radiators and the Supermarine S.4 was built with long-span Lamblin-type flat radiators partly recessed into the lower surface of the mainplanes. Even this latter installation created nearly 40 per cent of the total drag of the S.4. The first British racing seaplanes to have wing-surface radiators as an original design feature were the Supermarine S.5s, (N219, 220 and 221) the first of which first flew during June 1927. These aircraft also had longitudinal surface oil coolers on the sides of the fuselage. Wing and float surface radiators were used on the Gloster IVA, IVB and IV biplane racers (N222, 223 and 224) for the 1927 contest and on the Gloster VIs (N249 and N250) prepared for the penultimate contest in 1929. The combined oil cooler and oil tank on the Gloster IV, IVA and IVB formed part of the underside of the nose, while on the Gloster VI a surface oil cooler was fitted around the rear fuselage.

Almost all of the external surfaces of the Supermarine S.6 and S.6B were used to dissipate heat from the engine cooling water and oil. Newspapers of the day frequently referred to the S.6B as 'nothing more or less than a flying radiator' as the cooling surfaces were required to dissipate some 40,000 British thermal units of heat each minute to maintain normal engine running temperatures. A major problem with the oil cooling system was not only that of transferring heat from the oil cooler to the surrounding air but also that of transferring it from the oil itself to the surface of the cooler.

A major milestone in the development of aero-engines in the United States—and possibly in the world—was the flight testing in July 1918 of the evolutionary Curtiss K-12 engine. Based on the 300 hp Hispano-Suiza eight-cylinder vee engine, Kirkham embodied ideas of his own. He adopted twelve cylinders in order to obtain high power with a small frontal area, even though the demand from airframe designers at that time was for shorter engines which would adapt more readily to their concept of compact and manoeuvrable fighter aircraft. This engine employed the effective 'wet-sleeve' construction allied to a hollow monobloc crankcase containing cooling-water passages, which was, in itself, a triumph of engineering. But these features proved troublesome. The large crankcase was difficult to manufacture and to dismantle for servicing; the long crankshaft was unreliable, it tended to bow and often broke, as did the reduction gears.

Following some redesign including measures to simplify the crankcase construction, the new engine, designated C-12, was uprated to provide 427 hp. It proved more reliable but unfortunately Curtiss found no market for it. During 1920 Arthur Nutt, the company's new chief engineer, undertook another complete redesign of the engine, discarding the reduction gear to make it a direct-drive unit and derating it to produce only 405 hp. In this form and designated CD-12, it was the first Curtiss engine to pass a 50-hr running test. There followed yet another major redesign of most major components, and with the designation D-12 and an initial 375 hp power output this engine was the forerunner of a series which was to power many US military aircraft plus a number of outstandingly successful US Army and Navy racing aircraft. It helped to bring a world's speed record to the United States for the first time with an average speed of 223 mph (358·87 km/h), and powered Curtiss floatplanes to two first places, two seconds, and a fourth place, in Schneider Trophy contests in 1923, 1925 and 1926. It also powered a Macchi M.33 into third place in 1925.

The D-12 and its derivatives continued in Curtiss production until 1932, by which date a total of 1,192 had been built. It was described as a 'mechanical masterpiece', but it was also an aesthetically pleasing engine with a grace that stemmed from its simple, purposeful form. Its lines set a fashion for all high-power liquid-cooled engines until the late 1940s.

If the Curtiss D-12 was the outstanding United States inline racing engine of the 1920s, then in Great Britain the most successful engine in the Schneider series, as recorded earlier, was the Napier Lion which was used to power all but three of the British entrants in the Schneider contests from 1919 to 1929. Yet it is the Rolls-Royce R engine which is most remembered and has been most chronicled. It is true that this splendid engine played a major rôle in bringing the Trophy contests to a successful conclusion for Britain and in setting a new world speed record, but it was used only in 1929 and 1931. Even so, the most often remembered and recounted feature of the R engine was its relationship with the famed Merlin and the conjectured effect which this had on the course of the Second World War.

A Curtiss D-12 engine photographed in March 1922. This engine played a major role in the development of the high-performance aeroplane. (*Smithsonian Institution*)

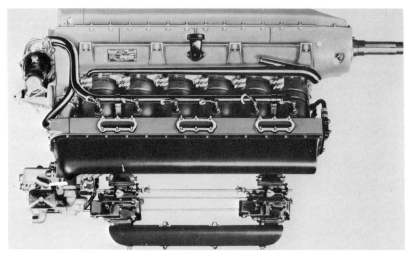

The 600 hp Packard Model 2A-1500 twelve-cylinder inverted-vee engine. An upright version was used to power the Curtiss R3C-3 in 1925. (*Smithsonian Institution*)

The 1,250 hp Packard X-2775 twenty-four cylinder engine comprised two 650 hp V-1500s mounted on a common crankcase. It was used in the Kirkham-Williams biplane of 1927 and Williams-Mercury monoplane of 1929. (*Smithsonian Institution*)

The Wright T-3A twelve-cylinder vee engine in the 650 hp category was typical of US liquid-cooled engines of the 1920s. A 680 hp example powered the Wright F2W-2 in 1924.
(*Smithsonian Institution*)

When R. J. Mitchell of Supermarine was setting about the initial design of a racing floatplane for the 1929 contest he decided that the ageing Lion had been stretched to its limit, and that a more powerful engine at the start of its development life was required. The Air Ministry asked Rolls-Royce to design and build this new engine, but the company's managing director, Basil Johnson, decided that, in spite of the success of its earlier aero-engines, there was a greater future for Rolls-Royce in the business of building fine motor-cars. However, Henry Royce took a very different view and quickly grasped the chance to produce a racing engine.

Because of the inevitable twin problems of shortage of time and money, this engine was to be based on an existing design rather than be a wholly new concept. The base engine was the H, or Buzzard, which was a comparatively new development. The Buzzard was an 825 hp twelve-cylinder liquid-cooled normally-aspirated vee engine.

The racing engine, known as the R engine, had the same stroke and bore as the Buzzard and embodied most of its moving parts. In its 1929 contest form, the R produced 1,850 hp achieved by the use of a super-charger of unusual design and pure benzole as a fuel. The supercharger air entered a forward-facing intake mounted in the vee between the two banks of cylinders. It was then led aft and down, through a trunking of gradually increased cross-sectional area, to the carburettor and thence to the supercharger which had a double-sided impeller to reduce the dia-meter. As the velocity of the air decreased in the growing area of the

262

trunking, so the pressure increased. This produced a comparatively light-weight but highly effective supercharging system. A 6:1 straight spur-type reduction gear was chosen to suit the high speed of a racing aircraft.

While the R engine retained many of the Buzzard's design features, the rocker covers, lower half of the crankcase, and reduction gear casing, were redesigned to produce a more streamlined shape and reduced frontal areas, and the front engine feet were repositioned to reduce the overall engine width.

On test Rolls-Royce experienced a number of problems, which was not altogether surprising in view of the high power output being achieved. They included loss of power, ignition difficulties as the plugs sooted up, and exhaust valves burning through and distorting. Rolls-Royce called in F. Rodwell Banks, a high-octane fuel specialist and pioneer in his field. Because of the small amount of time remaining before the contest at Calshot, Rod Banks diluted the 100 per cent benzole fuel with leaded gasoline and enabled the R engine to complete its test programme satisfactorily. The test programme consisted of the following: a 5–6 hours running-in under a light load on the water dynamometer, with a short full-throttle burst; 10 minutes full throttle to check the fuel consumption; a power curve run checking power against rpm. The engine was then stripped, checked and re-assembled, and a propeller was fitted ready for starting checks, carburettor adjustments, slow running and acceleration checks. With these all satisfactorily completed the engine was ready for delivery and installation in Mitchell's S.6.

Even then Rolls-Royce's problems with the R engine were not at an end, but in the contest it ran sweetly enough throughout, although slightly throttled back to maintain the correct temperatures.

View of the Rolls-Royce R engine showing the clean appearance of the valve rocker gear covers and the supercharger trunking of gradually increasing cross-sectional area. Note also the refined lines of the reduction gear casing and the lower crankcase. (*Rolls-Royce*)

The indecision about the British entry in the 1931 contest—which was not finally resolved until January of that year—left very little time for Rolls-Royce to increase the power of the R to the 2,350 hp which Mitchell decided would be required to give the S.6B a good chance of victory over the Italian aircraft. To keep the development costs as low as possible, Rolls-Royce undertook a number of tests by running a single-cylinder unit on one of the testbeds at Derby. The aim was to get as much power as possible through the development of valve cooling, valve and ignition timing, use of different plugs and fuels. An important feature of the 1931 R engine was the use of sodium-cooled valve stems. These valves had been developed by Sam Heron, an Englishman who had moved to the United States to work. Rod Banks obtained a set of sodium-cooled valves from a US manufacturer for test purposes and, as they proved successful in the R engine, Rolls-Royce negotiated a sub-licence from Bristol Aero-Engines—who held a British manufacturing licence for the valves—and produced the valves at Derby. Their design was modified to have sodium only in the hollow stem and not in the head, Rolls-Royce preferring to retain some 'meat' in that part of their valves.

As the weeks passed the major aim was to achieve a one-hour full-power run. During the first run the crankshaft fractured; on another occasion a connecting rod broke loose and came through the crankcase. By the end of April a 20-minute run was achieved, with 30 minutes nonstop being logged in mid-July. Just when it seemed that the magic hour-long run would be achieved on 3 August, the crankshaft broke again after 58 minutes. Eventually, after a redesign to reduce the amount of material machined off the forgings and so give greater strength, the R engine ran the hour at full throttle on 12 August. For these tests Heenan and Froude had installed a special water dynomometer designed to prevent blade erosion through cavitation and boiling. It had its own water supply tank to avoid the problem of changes in pressure experienced with the local Corporation supply system.

There were problems with recirculation of engine exhaust fumes through the test house which raised the engine running temperature by 10 deg C and also affected the testers. A 350 hp Kestrel engine mounted on a special stand drove a fan to blow air through the building; two more electrically-driven fans in the roof blew air onto the crankcase and small air jets led to the plugs located near the exhaust stubs.

Modifications to the 1929 R engine design including new connecting rods, provision of a larger sump and redesigned piston scraper-rings. This last improvement reduced the 112 gal (509 litres) per hour oil consumption of the test engine to a mere 14 gal (63·6 litres) per hour in the racing engine. Although these were some of the major design changes, in fact almost every component part of the engine right down to the bolts and nuts received careful scrutiny.

Although the time available to Rolls-Royce to create almost a new engine had been very limited and the changes made had been, in many cases, only expedients, the end product was of a sufficiently high engineering standard and reliability to enable the S.6B to push the Trophy-winning speed in the 1931 contest to 340·08 mph (547·297 km/h), while flying at only 97 per cent full throttle to avoid overheating.

It had become accepted that after a contest the RAF High Speed Flight made an attempt on the World Speed Record while the pilots and equipment were all at concert pitch. Thus Flt Lieut G. H. Stainforth, who had opted to make the attempt rather than make the contest fly-over, raised the record to 379·05 mph (610·02 km/h). But E. W. Hives, who was manager of Rolls-Royce experimental department, was not wholly satisfied and wanted to push this figure to 400 mph (643·72 km/h) or more . . . 'not 399·9 mph'. The Air Ministry was keen to oust the Flight from Calshot and hand back the station to the flying-boat squadron, No. 201, which had vacated it, but Sir Henry Royce took the lead in persuading the Ministry to stay its hand long enough for this final all-out attempt to be made.

There was no time to make mechanical improvements or changes to the R engine to produce even more power; the only measure which could be taken was to alter the fuel. Accordingly, Rod Banks' skill was in demand again and he proposed the use of a high alcohol-content fuel mixture allied to an increased supercharger gear ratio. With this fairly simple mechanical change and the Banks' 'cocktail', the engine produced 2,800 hp—but the cylinder holding-down bolts began to fail! When the original ratio was restored the engine provided some 2,600 hp and all was well. The final fuel mix for the 'sprint' engine enabled Stainforth in the S.6B S1595 to become the first man to fly at more than 400 mph over a measured distance when he established a new record of 407·5 mph (655·79 km/h).

With the end of the Schneider contests all further development on the R engines ceased, with the exception of some work to prepare them for installation in Sir Henry Segrave's high-speed boat *Miss England*, and in *Thunderbolt*, Capt George Eyston's land speed record-breaking car.

During 1915 the Brazil Straker Company, car manufacturers at Fish-ponds, Bristol, entered the aero-engine business. Its chief engineer was A. H. R. (later Sir Roy) Fedden and in 1917 the company won an order for 200 Mercury fourteen-cylinder air-cooled engines in which the cylinders were disposed along a two-turn helix, giving it almost a twin-row appearance. Later that year Brazil Straker was bought out by the Cosmos Engineering Company for whom Fedden and L. F. G. Butler, the chief designer, designed the 450 hp Jupiter nine-cylinder air-cooled direct-drive normally-aspirated single-row radial engine.

This was the engine chosen for the Sopwith Schneider G-EAKI for the 1920 contest, by which time Fedden had brought the Jupiter to a quite advanced stage of development. However, his programme of work on the Jupiter was halted abruptly when Cosmos went into liquidation during that year and was bought by Bristol Aeroplane Company. This engine was later built in very large quantities for very many types of British and foreign aircraft. It served as the basis for a series of Bristol radial engines, including the Mercury series of nine-cylinder air-cooled radial engines of which an 860 hp geared and supercharged unit powered the Short-Bristow Crusader (N226) built as a participant for the 1927 contest.

As with so many engines in Schneider contest aircraft, the Mercury was subject to carburetion problems, which, allied to shortcomings in the gas starting and ignition systems, made the pre-contest trials difficult and hazardous. In addition, during test-stand running of the Mercury at Bristol's Patchway factory, the crankshaft had been found to be too light in construction and the Jupiter III's crankshaft was substituted. Before the engine was fitted in the Crusader airframe, final running checks on the carburetion system were made at the RAE Farnborough.

A Bristol Mercury nine-cylinder radial of the type which powered the Short-Bristow Crusader. (*Rolls-Royce*)

The destruction of the Crusader in a pre-contest crash prevented any assessment of the Mercury's performance under the pressure of contest conditions.

In Italy the names of two engine manufacturers always will be associated with that country's Schneider Trophy seaplanes; La Fabbrica Automobili Isotta-Fraschini and Fabbrica Italiana Automobili Torino, the latter to become renowned as Fiat.

Both were incorporated during 1898, Isotta-Fraschini in Milan where, as its name implies, it was principally interested in the manufacture of motorcars, and internal combustion engines. Using Giustino Cattaneo's designs, production of aero-engines began in about 1908 and before the outbreak of war in 1914 Isotta-Fraschini engines were being used in Italian seaplanes, airships and landplanes. During the war the company produced some 5,000 engines and, it is recorded, 'nearly all the aero-

Close-up of the Isotta-Fraschini Asso engine at full throttle in a Macchi M.67. Note the oil coolers under the nose and along the fuselage sides. (*RAF Museum*)

engines made in Italy were under Isotta-Fraschini licence'. The majority of Macchi's seventeen seaplane types, between the L.1 of 1915 and the M.39 of 1926, were powered by this company's products, initially the V.4 and V.6 water-cooled inline engines and later the Asso with powers of between 150 and 260 hp. Yet for its Schneider contest floatplanes Macchi only once used an Isotta-Fraschini engine; this was the big 1,800 hp Asso 2-800 eighteen-cylinder water-cooled broad-arrow unit which equipped the fairly unsuccessful M.67s of 1929. However, an Isotta-Fraschini V.6 engine powered Jannello's S.13 in the 1919 contest; this was a 250 hp six-cylinder vertical inline engine which had been specifically produced, piece by piece with watch-like precision, and tuned for the contest.

Fiat, which was a major competitor of Isotta-Fraschini, was formed at Turin for the same express purpose as that company. While its interests were wide, they encompassed internal combustion engines, and the design and production of aero-engines began in 1908. Its automobile activities had brought Fiat in close contact with the products of the Mercedes company in Germany, and it was on this company's engines that Fiat based its early designs like the A.10 and 12. As recorded on page 11, the very large 650 hp twelve-cylinder A.14 was fitted in the M.19 for the 1921 contest, but a broken crankshaft almost certainly cost it the Trophy that year.

The British victory in 1922 and, more importantly, that by the United States in 1923, was a great spur to engine development in Italy. General Guidoni, the Government director of aircraft production, bought two Curtiss D-12 engines from the USA, and shipped them to Italy where

267

This 1,000 hp Fiat AS.3 engine was developed by Tranquillo Zerbi from the very successful AS.2, but was described as 'treacherous' when it forced both Macchi M.52s to retire before completing two laps of the 1927 contest course at Venice. (*Fiat Centro Storico*)

they were stripped, examined and test run after re-assembly. But in spite of his efforts the Italian manufacturers did not produce an indigenous high performance racing engine in time to power aircraft for the contest in 1925; instead the well worn D-12s were pressed into service yet again in the M.33.

Meanwhile, Tranquillo Zerbi, who had joined Fiat in 1919 and had spent a good deal of time developing the A.14, had used the old D-12 and Lion engines as design bases for his 400 hp A.20 from which he created the larger A.24. This latter engine was the plateau from which he began the design of the AS.2, a new twelve-cylinder direct-drive vee racing engine. Zerbi intended that it should produce some 800 hp and on a test stand the first engine exceeded this by more than ten per cent. When fitted in the M.39s for the 1926 contest, two AS.2s were high-compression engines and the third was a lower-compression engine in the M.39 charged with finishing the course at any cost.

The AS.3 engine, basically an AS.2 with increased bore, stroke, capacity, and compression ratio, was a major achievement for Fiat and Zerbi for he increased the power output by 220 hp, to reach 1,020 hp, but reduced the frontal area by more than two square feet. This output was helped by the use of a special fuel mixed from petrol, benzine and alcohol, and a new design of piston engineered in magnesium. The pressures of too little time and money to give the AS.3 the required amount of development test running resulted in the failure of the two high-compression engines in the contest. These failures only served to stimulate Zerbi for, almost Phoenix-like, from them came the 1,000 hp AS.5, a lightweight engine weighing only 340 grammes (12 ounces) for every horse power it delivered, giving it the best power-to-weight ratio of any racing engine then built.

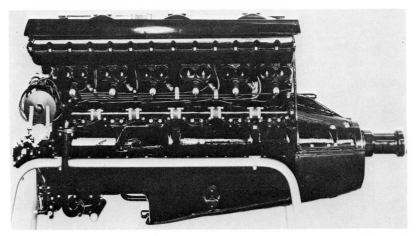

Zerbi pared away every excess ounce of metal in his design for the lightweight Fiat AS.5 which powered the Fiat C.29 floatplane. Only the later Rolls-Royce R and Fiat AS.6 engines had better power-to-weight ratios than the AS.5's, 0.34 kg/hp (0.77 lb/hp). (*Fiat Centro Storico*)

It was the giant AS.6, produced by bolting two AS.5s together in tandem on a common crankcase but driving two crankshafts and two separate co-axial propeller shafts, which ultimately helped Italy to secure for all time the world's speed record for floatplanes. This engine eventually was developed to produce 3,000 hp, achieved in part by raising the compression to more than 7:1 and by supercharging, the rear AS.5 having a centrifugal compressor with a down-draught intake to supercharge both halves of the power unit. Although physically the AS.6 was composed of two separate engines with the throttle linkage being the only mechanical link between them, Zerbi conceived the AS.6 as a single 50-litre unit.

Of Zerbi's design ingenuity and skill there was no doubt, the range of his engines which preceeded the AS.6 was testimony to this; there was not, however, the same levels of thoroughness in his company's test procedures which were to be found in those of other manufacturers, such as Rolls-Royce. As a consequence, the first series of bench tests were not sufficiently searching or representative of in-flight conditions and the apparently satisfactory results obtained were misleading in the extreme. Installed in the MC.72, the AS.6 performed badly, with the carburetion system being the principal problem; but before it could be pinpointed finally and cured, explosions in the carburettor air intake due to severe backfiring had caused two pilots to be killed in crashes, one immediately following an attempt by the pilot to demonstrate, audibly, his difficulties in engine handling by overflying his base and a gathering of Fiat and Macchi engineers. Investigations into the cause of the second crash revealed that the engine had backfired into the carburettor air intake and

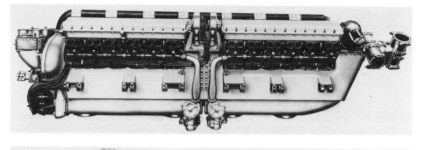

Basically two Fiat AS.5s bolted together, the giant twenty-four-cylinder AS.6 was 3·365 m (11 ft) long. Note the six rubber-bushed engine-mounting brackets along the crankcase, the air-intake duct between the cylinder banks, and the multiplicity of plug leads. (*Fiat Centro Storico*)

set fire to the gravity fuel tank, just behind it, which exploded, completely destroying the aircraft as it smashed into a low hill.

Apart from these carburetion problems Zerbi and his team were unable to balance the running speed of the two sections of the AS.6 because the rear one, driving the supercharger, produced less power for the propeller; in consequence the two propellers turned at different speeds if the blade pitch, which was adjustable, was not set at the correct angle.

Yet another snag was overheating and Mario Castoldi added more surface radiators to the aircraft in an effort to overcome this.

When the Schneider contests had ended and Italy decided to attempt to establish a new speed record, Zerbi invited Rod Banks, the British fuel expert, to help solve these difficulties. In Italy he quickly discovered that the engine had not been ground tested in conditions simulating those in the air.

While Zerbi had used Rolls-Royce's ram air intake and divergent duct to the supercharger's inlet side on the engine in the MC.72, he had not tested it on the bench. Thus, in the air, with the ram increasing with speed, the pressure differential across the carburettor was reduced below

270

that of anything experienced on the ground. In consequence the fuel/air mixture was weakened, causing severe backfiring in the induction pipe which was some 3 m (10 ft) long.

Banks persuaded Fiat to instal an engine-driven blower in the test house to provide ram air to the AS.6 to simulate in-flight conditions, and to undertake a programme of tests to include an hour's full-throttle run and a cyclic test to represent six runs up and down the three-kilometre speed course. With these completed and the engine installed in the MC.72, no further trouble was experienced and in 1933 and 1934 the MC.72 set world speed records of 682·078 km/h (423·822 mph) and 709·209 km/h (440·681 mph) respectively.

In 1921 Fiat had taken over the old Ansaldo-San Giorgio engine company, which had decided to cease aero-engine production, but before its demise it had produced the 550 hp 4E-28 twelve-cylinder water-cooled direct-drive vee engine for the S.12 flying-boat in the 1920 contest at Venice and the 475 hp variant for the S.21 of 1921.

The Società Piemontese Automobili, with a Turin factory, had built a number of wartime engines, and in 1922 the S.50 MVT floatplane was fitted with an SPA 230 hp six-cylinder water-cooled direct-drive inline engine. Although the S.50 was selected to represent Italy in the contest that year, it crashed during pre-contest trials. As recorded elsewhere in this book, the great efforts and achievements of the manufacturers of Schneider Trophy aircraft produced results and benefits which differed between companies and between nations, but it was in the field of aero-engine design development and production that most benefits accrued to those who best applied the knowledge, dearly won, through participation in the contests.

271

# The Rewards

Inevitably, both before and after each of the contests, the question was asked unceasingly 'What value is there in participating?'

In Britain many very senior people in the Government, the Royal Air Force and the aircraft industry were implacably opposed to British participation in the contest. In December 1925 Air Chief Marshal Sir Hugh Trenchard, Chief of the Air Staff, while ready to accept what benefits would accrue from the development of high-performance aircraft for the contests, said that neither Service pilots nor aircraft should fly in private races. Yet he went ahead and ordered the Supermarine and Gloster companies to produce special aircraft for a British team to fly. These opinions were shared by people in other countries too. Some remained obdurate in their beliefs; others changed their minds. Trenchard appeared to be sticking to his earlier views when, in 1929, he said that, from a Service point of view, he saw no advantage in the contest; then vacillation set in and he added '. . . although it may have been of benefit in the past'. There was, of course, a vast body of opinion among equally senior people that the Schneider contests were a vital part of the nation's overall aviation endeavour. They, too, remained obdurate in their opinion.

Of such a great and thrilling enterprise on so vast a canvas, it may have seemed invidious to seek for more reward than that of winning the Trophy, of participating in a great international sporting event, or of helping to create the unique spectacle of beautiful seaplanes being flown fast and low, over water, in pursuit of an equally handsome piece of silver statuary. But even in those far off and tranquil days between the wars, investments of any kind were required to return a dividend in some form. The investment in the Schneider contests by the participating nations and companies was very substantial.

It is impossible to measure the total value of the material content, the man-hours, the amount of physical effort or skill, and equally immeasurable must be the many intangible benefits which emanated from this grand aero-maritime adventure.

Rewards there certainly were; without them the contests would have ceased much earlier than they did. Each nation approached participation from a slightly different standpoint, each was differently motivated. Like all forms of air racing and competitive flying of that era, the Schneider contests ultimately were recognized as unique and valuable proving grounds for high-performance aeroplanes and their equipment. This was apparent in the United States where the battle between the Army Air Service and the Navy Bureau of Aeronautics created a climate in which development of this type of aeroplane could flourish—at a price. Thus to suit contemporary political needs military prototypes were passed off as racing aeroplanes—and vice versa, for it was necessary to resort to subterfuges of this kind to get funds approved for the development of racing aircraft, however much they may have added pace to the advancement of aircraft engineering.

When the United States finally decided in 1927 that the rewards would not match the investment, it pulled out to concentrate on the development of conventional transport landplanes rather than pursue Jacques Schneider's aims and hopes of developing advanced transport seaplanes. In the shrewd eyes of the Secretary of the Navy Department and of the chiefs of the Army Aviation Department, enough was enough. Yet the United States left the Schneider arena more technically enriched than when it had entered it only four years previously.

The reasons for Italy's long-sustained attempts to become the permanent holder of the Trophy are legion, beginning with pure sporting instincts, which grew into a passionate desire to wipe out the memory of the mistake in the 1919 contest which cost Italy the Coppa Schneider, and finally the need for Fascism to prove itself superior to all comers in the air. So keen was Italian aviation to win that its facilities, planning and preparations were far in excess of those of any other country. It seemed that securing the Trophy was all the reward which was sought and that the advancement of aviation technology was secondary. Nevertheless, apart from prestige, the Macchi, Fiat and Savoia companies drew much benefit from creating specialized high-performance aeroplanes. An interesting sidelight is that more than half a century after the last Schneider contest, Aeronautica Macchi, SIAI Marchetti and Fiat are still among the major aviation companies in Italy.

For Great Britain, a maritime nation with 'an Empire on which the sun never set', participation in the Schneider contests was part of a natural process of advancing its aviation development, and it continued to believe that there were both technical and commercial benefits to be had. Eventually, stubborn persistence allied to great feats of engineering and flying skill paid the ultimate dividend, so important in an increasingly competitive world.

France can hardly be recognized as a major contender for the Trophy. After launching the whole series and both winning and taking second place in the first contest, no other French aircraft completed the course in any of the five contests in which they entered. In 1909 France was host to the world's first international air race and was deeply devoted to promoting competitive flying, so that competing in the new contest for seaplanes was a natural process. Thus the Schneider Trophy, in spite of being French, was just another prize, and perhaps France's initial failure to assess the importance of the contest was a major setback to its aviation aspirations. In later years, despite some splendid engineering achievements by the Société des Avions Bernard, the French challenge, if it ever existed, faded away.

273

So what were the rewards which resulted from each country's participation? In general terms, the four main competing nations all gained the same things in different measure; it was the use to which they put these results—whatever they were—which made the investment of value or not.

In the event it was in the field of military aviation that the rewards were applied. The easiest to quantify was the comparatively rapid development of reliable high-power and efficient aero-engines. The first Gnome rotary engines of 1913 had specific weights of about 2·7 lb/horse power (1·2 kg/hp); by 1931 this had become 0·61 lb/ horse power (0·27 kg/hp), in the Rolls-Royce R engine, the lowest of any Schneider engine. During the same period specific power jumped from around 5 hp/litre in the rotaries to 75 hp/litre in the R engine, the highest of any Schneider engine. These improvements, particularly in later years, were produced by using special fuel mixtures for more efficient combustion, at the elevated brake mean effective pressures in the cylinders, by supercharging to obtain high power at low-level, and the use of special materials, ignition and combustion system equipment. All this was allied to a steady reduction in engine frontal area.

Arthur A. Rubbra, CBE, BSC, CEng, FRAeS, FIMechE, who joined Rolls-Royce Experimental Department in 1925 and was chief designer during 1940–44 and technical director from 1954 until 1966, said: 'I think there are a number of areas where the development of the Merlin was helped by the work done on the R engine, although the target of completion of an hour's run in one piece at full output was rather different from that of completing the official Service type test. For this reason, the satisfactory solution of such troubles by this method does not always read across to those met with in service life.

However, there is no doubt that such running at high output for short duration does help considerably in pin-pointing quickly the likely trouble spots and was used extensively and successfully as a general test procedure in the development of the Merlin'.

Mr Rubbra went on to say that among the areas of R engine development which benefited the Merlin were the development of the mechanical parts, the sodium-cooled exhaust valves, the sparking plugs to withstand the combustion conditions at high boost pressures, and the use of exhaust gas discharge to augment total thrust. This last feature was subsequently widely adopted on Merlin-powered British and Allied aircraft.

Ignoring the engines used before the First World War, the development effort stemming from the need to create engines for Schneider Trophy aircraft can be said to have increased, by three times, the power developed per lb of engine weight; by four times, the power developed per unit volume; and by five times the power per unit of frontal area. It is almost impossible to believe that, but for the spur of competition, this work would have advanced as quickly as it did. After Great Britain had won the last contest in September 1931, a very critical letter regarding the worth of the Schneider contests appeared in *The Daily Telegraph*. It was answered at length by Arthur F. Sidgreaves, then managing director of Rolls-Royce. He wrote, 'As a result of the test this year, all main components of these engines have undergone a definite improvement and, in consequence, the life of the standard engine in service will be much longer than it would otherwise have been. The second chief advantage is the amount of information obtained in the matter of design of such components as superchargers. Valuable lessons have been learned, too, in the reduction of wind resistance. It is not too much to say that the research for the Schneider Trophy over the past two years is what our aero-engine department would otherwise have taken six to ten years to learn'. In other words, it could have been 1941 before this wealth of information was available to Rolls-Royce. By then it would have been too late.

Of the four main competing nations, Great Britain capitalized upon this great technical and engineering achievement to most effect. Italy soon abandoned the development of liquid-cooled inline engines for use in military aircraft and in 1933–34 turned to air-cooled radial engines instead. Only a handful of Italian aeroplanes which operated in the Second World War had anything but this type of engine, and two of the inline-engined types had German-built power units. The United States' financial crisis in the mid-thirties, allied to its political stance of isolation from Europe, plus the rivalry which continued to grow between its Army and Navy air arms, all contributed to the fact that much of the spin-off benefit from Curtiss' Schneider contest achievements lay dormant. France, which soon fell by the wayside in the contests, drew only limited benefit from whatever engine development it undertook. Hispano-Suiza concentrated on liquid-cooled engines, which rarely reached the peaks of design and performance achievement attained by the earlier models.

Happily, although some Rolls-Royce engineers believed that the company's intensive work on the R engine had delayed progress on the more modest Kestrel—which was being widely adopted for British military aircraft—the later PV.12, a private venture liquid-cooled inline engine which became the renowned Merlin, certainly gained much from the big racing engine's development programme. This had shown the way in which high anti-knock fuels and supercharging could be employed to produce more from a given cylinder capacity and without markedly increasing the size or weight of the engine.

One of the early post-Schneider Trophy era benefits was the manner in which the experience and expertise of Rodwell Banks, the British fuels expert who had formulated these exotic fuel mixtures for the R engine, was invited to solve some development problems on Italy's new Fiat AS.6 engine. So successful was he and the Fiat engineering team that an MC.72 floatplane powered by the AS.6 established a world speed record in 1933, attaining 432·822 mph. A year later this same aircraft raised this record to 440·681 mph. Much later, during 1944, when the German V1 flying bombs were threatening to swamp Britain's air defences and outpace the RAF's Spitfires and Tempests, the Royal Aircraft Establishment developed a similarly-based fuel to give these aircraft a vital extra 30 mph (48 km/h) at sea-level.

Of the engine-associated systems, liquid cooling was the one which became most highly developed. From the effective but drag producing Lamblin-type radiators Curtiss moved quickly during 1922 to produce the first minimum-drag wing-surface radiators. This type of radiator of various designs subsequently was used almost universally on Schneider contest aircraft—with a few notable exceptions—but because of its long-term unreliability and its complexity plus its potential vulnerability to battle damage, its use was confined to these and other specialized racing aeroplanes.

Similarly, the advance of fuel system design was slow, occasioned by the few and simple demands made upon it during the limited duration contest flights made at low levels.

Any benefits from these development programmes was, therefore, small, but there was a direct read-across to the, admittedly short, development history of the Rolls-Royce Goshawk evaporative-cooled in-line engine and its installation in a number of fighters to meet specification F.7/30, which employed wing surface condensers. Strangely, on the question of vulnerability to damage there was a body of authoritative opinion which said that the loss of steam from the condenser resulting from bullet strikes would enable the engine to run longer than with loss of liquid coolant from a radiator.

One final long-term beneficial result from Britain's Schneider Trophy investment was the centrifugal compressor of Frank Whittle's W.1 turbo-jet engine of 1938, which was reputed to have been based on the unit used in the R engine's superchargers.

Curtiss again led the field with the introduction of the Reed metal-bladed propeller with thin blade sections. These, in one step, overcame the fundamental weaknesses of the conventional wooden propeller—the strong but thick sections which caused compressibility losses and had low overall efficiency at high speed and had low resistance to water damage. By 1925 all Schneider contest aircraft had metal propellers; later units produced in Italy had ground-adjustable-pitch blades. But these thin blades set at very coarse pitch had shortcomings at take-off where they provided low thrust, as the blades were partially stalled and their efficiency correspondingly low. The Italian coaxial counter-rotating propellers on the AS.6-powered MC.72 was another quantum jump forward, overcoming torque reaction, enabling smaller floats to be used and providing high thrust at take-off.

Turning to advances in airframe design during the eighteen years of the Schneider series, these were as dramatic as that of the engines. From the wood, wire and fabric structures of 1913, airframe construction moved rapidly to wood and later to metal monocoque structures, machined metal spars, metal clad mainplanes and floats. Airframe configuration initially moved backward from the monoplane to the biplane, before advancing again with the Italian and British re-introduction of the monoplane in the 1925 contest.

Perhaps the most significant developments came with the refinements in aerodynamic design which were aimed principally at increasing speed. Reduction of drag was achieved by decreasing the frontal area, the wetted area and the engine installation drag. The contests' fiercely competitive element stimulated great progress in the steady reduction in parasite area, from the 13 sq ft (1·2 sq m) of the 1922 Sea Lion II down to the 3·4 sq ft (0·31 sq m) of the S.5 in 1927.

Streamlining became almost an exact science in design offices on both sides of the Atlantic and was practiced assiduously, particularly in biplane configurations, and this experience paid great dividends in the creation processes of military aircraft.

As the design of the Schneider aircraft advanced up the speed scale under the twin influences of increased engine power and aerodynamic refinement, so did wing loading creep ever upwards until in the MC.72 it reached the alarmingly high figure of 41 lb/sq ft (201 kg/sq m). As a comparison the figure for the Spitfire I of 1938 was 25 lb/sq ft (122 kg/sq m) and 41 lb/sq ft for the Meteor 4 of 1945. This increase in wing loading inevitably resulted in much higher take-off and alighting speeds, but only the S.4 was fitted with flaps to help reduce these. Certainly a comparatively small number of pilots in each competing country learned how to handle their aircraft in these flight regimes, but it is doubtful whether their experience was of general benefit.

Flying these often temperamental racing machines was not always easy as their handling characteristics often differed from any other type of aircraft. Almost without exception the floatplanes had only marginal directional stability, which required them to be equipped with a variable gear-ratio control system for the rudder. None of the Schneider Trophy aircraft had ailerons with aerodynamic balance and pilots were forced to accept quite high lateral stick forces. However, during the contest the aircraft flew either straight and level between the turning points or rounded the pylons at a constant height and acceleration of some 4g, and so these stick forces were acceptable. In contrast, longitudinal stick forces were reputed to be light and these contrasting characteristics must have made the handling of the floatplanes quite difficult for the less experienced pilots.

In view of the comparatively few types of military or civil floatplanes which were produced subsequently, they could have benefited only marginally from data provided by flight trials of the Schneider aircraft. In the same way that the United States' experience with its Curtiss racing aircraft influenced and benefited the military pursuit aircraft of the Army and Navy during the 1920s and early 1930s, so Great Britain's development of the victorious Supermarine floatplanes and their Rolls-Royce engines led on to even greater and more important glory with their contribution to the creative processes of the Spitfire and the Merlin. Not that the benefits derived from the production and operation of the S.4, S.5, S.6 and S.6B passed in one giant leap to Reginald Mitchell's drawing board, for he schemed a variety of projects to meet Air Ministry specification F.5/34. Rather did they bridge the design gap by way of the Supermarine Type 224, built to meet the requirements of specification F.7/30, and a number of design projects which preceded the Type 300 which became the immortal Spitfire. Similarly, the PV.12, a private venture engine which became known as the Merlin, was created by evolution from its illustrious forebears, the R racing engines.

For Italy, its decision to opt out of inline engine development was disastrous for when Mario Castoldi was seeking to improve his well-proved radial-engined Macchi C.200 single-seat fighter in 1939, he was forced to rely on stuttering deliveries of German-built Daimler-Benz DB.601 inline engines for the C.202.

Without doubt, the greatest and most traceable dividends from any country's Schneider contest investment were the Merlin-powered Spitfires which, with the similarly engined Hawker Hurricanes, played an early and absolutely vital rôle in the defence of the British Isles during the summer of 1940. Without the stimulus of the regular Schneider Trophy contests it is most unlikely that this airframe/engine combination would have been developed in time.

Some 30 years after the Battle of Britain, Sir George Edwards, then chairman and managing director of British Aircraft Corporation, wrote, 'If the industry had been limited, during these inter-war years, to design studies alone and had not been able to translate ideas into hardware by actually building aeroplanes, it is certain that such successful fighters as the Spitfire and Hurricane would not have emerged.'

# The Results

The following tables give basic information about the results of each of the twelve Schneider Trophy contests, the entrants which reached the starting and finishing lines and those which fell by the wayside en route between the two. Other data help to provide a general comparative picture of the contests.

Maurice Prévost, pilot of the winning Deperdussin in 1913, is pictured with his mother and the aircraft's designer Louis Béchereau. (*Musée de l'Air*)

# First Contest, at Monaco — 16 April, 1913

Course: 28 laps of 10 km left-hand circuit round four-leg course, with start and finish off Monaco
Weather: Bright sun, light southwest breeze, water calm

| Aircraft | Engine | Pilot | Nationality | Contest number | Start order | Final placing | Average speed |
|---|---|---|---|---|---|---|---|
| Deperdussin | 160 hp Gnome | Maurice Prévost | France | 19 | 1 | 1 | 73·6 km/h* (45·75 mph) |
| Morane-Saulnier | 80 hp Gnome | Roland Garros | France | 2 | 2 | 2 | About 92 km/h (57 mph) |
| Nieuport | 100 hp Gnome | Gabriel Espanet | France | 6 | 3 | Retired on lap 8 | — |
| Nieuport | 100 hp Gnome | Charles Weymann | USA | 5 | 4 | Retired on lap 25 | — |

* This includes time spent on surface after incorrect finish. Average would have been 98·1 km/h (60·95 mph).

# Second Contest, at Monaco — 20 April, 1914

Course: 28 laps of 10 km left-hand circuit round four-leg course, with start and finish off Monaco
Weather: Cloudy-bright, freshening southwest breeze, water rippled

| Aircraft | Engine | Pilot | Nationality | Contest number | Start order | Final placing | Average speed |
|---|---|---|---|---|---|---|---|
| Nieuport | 160 hp Gnome | Pierre Levasseur | France | 6 | 1 | Retired on lap 18 | — |
| Nieuport | 160 hp Gnome | Gabriel Espanet | France | 5 | 2 | Retired on lap 17 | — |
| FBA | 100 hp Gnome Monosoupape | Ernest Burri | Switzerland | 7 | 3 | 2 | 82·35 km/h (51·17 mph) |
| Tabloid | 100 hp Gnome Monosoupape | Howard Pixton | Great Britain | 3 | 4 | 1 | 139·66 km/h (86·78 mph) |
| Deperdussin | 160 hp Le Rhône | Lord Carbery | Great Britain | — | 5 | Retired on lap 3 | — |
| Deperdussin | 200 hp Gnome | Maurice Prévost | France | — | 6 | — | — |

# Third Contest, at Bournemouth — 10 September, 1919

Course: Ten laps of 20 nautical miles left-hand circuit round three-leg course, with start and finish off Bournemouth

Weather: Thick sea fog, no wind, flat calm sea

| Aircraft | Engine | Pilot | Nationality | Contest number | Start order | Final placing |
|---|---|---|---|---|---|---|
| Fairey III (G-EALQ) | 450 hp Napier Lion | Vincent Nicholl | Great Britain | 1 | 1 | Retired on lap 1 |
| Supermarine Sea Lion I (G-EALP) | 450 hp Napier Lion | Basil Hobbs | Great Britain | 5 | 2 | Crashed on lap 1 |
| Sopwith Schneider (G-EAKI) | 450 hp Cosmos Jupiter | Harry Hawker | Great Britain | 3 | 3 | Retired on lap 1 |
| Savoia S.13 | 250 hp Isotta-Fraschini | Guido Jannello | Italy | 7 | 4 | —* |

* Jannello completed 11 laps flying in fog, but mistook position of first turning point, turned at reserve marker boat instead of at correct point in Swanage Bay, and was disqualified. Contest was declared void.

## Fourth Contest, at Venice — 20 September, 1920

Course: Ten laps of 37·117 km left-hand circuit round three-leg course, with start and finish at San Andrea naval air station
Weather: Strong northeast wind, cloudy and rough water

| Aircraft | Engine | Pilot | Nationality | Contest number | Start order | Final placing | Average speed |
|---|---|---|---|---|---|---|---|
| Savoia S.12 (3011) | 550 hp Ansaldo 4E | Luigi Bologna | Italy | 7 | 1 | 1 | 172·561 km/h (107·224 mph) |

## Fifth Contest, at Venice — 11 August, 1921

Course: 16 laps of 24·6 km left-hand circuit round three-leg course, with start and finish off Excelsior Hotel, Venice Lido
Weather: Sunny, fresh breeze, water rippled

| Aircraft | Engine | Pilot | Nationality | Contest number | Start order | Final placing | Average speed |
|---|---|---|---|---|---|---|---|
| Macchi M.7 | 250 hp Isotta-Fraschini | Giovanni de Briganti | Italy | 1 | 1 | 1 | 189·677 km/h (117·859 mph) |
| Macchi M.19 (3098) | 650 hp Fiat A.14 | Arturo Zanetti* | Italy | 4 | 2 | Retired on lap 12 | — |
| Macchi M.7 | 250 hp Isotta-Fraschini | Piero Corgnolino | Italy | 14 | 3 | Retired on lap 16 | — |

* M.19 was the only aircraft to compete in a Schneider contest with a two-man crew. The mechanic was named Pedetti.

## Sixth Contest, at Naples — 12 August, 1922

Course:  13 laps of 28·5 km left-hand circuit round three-leg course, with start and finish off Naples
Weather: Brilliant sunshine, clear skies, light breeze, water calm

| Aircraft | Engine | Pilot | Nationality | Contest number | Start order | Final placing | Average speed |
|---|---|---|---|---|---|---|---|
| Supermarine Sea Lion II (G-EBAH) | 450 hp Napier Lion | Henri Biard | Great Britain | 14 | 1 | 1 | 234·516 km/h (145·721 mph) |
| Macchi M.7 (I-BAFV) | 260 hp Isotta-Fraschini | Piero Corgnolino | Italy | 10 | 2 | 4 | 199·607 km/h (124·029 mph) |
| Macchi M.17 (I-BAHG) | 260 hp Isotta-Fraschini | Arturo Zanetti | Italy | 9 | 3 | 3 | 213·63 km/h (132·75 mph) |
| Savoia S.51 (I-BAIU) | 300 hp Hispano-Suiza | Alessandro Passaleva | Italy | 8 | 4 | 2 | 230·93 km/h (143·5 mph) |

## Seventh Contest, at Cowes, Isle of Wight — 28 September, 1923

Course: Five laps of 37·2 nautical miles left-hand circuit round three-leg course, with start and finish off Cowes*
Weather: Bright sunshine, fresh southwest wind, water calm

| Aircraft | Engine | Pilot | Nationality | Contest number | Start order | Final placing | Average speed |
|---|---|---|---|---|---|---|---|
| Curtiss CR-3 (A6080) | 465 hp Curtiss D-12 | Lieut Rutledge Irvine | USA | 3 | 1 | 2 | 278·97 km/h (173·35 mph) |
| Curtiss CR-3 (A6081) | 465 hp Curtiss D-12 | Lieut David Rittenhouse | USA | 4 | 2 | 1 | 285·457 km/h (177·374 mph) |
| Supermarine Sea Lion III (G-EBAH) | 525 hp Napier Lion III | Henri Biard | Great Britain | 7 | 3 | 3 | 252·93 km/h (157·17 mph) |
| CAMS 38 (F-ESFD) | 360 hp Hispano-Suiza modèle 42 | Lieut de Vaisseau Maurice Hurel | France | 9 | 4 | Retired on lap 2 | — |

* The first leg of this course, eastward from the Cowes starting line to the first turn round a large white cross at Selsey on the mainland, was the longest in the entire contest series. This contest also was flown over the smallest number of laps.

285

## Eighth Contest, at Baltimore — 26 October, 1925

Course: Seven laps of 50 km left-hand circuit round three-leg course with start and finish off Bay Shore Park
Weather: Bright sunshine, fresh south-southwest wind, water choppy

| Aircraft | Engine | Pilot | Nationality | Contest number | Start order | Final placing | Average speed |
|---|---|---|---|---|---|---|---|
| Curtiss R3C-2 (A7054) | 565 hp Curtiss V-1400 | Lieut James Doolittle | USA | 3 | 1 | 1 | 374·274 km/h (232·562 mph) |
| Gloster IIIA (N194) | 700 hp Napier Lion VII | Hubert Broad | Great Britain | 5 | 2 | 2 | 320·53 km/h (199·17 mph) |
| Curtiss R3C-2 (A6979) | 565 hp Curtiss V-1400 | Lieut George Cuddihy | USA | 2 | 3 | Retired on lap 7 | — |
| Curtiss R3C-2 (A6978) | 565 hp Curtiss V-1400 | Lieut Ralph Ofstie | USA | 1 | 4 | Retired on lap 6 | — |
| Macchi M.33 (MM.49) | 500 hp Curtiss D-12A | Giovanni de Briganti | Italy | 7 | 5 | 3 | 271·08 km/h (168·44 mph) |

# Ninth Contest, at Hampton Roads, Norfolk, Virginia — 13 November, 1926

Course: Seven laps of 50 km left-hand circuit round three-leg course, with start and finish off Norfolk Naval Air Station
Weather: Bright, fresh northwest wind, water choppy

| Aircraft | Engine | Pilot | Nationality | Contest number | Start order | Final placing | Average speed |
|---|---|---|---|---|---|---|---|
| Macchi M.39 (MM.74) | 800 hp Fiat AS.2 | Lieut Adriano Bacula | Italy | 1 | 1 | 3 | 350·845 km/h (218·00 mph) |
| Curtiss F6C-3 Hawk (A7128) | 507 hp Curtiss D-12A | Lieut William Tomlinson | USA | 2 | 2 | 4 | 220·406 km/h (136·953 mph) |
| Curtiss R3C-4 (A6979) | 685 hp Curtiss V-1550 | Lieut George Cuddihy | USA | 4 | 3 | Retired on lap 7 | — |
| Macchi M.39 (MM.75) | 800 hp Fiat AS.2 | Capt Arturo Ferrarin | Italy | 3 | 4 | Retired on lap 4 | — |
| Macchi M.39 (MM.76) | 800 hp Fiat AS.2 | Maj Mario de Bernardi | Italy | 5 | 5 | 1 | 396·698 km/h (246·496 mph) |
| Curtiss R3C-2 (A7054) | 565 hp Curtiss V-1400 | Lieut Christian Frank Schilt | USA | 6 | 6 | 2 | 372·34 km/h (231·36 mph) |

# Tenth Contest, at Venice — 26 September, 1927

Course: Seven laps of 50 km left-hand circuit round three-leg course, with start and finish off Excelsior Hotel, Venice Lido
Weather: Overcast, cloudy-bright, light breeze, water calm with slight swell

| Aircraft | Engine | Pilot | Nationality | Contest number | Start order | Final placing | Average speed |
|---|---|---|---|---|---|---|---|
| Gloster IVB (N223) | 875 hp Napier Lion VIIB | Flt Lieut S. M. Kinkead | Great Britain | 1 | 1 | Retired on lap 6 | — |
| Macchi M.52 | 1,000 hp Fiat AS.3 | Maj Mario de Bernardi | Italy | 2 | 2 | Retired on lap 2 | — |
| Supermarine S.5 (N220) | 875 hp Napier Lion VIIB | Flt Lieut S. N. Webster | Great Britain | 4 | 3 | 1 | 453·282 km/h (281·655 mph) |
| Macchi M.52 | 800 hp Fiat AS.2 | Capt Frederico Guazetti | Italy | 5 | 4 | Retired end of lap 6 | — |
| Supermarine S.5 (N219) | 900 hp Napier Lion VIIA | Flt Lieut O. E. Worsley | Great Britain | 6 | 5 | 2 | 439·45 km/h (273·07 mph) |
| Macchi M.52 (MM.82) | 1,000 hp Fiat AS.3 | Capt Arturo Ferrarin | Italy | 7 | 6 | Retired on lap 1 | — |

288

## Eleventh Contest, at Calshot — 7 September, 1929

Course: Seven laps of 50 km left-hand circuit round three-leg course, with start and finish off Ryde, Isle of Wight
Weather: Bright sunshine, light south-southeast breeze, water rippled

| Aircraft | Engine | Pilot | Nationality | Contest number | Start order | Final placing | Average speed |
|---|---|---|---|---|---|---|---|
| Supermarine S.6 (N247) | 1,900 hp Rolls-Royce R. | Flg Off H. R. D. Waghorn | Great Britain | 2 | 1 | 1 | 528·879 km/h (328·629 mph) |
| Macchi M.52R | 1,000 hp Fiat AS.3 | Warrant Officer Dal Molin | Italy | 4 | 2 | 2 | 457·38 km/h (284·20 mph) |
| Supermarine S.5 (N219) | 875 Napier Lion VIIB | Flt Lieut D. D'Arcy Greig | Great Britain | 5 | 3 | 3 | 454·02 km/h (282·11 mph) |
| Macchi M.67 (MM.105) | 1,800 hp Isotta-Fraschini | Lieut Remo Cadringher | Italy | 7 | 4 | Retired on lap 2 | — |
| Supermarine S.6 (N248) | 1,900 hp Rolls-Royce R | Flg Off Richard Atcherley | Great Britain | 8 | 5 | — | 523·89 km/h (325·54 mph)* |
| Macchi M.67 (MM.103) | 1,800 hp Isotta-Fraschini | Lieut Giovanni Monti | Italy | 10 | 6 | Retired on lap 2 | — |

* Disqualified for cutting a pylon.

## Twelfth Contest, at Calshot — 13 September, 1931

Course: Seven laps of 50 km left-hand circuit round three-leg course, with the start and finish off Ryde, Isle of Wight
Weather: Clear, bright sunshine, light north wind, water choppy with some swell

| Aircraft | Engine | Pilot | Nationality | Contest number | Start order | Final placing | Average speed |
|---|---|---|---|---|---|---|---|
| Supermarine S.6B (S1595) | 2,300 hp Rolls-Royce R | Flt Lieut John Boothman | Great Britain | 1 | 1 | 1 | 547·297 km/h (340·08 mph) |

There were no other challengers in this contest. Boothman 'flew over' the course to retain the Schneider Trophy for Great Britain and to win it outright with a third consecutive British victory.

# APPENDIX II

# The Fatalities

Inevitably victory in the Schneider Trophy contests and the establishment of world speed records was dearly bought, often with the lives of brave young pilots. In this respect, Italy paid more dearly than any other nation. The following list of those who died pays special tribute to their individual achievements and to their memory.

1922 SIAI test pilot killed in S.50 seaplane prototype.

1926 US Marine Corps Lieut H. J. Norton in Curtiss CR-3 (A6081). Stalled in turn and crashed into the Potomac River, near Anacostia, USA. 13 September.

Commandant Marchese Vittorio Centurione in Macchi M.39 practice aircraft. Stalled and crashed into Lake Varese near Schirana Air Station, Italy. 21 September.

US Navy Lieut F. Conant in a Navy training aircraft. Hit pole sticking out of shallow water when low flying over Winter Harbor, 30 miles (48 km) north of Norfolk, Virginia, and crashed. 30 October.

1927 Lieut S. Borra, in Macchi M.39 practice aircraft. Stalled while cornering and crashed into Lake Varese. 16 June.

1928 Flt Lieut S. M. Kinkead in Supermarine S.5 N221. Flew into the sea at Calshot while attempting to establish new world speed record. 12 March.

1929 Capt G. Motta in Macchi M.67. Dived into Lake Garda after fast low-level test run. 22 August.

1930 Warrant Officer T. Dal Molin in Savoia Marchetti S.65. Crashed into Lake Garda while attempting to establish new world speed record. 18 January.

1931 Lieut G. Bougault in Bernard H.V.120. Crashed at Berre. Cause not definitely established but propeller disintegration or sparking plug blown through windscreen killing pilot could have been primary reason. 30 July.

Capt G. Monti in Macchi MC.72. Crashed into Lake Garda after low-level run over Desenzano training base to demonstrate irregular running of engine to engineers on ground. 2 August.

RN Lieut J. Brinton in Supermarine S.6A N248. Dived into the sea off Calshot while taking off for practice flight. 18 August.

Lieut S. Bellini in second Macchi MC.72. Flew into hillside near Lake Garda after gravity fuel tank fire. 11 September.

# APPENDIX III

# A Pilot's View

Air Vice-Marshal S. N. Webster, CBE, who, as a young Flight Lieutenant, flew the Supermarine S.5 to victory in the 1927 Schneider contest in Venice, said:
'I was test flying at Martlesham Heath when I was sent off to Felixstowe, which wasn't far away, to join the High Speed Flight. I had never flown a seaplane but took to it like a duck to water! We were flying everything at Martlesham—the Inflexible, the Vixen, a Gamecock, the Hinaidi and a Sidestrand—so we tended to take everything in our stride. I had over one hundred and twenty types in my log book. We had a Flycatcher on floats for practice flying and my first flight in that was on 17 February, 1927; then we moved on to the old Bamel and the Gloster IIIs. I did quite a lot of flying in the Bamel. We used to pop back to Martlesham to do normal testing in between practice flights. I also had three flights in the Crusader at Felixstowe.'

On the question of whether Reginald Mitchell consulted the High Speed Flight pilots on such matters as cockpit layout, the Air Marshal said that that was all finalized by the time he first flew the S.5 on 14 July. He found the aircraft very responsive and his log book comments were 'very, very nice. No snags!'

Pre-contest flying was limited and the young pilot got airborne in the S.5 only twice at Calshot and four times in Venice.

Of the contest itself Webster said: 'I was pretty sure it was in the bag. I knew I had the legs on Worsley.'

One personal memory concerned the Italian poet and patriot D'Annunzio. 'He came to the Lido to watch the contest but on my first lap, the old Lion and its propeller made such a noise he went home again'!

In response to a question about the benefits of the contest, Air Marshal Webster believed that it was the designers and engineers rather than the pilots who learned most about high speed flying. He also believed that the British victories had little or no effect on overseas sales of British aircraft.

Was there any personal benefit from his splendid victory so far from home? 'Certainly not. We were all professional pilots and it was regarded as just another job.'

# APPENDIX IV

# The Timing

As is recorded elsewhere in this book, the average speeds attained by the winning aircraft in the contest series rose, during the eighteen years and five months between the first Schneider Trophy contest at Monaco on 16 April, 1913, and the twelfth and final contest at Calshot on 13 September, 1931, from the 73·6 km/h (45·75 mph) of Maurice Prévost's Deperdussin monoplane to the 547·297 km/h (340·08 mph) attained by the Supermarine S.6B S1595 flown by Flt Lieut John Boothman. It should be noted that due to an incorrect finish, which had to be completed correctly, Prévost's time was a true average of 98·1 km/h (60·95 mph).

Maximum indicated airspeeds during these years of the contest rocketed from the alleged 157·7 km/h (98 mph) of Weymann's Nieuport monoplane to the optimistic 608 km/h (378 mph) recorded by John Boothman in the S.6B on the 7¼ mile (11·6 km) leg of the 1931 contest course from St Helen's Point, Isle of Wight, to West Wittering on the mainland. And even these speeds were exceeded by Flt Lieut George Stainforth in the S.6B S1596 on the same day. Four runs—two with the wind and two in the opposite direction—over a three kilometre course off Lee-on-Solent enabled him to establish a new world speed record at an average speed of 610·02 km/h (379·05 mph). On 29 September, Stainforth broke this 16-days-old record when, flying the second S.6B, S1596, with a specially prepared racing R engine using exotic high alcohol content fuel, he became the first person to exceed 400 mph (643·72 km/h) over a measured run in establishing the new world record at an average speed of 655·79 km/h (407·5 mph). The record was pushed even higher by Agello and the MC.72 on 23 October, 1934, with a speed of 709·209 km/h (440·681 mph). This world record is still Italy's after more than 40 years.

Clearly, none of these records could have been homologated, nor, indeed, could a winner have been established without quite accurate time-keeping. Everything is relative, of course, and at the speeds attained in record attempts and in the contests up until 1927, the split-second stop-watch in the hand of a trained and experienced time-keeper, the method used for motorcar and motorcycle speed contests, was considered sufficiently accurate. But it was becoming increasingly apparent that at the very high speeds then being achieved, any delay in pressing the button of the stop watch, however fractional, was enough to cause serious miscalculations in the final speed. However, in that year on 4 November, camera experts and observers from the Royal Aircraft Establishment at Farnborough had used ciné camera guns to time the Supermarine S.5 N220, winner of the recent Schneider Trophy contest, flying over a 3 km straight course at Calshot.

Two camera guns were used and were set up, one at each end of the measured course, and aimed approximately at the point in the sky through which the S.5

293

would pass. As the aircraft completed the course, its passage was recorded by several exposures. Simultaneously, a corresponding photograph was taken of a stop-watch inside the camera-gun. Before and after the timing operations the two watches were synchronized by photographing them together so that the times thus recorded could be corrected to a common standard.

By removing the human element in the timing mechanism's control loop, this method was a great advance on earlier methods of timing. It was, however, still imperfect as it relied upon the accuracy of the stop watch which had $\frac{1}{5}$ second increments. While this fraction of time was so small as to be disregarded in the assessment of earlier speed trials, it could, for example, create an error of up to ·37 mph (·59 km/h) when measuring a speed of 380 mph (611 km/h) over a 3 km (1·86 mile) course. As the RAE system employed two stop watches, a combined inaccuracy of up to ·75 mph (1·2 km/h) was possible.

Inaccuracies of this order were completely unacceptable and further development of photographic timing techniques and equipment was put in hand. As a result, in 1929 a new system was devised by the Scientific Research Department of the Air Ministry, which eliminated the human and instrument errors inherent in the earlier systems. The basic principle of this highly accurate timing system was essentially the same as the earlier camera-gun method; the main difference lay in the fact that the stop-watches were replaced by electrically-operated counters controlled by a single tuning fork. The fork was maintained in a steady vibratory condition transmitting electrical impulses at each end of the measured course. These counters were photographed simultaneously with the aircraft as it crossed the line of sight. In this way, the time of the transit of the starting and finishing lines was photo-recorded in terms of tuning-fork vibrations rather than $\frac{1}{5}$ seconds on independent stop-watches.

Each camera had two counters, operating alternately, and each counter was connected in series with its corresponding counter in the other camera. The pairs of counters were operated approximately ten times per second, the two electrical circuits being interrupted alternately by the tuning-fork vibrations.

Working in conjunction with the fork were the two cine-cameras, in the back of which were fitted the two counters illuminated by two lamps. The image of the counters was projected through a lens and was printed on each film as it was exposed.

This system was approved by the Fédération Aéronautique Internationale for recording speed record attempts and was used for those made by the S.6B S1596 flown by Flt Lieut George Stainforth, to establish a new world speed record for Great Britain in September 1931. On that occasion two wooden huts were built on the shore at each end of the speed course between Lee-on-Solent and Hill Head. The camera in each hut was lined up with the sighting posts at the course ends. At the 'home' hut a concrete pedestal supported the tuning fork, and the two stations were connected by a telephone cable and a submarine cable, the latter forming part of the counter circuit.

When the S.6 became airborne, the tuning fork was started and maintained in a vibratory state. The two cameras were directed on the respective sighting posts and a strip of film was exposed to record the initial counter readings. When the S.6 approached the course, the counters and stop-watches were started and the camera was tracked horizontally to the correct position and then switched on until the aircraft had passed through the field of vision. A similar process was used at the finishing line.

John Boothman in S.6B S1595 (No. 1) out on the course winning the Schneider Trophy for Great Britain in 1931. (*Flight*)


This procedure was repeated for the four runs, the counters being continuously in operation. They were stopped at the end of the flight and were photographed again, as were the sighting posts. The watch time during which the counters were operating was noted to check the rate of the tuning fork.

When the films were processed and printed, the distance of the aircraft from the centre line of the film was plotted against the counter readings for each frame and a mean line was drawn through the points. The sighting post was marked in and the readings at this point were taken. By subtracting the initial counter reading from this figure, the number of tuning-fork vibrations from the starting of the counters was established. In this way, the time of each run as measured in fork vibrations could be calculated, and as the rate of the fork was known, it was then possible to determine the time taken for each run in seconds.

It was calculated that this method of timing was accurate to $\frac{1}{20}$ second. At speeds around 400 mph (643 km/h) over a 3 km (1·86 mile) course, any error could be limited to ·01 mph (·016 km/h).

# APPENDIX V

# The Extant Aircraft

Of the total of 47 aeroplanes which flew in the Schneider Trophy contests (three flew in two contests) only five still exist. The remainder either crashed or were broken up by wreckers seeking space, souvenirs or money.

The oldest of these is the Curtiss R3C-2, which was later serialled A7054, and is the one in which Lieut James H. Doolittle flew to victory in the 1925 contest. It can be seen at the National Air and Space Museum in Washington, D.C.

The following list shows the other aircraft still in existence at December 1980.

| Type | Serial | Location | Remarks |
|---|---|---|---|
| Macchi M.39 | MM.76 | Centro Storico Scientifico de Volo, Turin. | Winning aircraft in 1926 contest flown by Maj M. de Bernardi. |
| Supermarine S.6B | S1595 | Science Museum, London. | Winning aircraft in 1931 contest flown by Flt Lieut J. Boothman. |

The Macchi-Castoldi MC.72 on exhibition in Brussels in June 1950. (*John Stroud*)

296

World speed record setter S.6B S1596 on Horse Guards Parade, London, during 1968. In front of the aircraft Air Marshal Sir Richard 'Batchy' Atcherley is interviewed for television by Shaw Taylor. (*Kenneth Brookes*)

| | | | |
|---|---|---|---|
| Supermarine S.6B | S1596 | Mitchell Memorial Hall, Southampton. | Aircraft in which Flt Lieut G. H. Stainforth set world speed record of 407·5 mph, 29 September, 1931. |
| Macchi-Castoldi MC.72 | | Centro Storico Scientifico de Volo, Turin. | Established world speed record for floatplanes of 440·681 mph 23 October, 1934. |

The replica Supermarine S.5 which first flew in 1975. (*Flight International*)

## APPENDIX VI

# The Replicas

Among a number of replica aircraft at Thorpe Park, Chertsey, in Surrey, which features British maritime history, are a Curtiss R3C-2, a Macchi M.52, a Deper-dussin, and a Supermarine S.6B. All are full-sized and float on one of several lakes in the Park. A fifth Schneider Trophy aircraft is a flying Supermarine S.5 replica which is accorded proper hangarage.

The four non-flying replicas are built of marine ply on hardwood frames and are almost entirely of wood, some metal fittings being used in the basic structure. In effect, they are mock-ups to reproduce the original lines and appearance of the original aircraft.

When the author visited the Park in September 1980, the Macchi M.52 was equipped with an old de Havilland Gipsy Queen engine to enable it to taxi on the water. It was finished in red overall, with vertical green, white and red national rudder stripes. There were no other markings. The surface radiators were painted on the mainplanes but due to weathering were not readily apparent. Plans were then in hand to rebuild the Curtiss R3C-2 and instal an engine for taxi-ing. It was finished in black overall, with vertical blue, white and red rudder stripes, US ARMY in white on the fin and the contest number 3 on the fuselage as carried by Doolittle's R3C-2 in which he won the 1925 contest.

The S.6B was finished as Boothman's Trophy-winning S1595 of 1931. Due to weathering, the mainplanes were to be re-covered and a taxi-ing engine fitted. It was suggested that at one stage it had been hoped that a Merlin would be used.

The Deperdussin had a blue fuselage with the remainder of the airframe finished in brown. It carried a contest number 19 on the fuselage, the number allocated to Maurice Prévost's Deperdussin in which he won the first Schneider contest in 1913.

The most interesting replica at the Park was the flying example of the S.5. A decision to include this aeroplane, rather than an S.6, was made in 1972. Leisure Sport Ltd, which owns the Park and is a member of the Ready Mixed Concrete Ltd Group of Companies, asked Ray Hilborne to examine the possibility of producing a design for one or other of these Supermarine aeroplanes. With his experience of completing other replicas, such as the Avro Triplane and Pfalz D III, Hilborne believed that an all-wood wire-braced S.5 could be built more easily as the Rolls-Royce Continental IO-360 flat-six engine chosen to power it could be housed more readily and realistically under an S.5 cowling.

The Macchi M.52 replica taxi-ing at Thorpe Park. (*Vivienne Sparrow*)

Inevitably there were some small design and configuration differences between the replica and Webster's N220 of the 1927 contest. The loaded weight was reduced from the 3,242 lb (1,470 kg) of the original to 1,500 lb (680 kg); this lower weight and the reduced engine torque allowed the use of slightly narrower floats with water rudders. Always a tight fit in the original, the cockpit width of the replica was increased by two inches. The almost symmetrical RAF 30 wing section also was changed to one which reduced the stalling speed to around 55 mph (88·5 km/h).

Construction began in autumn 1972 and, after some extensive taxi-ing trials, a first flight was made on 28 August, 1975, piloted by John Hall. As in the original S.5, there was a knack to taking-off to avoid porpoising; some concentration was also required to keep straight when running on the step, as the forward view is restricted. The replica S.5 has a wide speed range in the air, stalling at 55 mph (88·5 km/h) but with a 180 mph (289·6 km/h) maximum speed. While this may compare unfavourably with Webster's S.5, which returned a speed of 319·57 mph (514·29 km/h), the geared Napier Lion VIIB twelve-cylinder engine developed 875 hp while the little Rolls-Royce Continental produces only 210 hp at sea level. For alighting, an 80 mph (128·7 km/h) powered approach is made and the aircraft is gently flown onto the water. This beautiful replica was flown during the public day displays at the 1976 SBAC Exhibition and Flying Display at Farnborough.

# Bibliography

The following list of books, reference sources, and periodicals, consulted by the author is provided in the belief that it will be of interest and value to researchers and those wishing to acquire a wider and more detailed knowledge of aero-maritime activities, air racing, and engineering achievements, related to them during the past 75 years.

*Books*
*Aeroplane Structures,* A. J. S. Pippard and J. L. Pritchard (Pitman, 1919)
*Handbook of Aeronautics,* edited by J. L. Pritchard (Pitman, 1931)
*Handbook of Aeronautics (Aero-Engines),* Andrew Swan (Pitman, 1934)
*British Seaplanes' Triumph in the International Schneider Trophy Contest 1913–1931,* Ellison Hawks (Real Photographs, 1945)
*Benefits of War,* Prof A. M. Low (Scientific Book Club, 1945)
*Aircraft—from Airship to Jet Propulsion,* Bonner W. A. Dickson (Vickers-Armstrongs Ltd, 1949)
*Fellowship of the Air 1901–1951,* B. J. Hurren ( Iliffe & Sons for 'Flight', 1951)
*Men and Machines,* C. H. Wilson and W. J. Reader (Weidenfeld and Nicholson, 1958)
*British Civil Aircraft 1919–59 Vol 1,* A. J. Jackson (Putnam, 1959)*
*British Civil Aircraft 1919–59 Vol 2,* A. J. Jackson (Putnam, 1960)*
*The Blackburn Story* (Blackburn Aircraft Ltd, 1960)
*Spitfire—the story of a famous fighter,* Bruce Robertson (Harleyford, 1960)
*Velivoli Macchi dal 1912 al 1963,* Rosario Abate and Giulio Lazzati (Aermacchi, 1963)
*Avro Aircraft since 1908,* A. J. Jackson (Putnam, 1965)
*The British Fighter since 1912,* Peter Lewis (Putnam, 1965)
*Supermarine S.4–S.6B,* C. F. Andrews and W. G. Cox (Profile Publications, 1965)
*Curtiss Army Hawks,* Peter M. Bowers (Profile Publications, 1965)
*British Flying-Boats and Amphibians,* G. R. Duval (Putnam, 1966)
*Aeromarine Origins,* H. F. King (Putnam, 1966)
*Curtiss Navy Hawks,* Peter M. Bowers (Profile Publications, 1966)
*Racing Planes and Air Races,* Reed Kinert (Aero Publishers, USA, 1967)
*Aircraft of the Royal Air Force since 1918,* Owen Thetford (Putnam, 1968)
*Pioneer Aircraft 1903–1914,* Kenneth Munson (MacMillan, 1969)
*Battle over Britain,* F. K. Mason (McWhirter Twins, 1969)
*History of Marine Aviation,* John Killen (Muller, 1969)
*Veteran and Vintage Aircraft,* Leslie Hunt (Garnstone Press, 1970)
*Sopwith—the man and his aircraft,* Bruce Robertson (Harleyford, 1970)
*Gloster Aircraft since 1917,* Derek N. James (Putnam, 1970)
*The Schneider Trophy Races,* Ralph Barker (Chatto and Windus, 1971)
*Bristol Aircraft since 1910,* C. H. Barnes (Putnam, 1971)
*British Racing and Record-Breaking Aircraft,* Peter Lewis (Putnam, 1971)

*Later revised in three volumes.

*Flying Boats and Seaplanes since 1910*, Kenneth Munson (MacMillan, 1971)
*Avro—An Aircraft Album*, Harlin Jenks (Ian Allan, 1973)
*Fairey Aircraft since 1915*, H. A. Taylor (Putnam, 1974)
*The Speed Seekers*, Thomas G. Foxworth (Macdonald and Jane's 1975)
*Rolls-Royce From the Wings*, R. W. Harker (Oxford Illustrated Press, 1976)
*International Encyclopaedia of Aviation* (Crown Publishers, USA, 1977)
*I kept no Diary*, Air Commodore F. R. Banks (Airlife Publications, 1978)
*The Air Racer*, Charles A. Mendenhall (Speciality Press, USA, 1979)
*The Wooden Wonder*, James G. Robins (J. G. Robins, 1980)

*References*
*Jane's All the World's Aircraft* (Sampson Low 1912–33)
*Luftschau* (10 December, 1928)
*Flugsport* (No. 19, 1931)
Royal Aero Club Schneider Trophy press announcements (1931)
*Zeitschrift für Flugtechnik und Motorluftschiffart* (27 August, 1932)
*Triebwerksanordnungen bei Dornier-Flugzeugen* (*Der Flieger*, April 1942)
*The two Rs 1904–1954* (*Flight*, 7 May, 1954)
*The Centenary Journal of the Royal Aeronautical Society* (1966)
*Glosters and the Schneider Trophy*, Basil Fielding (*R.A.E. News*, November 1968)
*Technical Aspects of the Schneider Trophy Races*—lecture by Dr Ing Ermanno Bazzocchi to the Coventry and Southampton branches of the Royal Aeronautical Society on 17/18 March, 1971
*The Curtiss D-12 Aero-Engine*, Hugo T. Byttebier (Smithsonian Institution Press, Washington, D.C., 1972)

*Periodicals*
*Aero, The*
*Aeronautics*
*Aeroplane, The*
*Aeroplane Monthly*
*Aerospace*
*Aircraft Engineering*
*Aircraft Illustrated*
*Fanatique de l'Aviation, Le*
*Flight/Flight International*
*Koku Fan*
*Monitor, The*
*Royal Aero Club Gazette*
*Royal Aeronautical Society Journal*
*Royal Aircraft Establishment News*

# INDEX OF AIRCRAFT,
# ENGINES AND CONTESTS